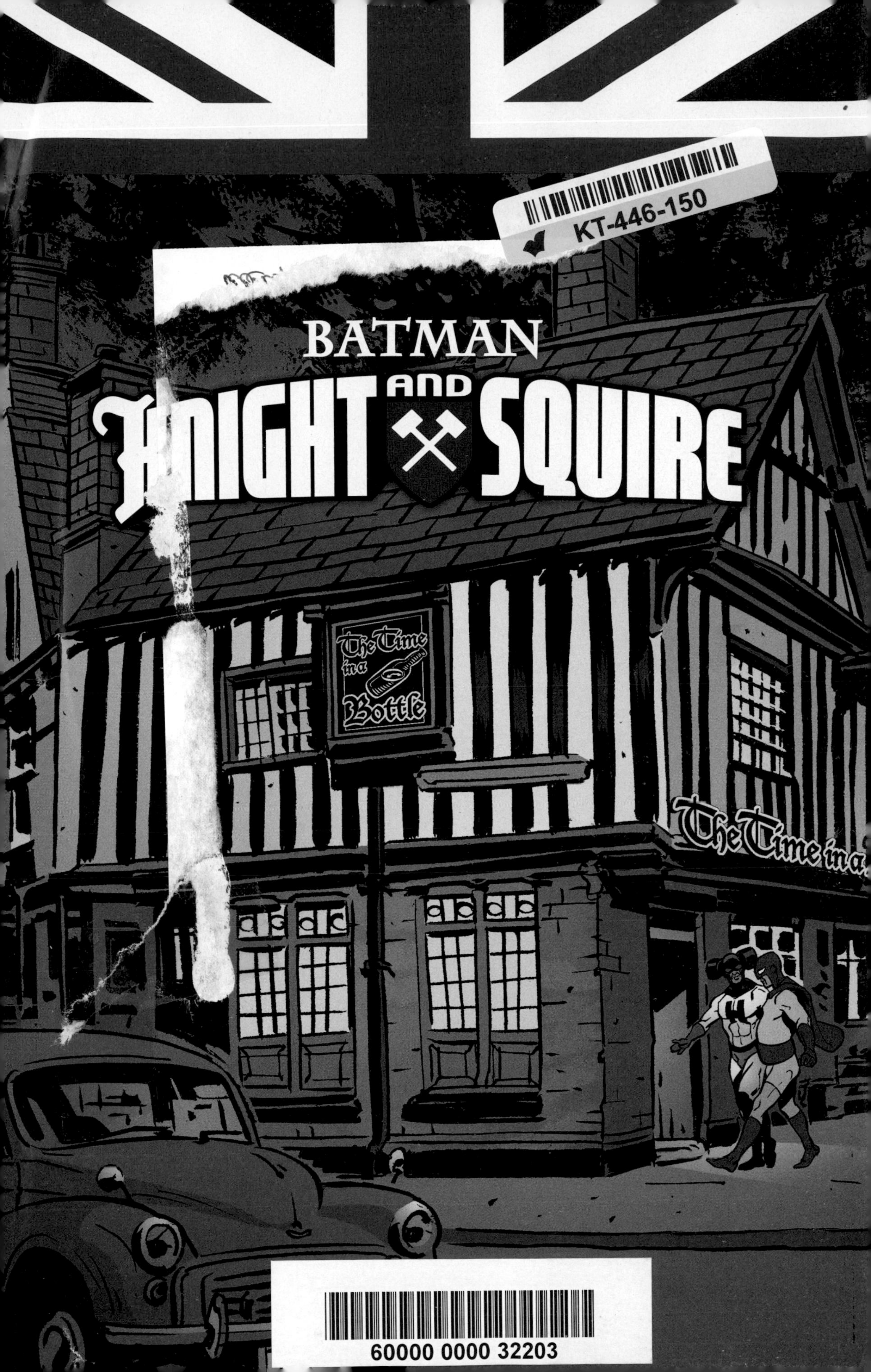
BATMAN
KNIGHT AND SQUIRE
The Time in a Bottle
The Time in a

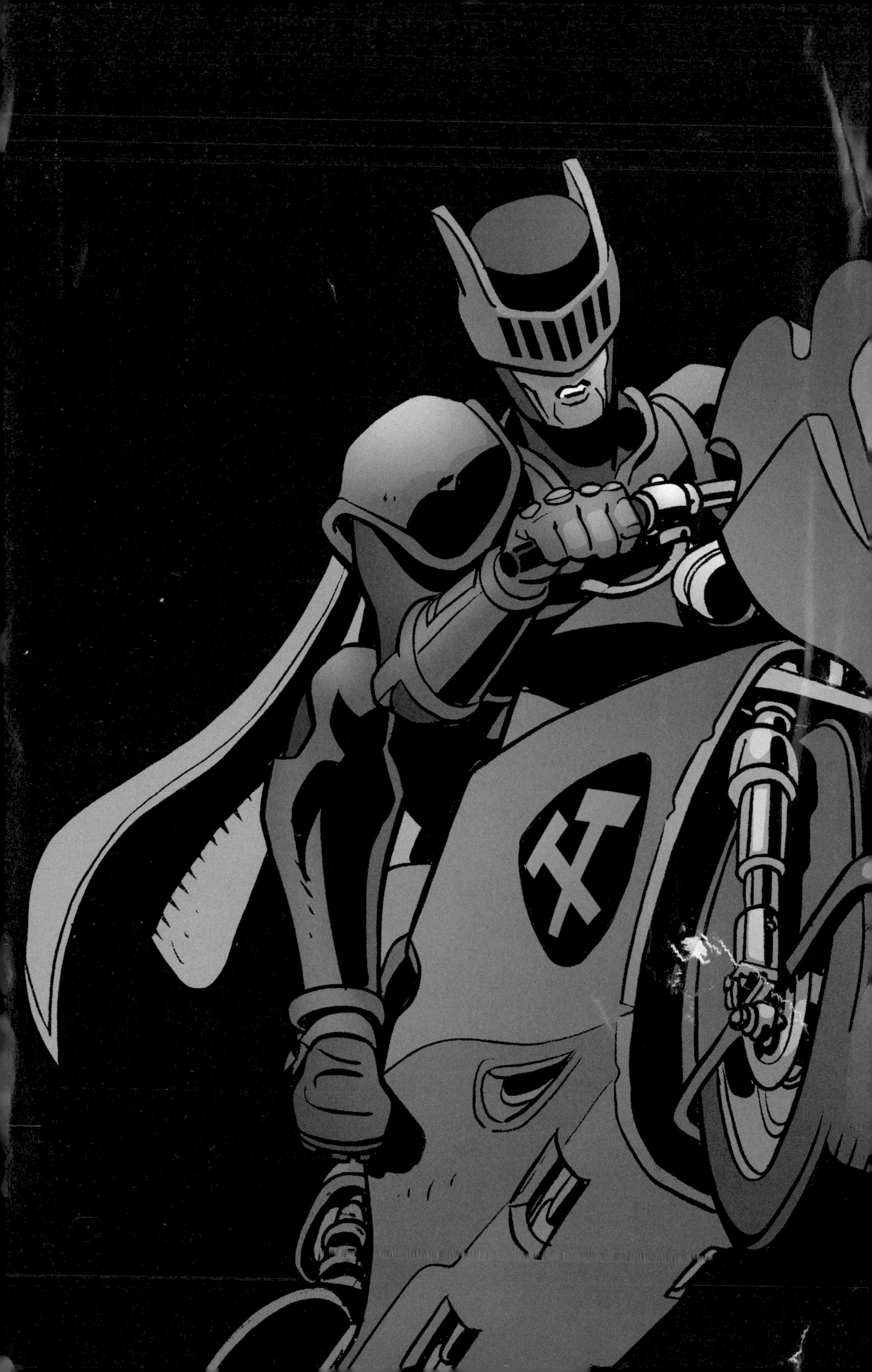

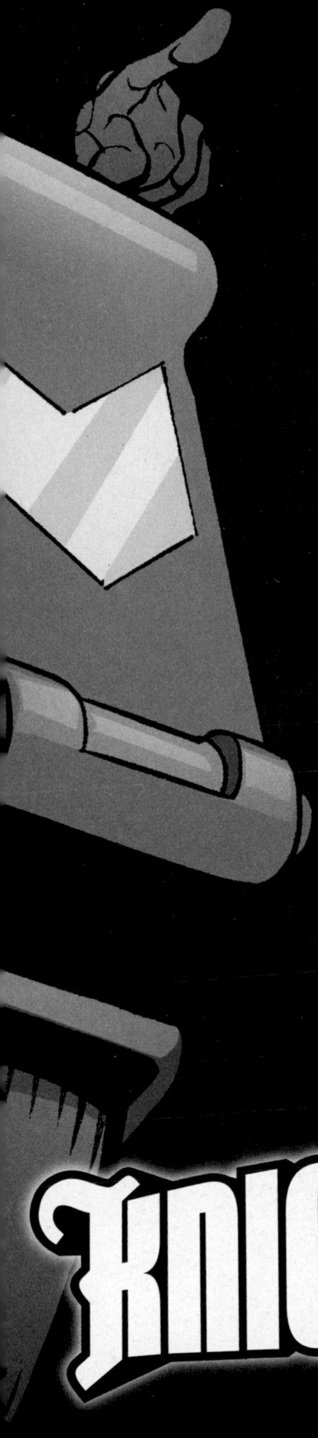

Paul Cornell
Writer

Jimmy Broxton
Artist

Staz Johnson
Issue #4 Layouts

Guy Major
Colorist

Steve Wands
Letterer

Yanick Paquette and **Michel Lacombe**
Cover Artists

Nathan Fairbairn
Cover Colorist

Billy Tucci
Issue #1 Variant Cover Artist

Hi-Fi
Issue #1 Variant Cover Colorist

BATMAN KNIGHT AND SQUIRE

Batman *created by* **Bob Kane**

BATMAN: KNIGHT AND SQUIRE

Published by DC Comics. Cover and compilation Copyright © 2011 DC Comics. All Rights Reserved.

Originally published in single magazine form in KNIGHT AND SQUIRE 1-6. Copyright © 2010, 2011 DC Comics.
All Rights Reserved. All characters featured in this issue, the distinctive likenesses thereof and related elements are trademarks of DC Comics.
The stories, characters and incidents mentioned in this magazine are entirely fictional.
DC Comics does not read or accept unsolicited submissions of ideas, stories or artwork.

DC Comics, 1700 Broadway, New York, NY 10019
A Warner Bros. Entertainment Company
Printed by Quad/Graphics, Dubuque, IA, USA. 5/27/11. First Printing.
ISBN: 978-1-4012-3071-5

SUSTAINABLE
FORESTRY
INITIATIVE
Certified Chain of Custody
Promoting Sustainable
Forest Management

Fiber used in this product line meets the
sourcing requirements of the SFI program.
www.sfiprogram.org SGS-SFI/COC-0130

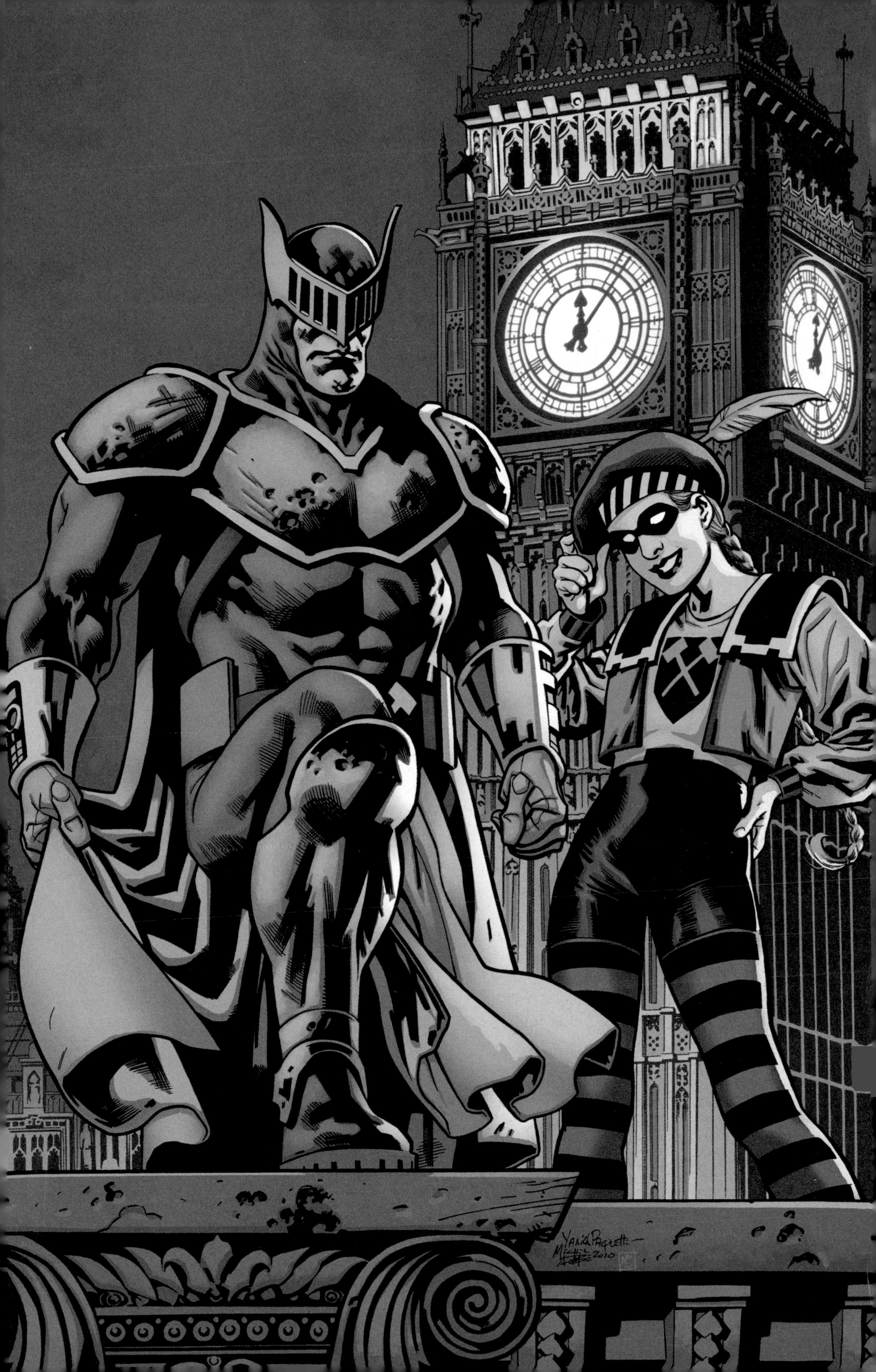

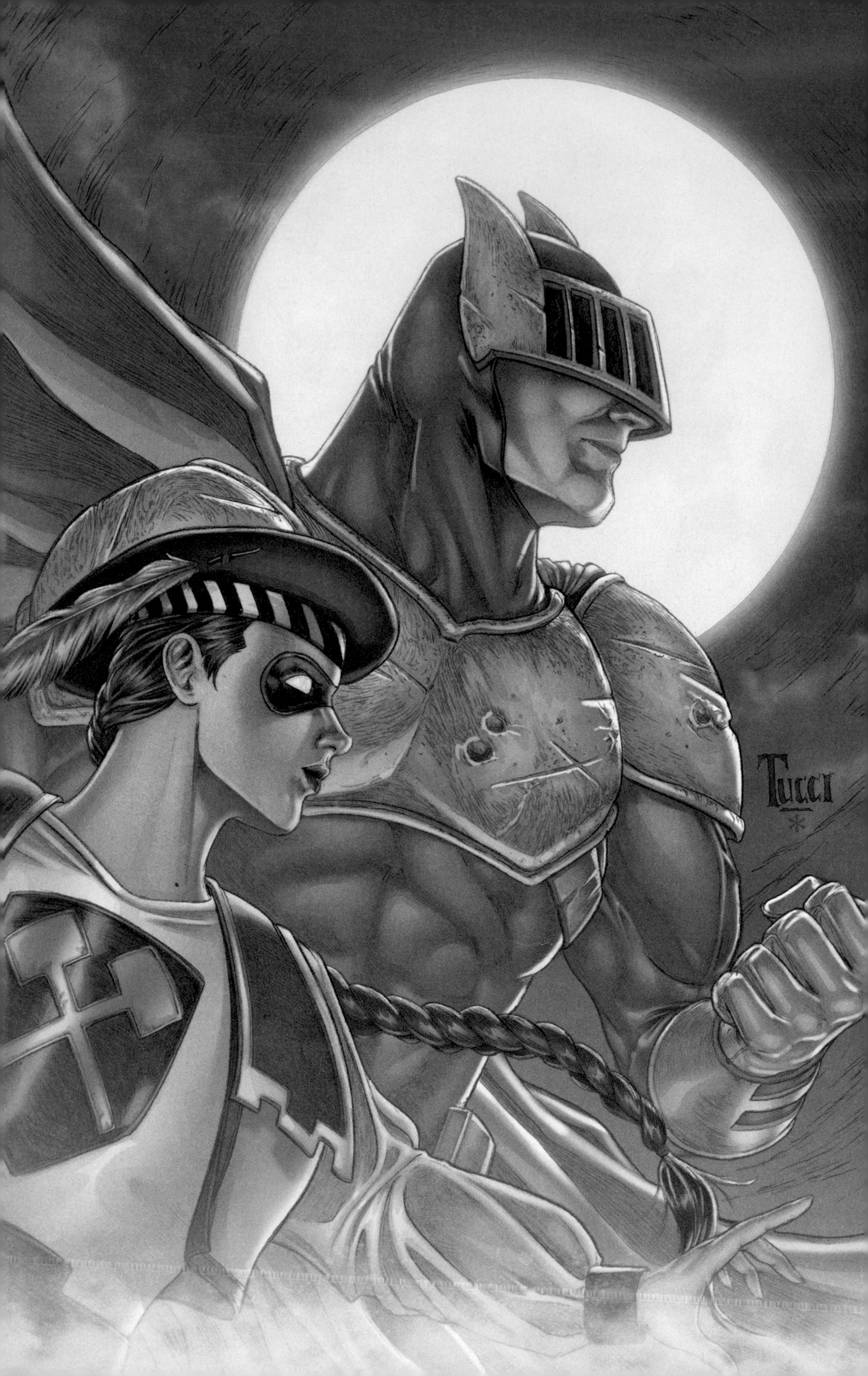
TUCCI

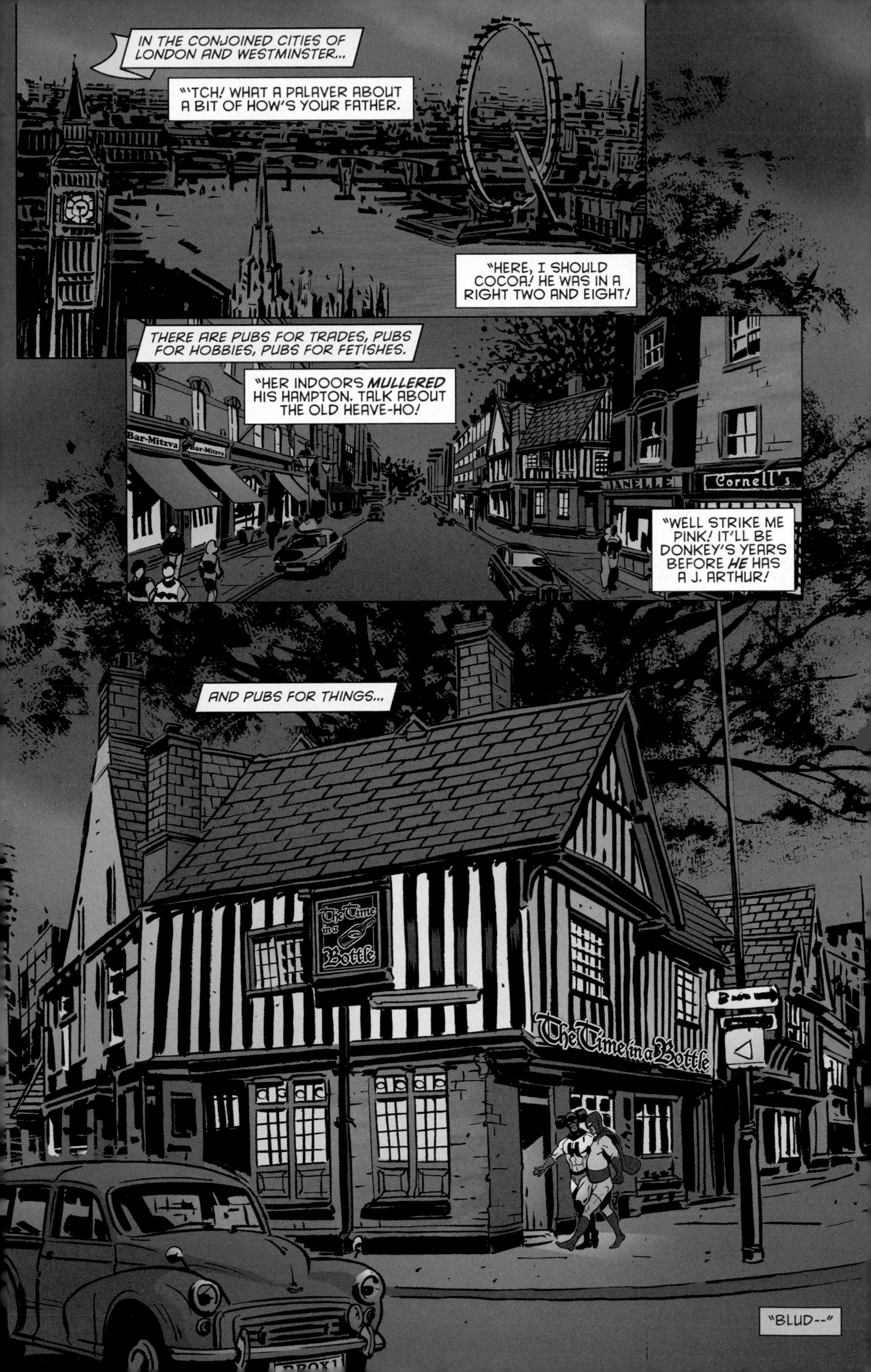
IN THE CONJOINED CITIES OF LONDON AND WESTMINSTER...
"'TCH! WHAT A PALAVER ABOUT A BIT OF HOW'S YOUR FATHER.
"HERE, I SHOULD COCOA! HE WAS IN A RIGHT TWO AND EIGHT!
THERE ARE PUBS FOR TRADES, PUBS FOR HOBBIES, PUBS FOR FETISHES.
"HER INDOORS MULLERED HIS HAMPTON. TALK ABOUT THE OLD HEAVE-HO!
Bar-Mitzva
Bar-Mitzva
Cornell's
"WELL STRIKE ME PINK! IT'LL BE DONKEY'S YEARS BEFORE HE HAS A J. ARTHUR!
AND PUBS FOR THINGS...
The Time in a Bottle
The Time in a Bottle
"BLUD--"

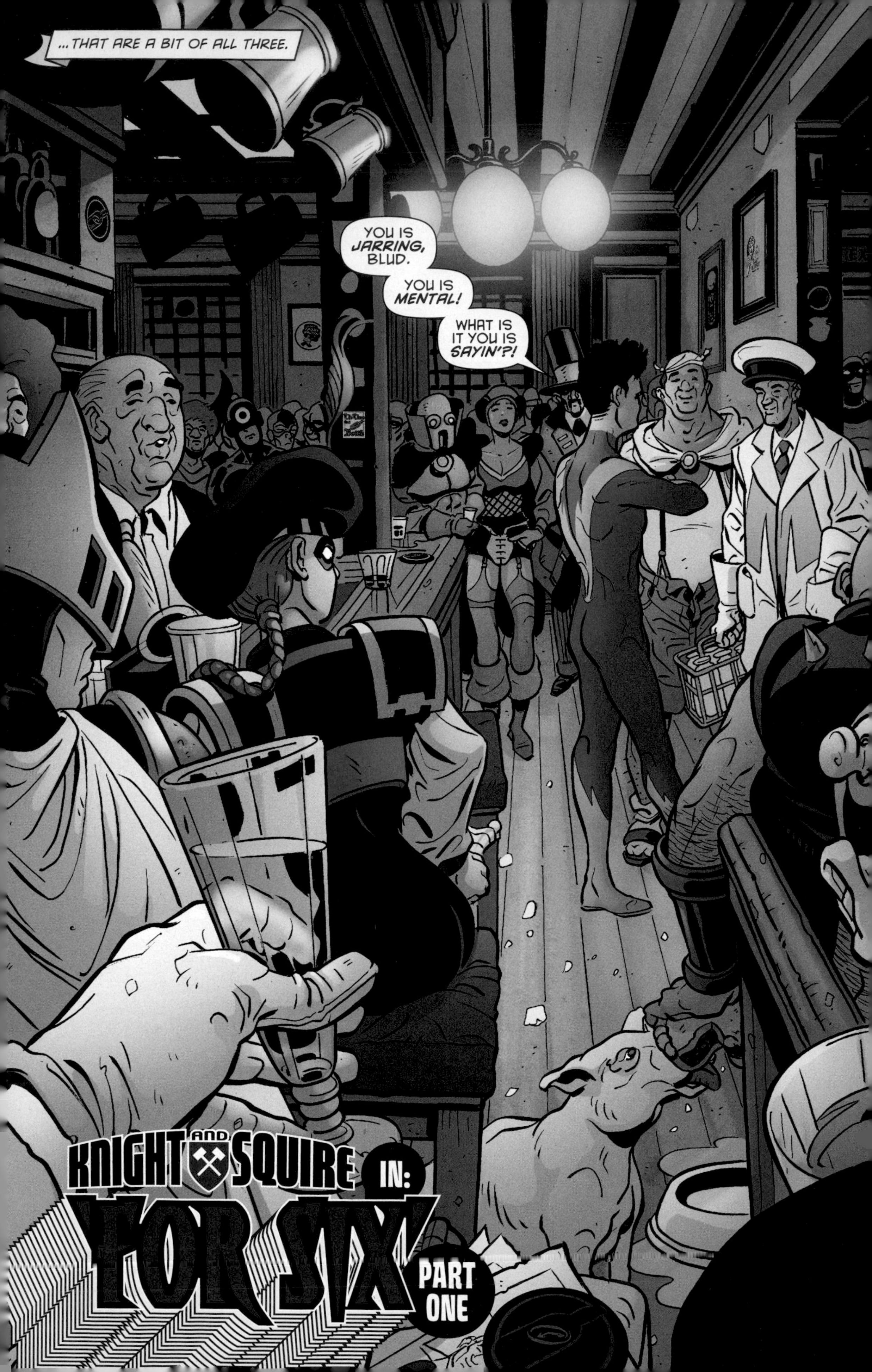
...THAT ARE A BIT OF ALL THREE.
YOU IS JARRING, BLUD.
YOU IS MENTAL!
WHAT IS IT YOU IS SAYIN'?!
KNIGHT AND SQUIRE IN:
FOR SIX
PART ONE

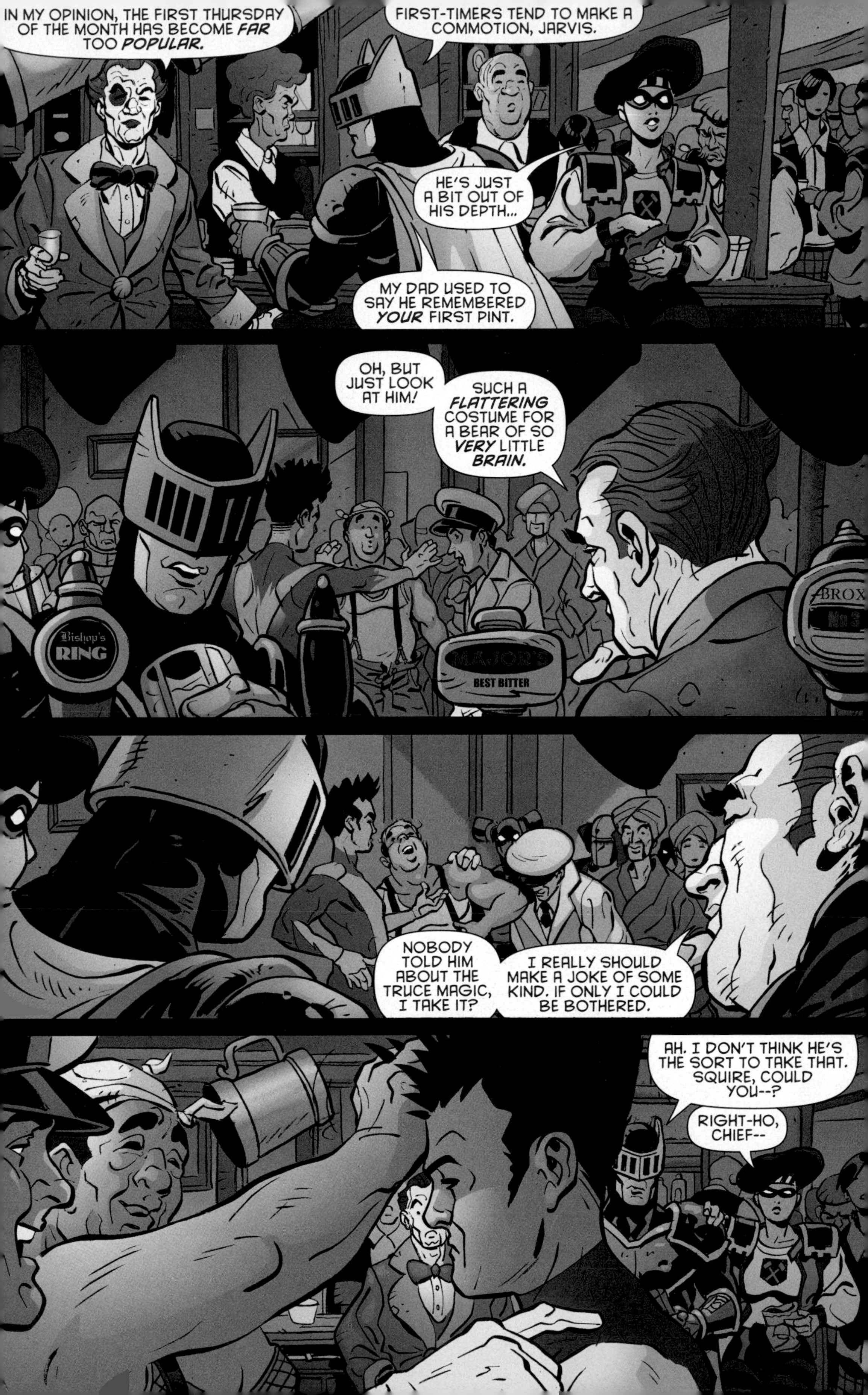

IN MY OPINION, THE FIRST THURSDAY OF THE MONTH HAS BECOME FAR TOO POPULAR.
FIRST-TIMERS TEND TO MAKE A COMMOTION, JARVIS.
HE'S JUST A BIT OUT OF HIS DEPTH...
MY DAD USED TO SAY HE REMEMBERED YOUR FIRST PINT.
OH, BUT JUST LOOK AT HIM!
SUCH A FLATTERING COSTUME FOR A BEAR OF SO VERY LITTLE BRAIN.
Bishop's RING
BEST BITTER
BROX
NOBODY TOLD HIM ABOUT THE TRUCE MAGIC, I TAKE IT?
I REALLY SHOULD MAKE A JOKE OF SOME KIND. IF ONLY I COULD BE BOTHERED.
AH. I DON'T THINK HE'S THE SORT TO TAKE THAT. SQUIRE, COULD YOU--?
RIGHT-HO, CHIEF--

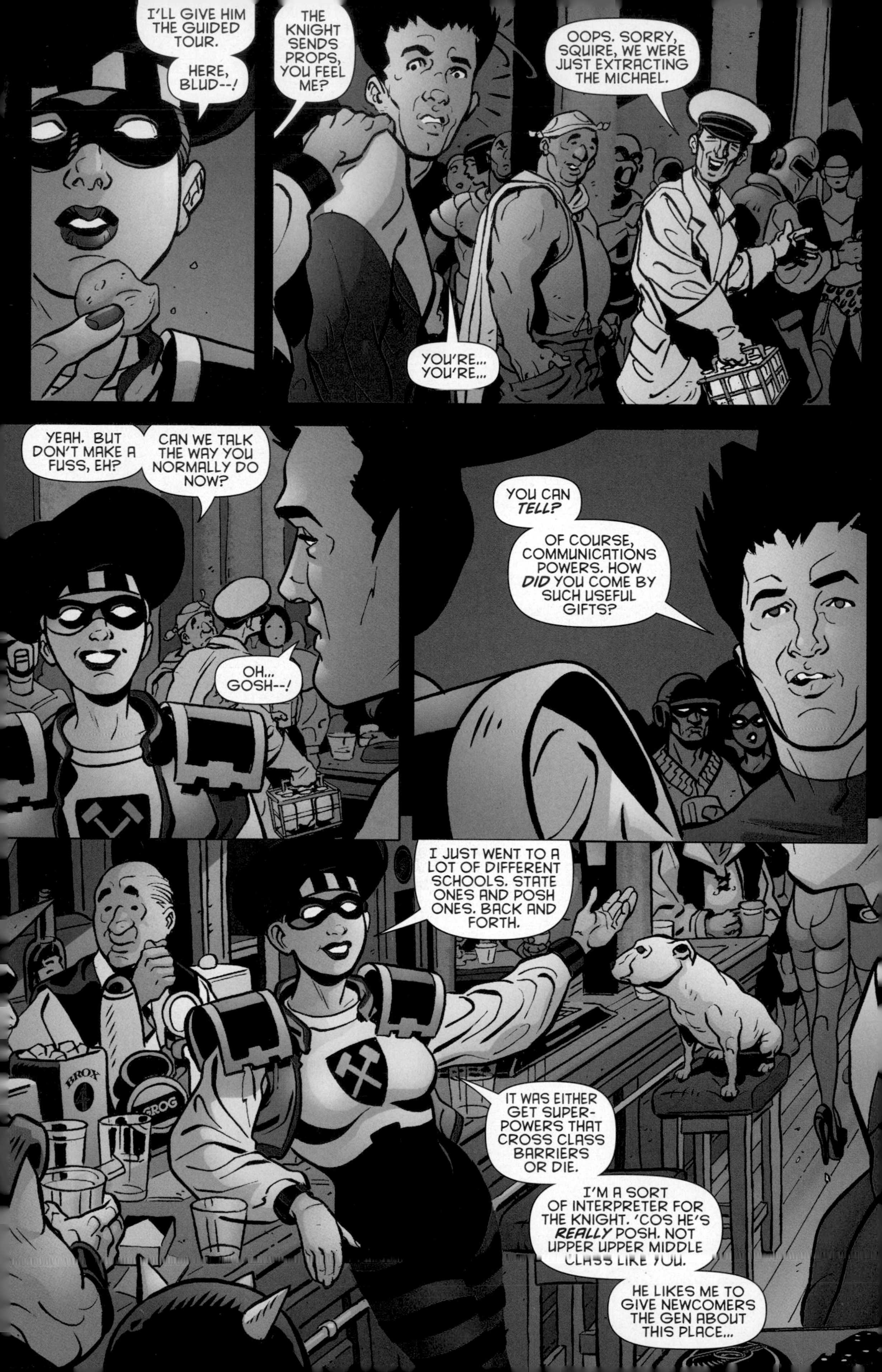
I'LL GIVE HIM THE GUIDED TOUR.
HERE, BLUD--!
THE KNIGHT SENDS PROPS, YOU FEEL ME?
OOPS. SORRY, SQUIRE, WE WERE JUST EXTRACTING THE MICHAEL.
YOU'RE... YOU'RE...
YEAH. BUT DON'T MAKE A FUSS, EH?
CAN WE TALK THE WAY YOU NORMALLY DO NOW?
OH... GOSH--!
YOU CAN TELL?
OF COURSE, COMMUNICATIONS POWERS. HOW DID YOU COME BY SUCH USEFUL GIFTS?
I JUST WENT TO A LOT OF DIFFERENT SCHOOLS. STATE ONES AND POSH ONES. BACK AND FORTH.
IT WAS EITHER GET SUPER-POWERS THAT CROSS CLASS BARRIERS OR DIE.
I'M A SORT OF INTERPRETER FOR THE KNIGHT. 'COS HE'S REALLY POSH. NOT UPPER UPPER MIDDLE CLASS LIKE YOU.
HE LIKES ME TO GIVE NEWCOMERS THE GEN ABOUT THIS PLACE...
BROX
GROG

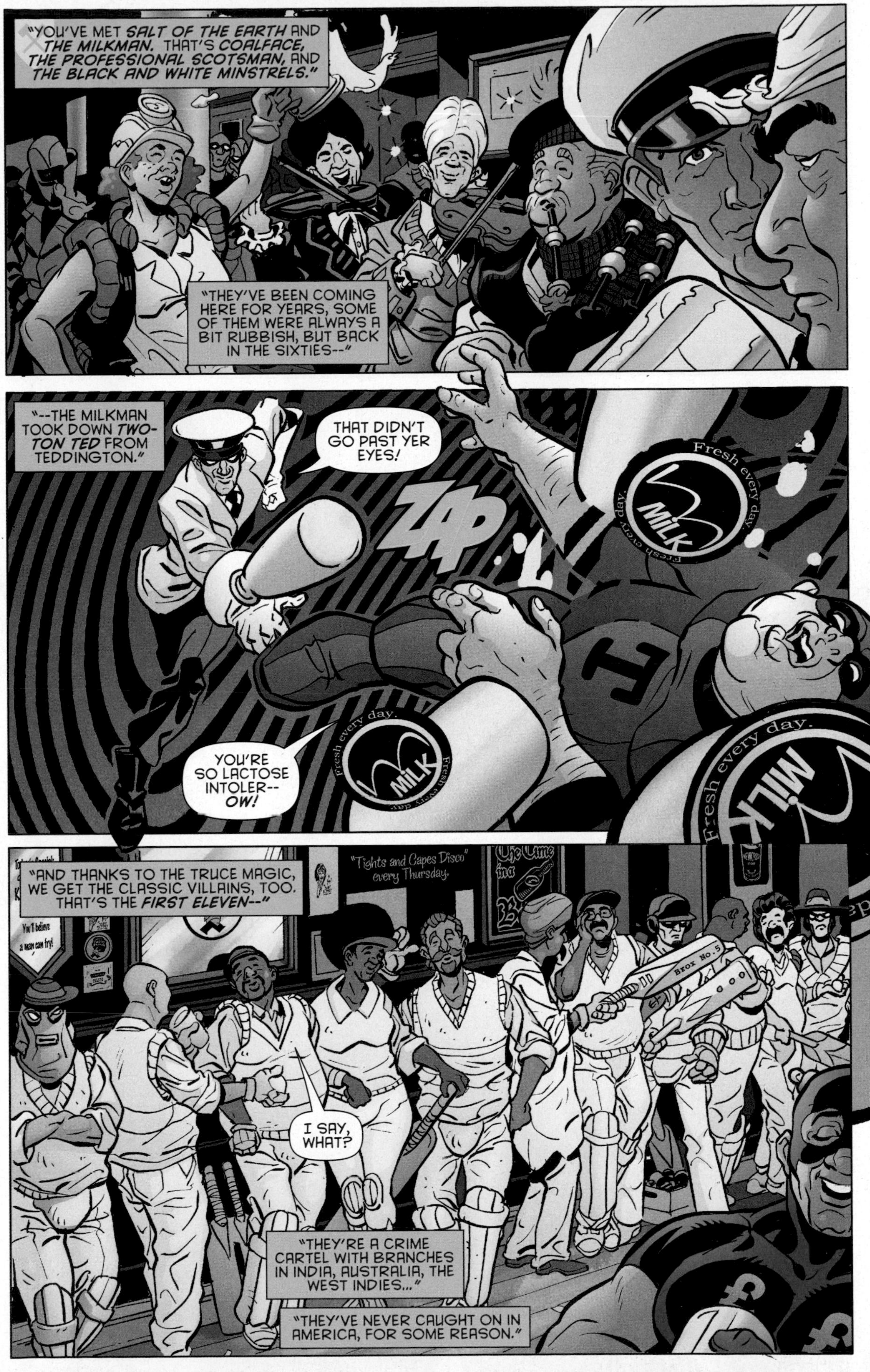
"YOU'VE MET SALT OF THE EARTH AND THE MILKMAN. THAT'S COALFACE, THE PROFESSIONAL SCOTSMAN, AND THE BLACK AND WHITE MINSTRELS."
"THEY'VE BEEN COMING HERE FOR YEARS, SOME OF THEM WERE ALWAYS A BIT RUBBISH, BUT BACK IN THE SIXTIES--"
"--THE MILKMAN TOOK DOWN TWO-TON TED FROM TEDDINGTON."
THAT DIDN'T GO PAST YER EYES!
ZAP
Fresh every day.
MILK
YOU'RE SO LACTOSE INTOLER-- OW!
"AND THANKS TO THE TRUCE MAGIC, WE GET THE CLASSIC VILLAINS, TOO. THAT'S THE FIRST ELEVEN--"
"Tights and Capes Disco" every Thursday.
You'll believe a man can fry!
Brox No. 5
I SAY, WHAT?
"THEY'RE A CRIME CARTEL WITH BRANCHES IN INDIA, AUSTRALIA, THE WEST INDIES..."
"THEY'VE NEVER CAUGHT ON IN AMERICA, FOR SOME REASON."

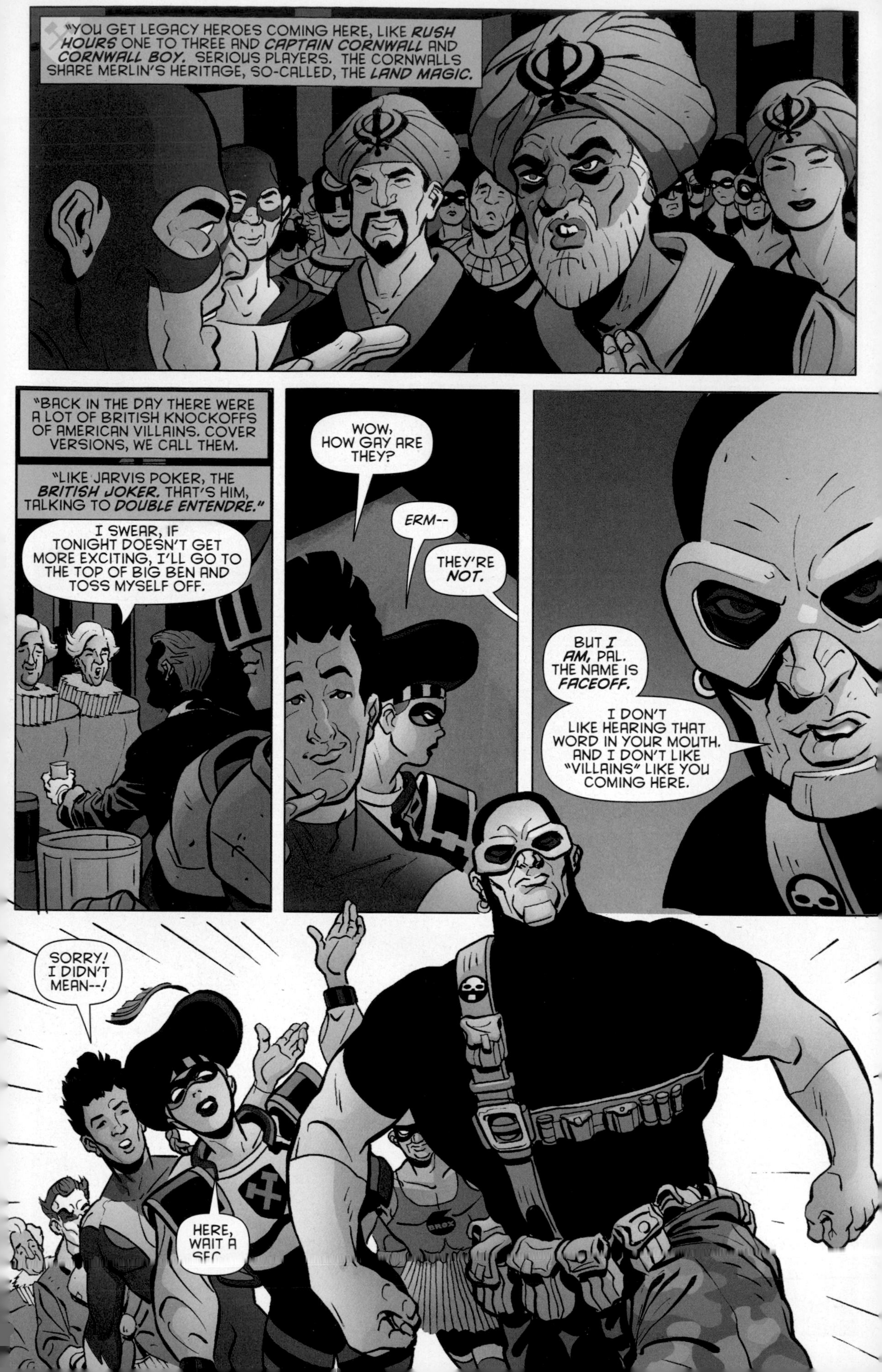
"YOU GET LEGACY HEROES COMING HERE, LIKE RUSH HOURS ONE TO THREE AND CAPTAIN CORNWALL AND CORNWALL BOY. SERIOUS PLAYERS. THE CORNWALLS SHARE MERLIN'S HERITAGE, SO-CALLED, THE LAND MAGIC.
"BACK IN THE DAY THERE WERE A LOT OF BRITISH KNOCKOFFS OF AMERICAN VILLAINS. COVER VERSIONS, WE CALL THEM.
"LIKE JARVIS POKER, THE BRITISH JOKER. THAT'S HIM, TALKING TO DOUBLE ENTENDRE."
I SWEAR, IF TONIGHT DOESN'T GET MORE EXCITING, I'LL GO TO THE TOP OF BIG BEN AND TOSS MYSELF OFF.
WOW, HOW GAY ARE THEY?
ERM--
THEY'RE NOT.
BUT I AM, PAL. THE NAME IS FACEOFF.
I DON'T LIKE HEARING THAT WORD IN YOUR MOUTH. AND I DON'T LIKE "VILLAINS" LIKE YOU COMING HERE.
SORRY! I DIDN'T MEAN--!
HERE, WAIT A SEC

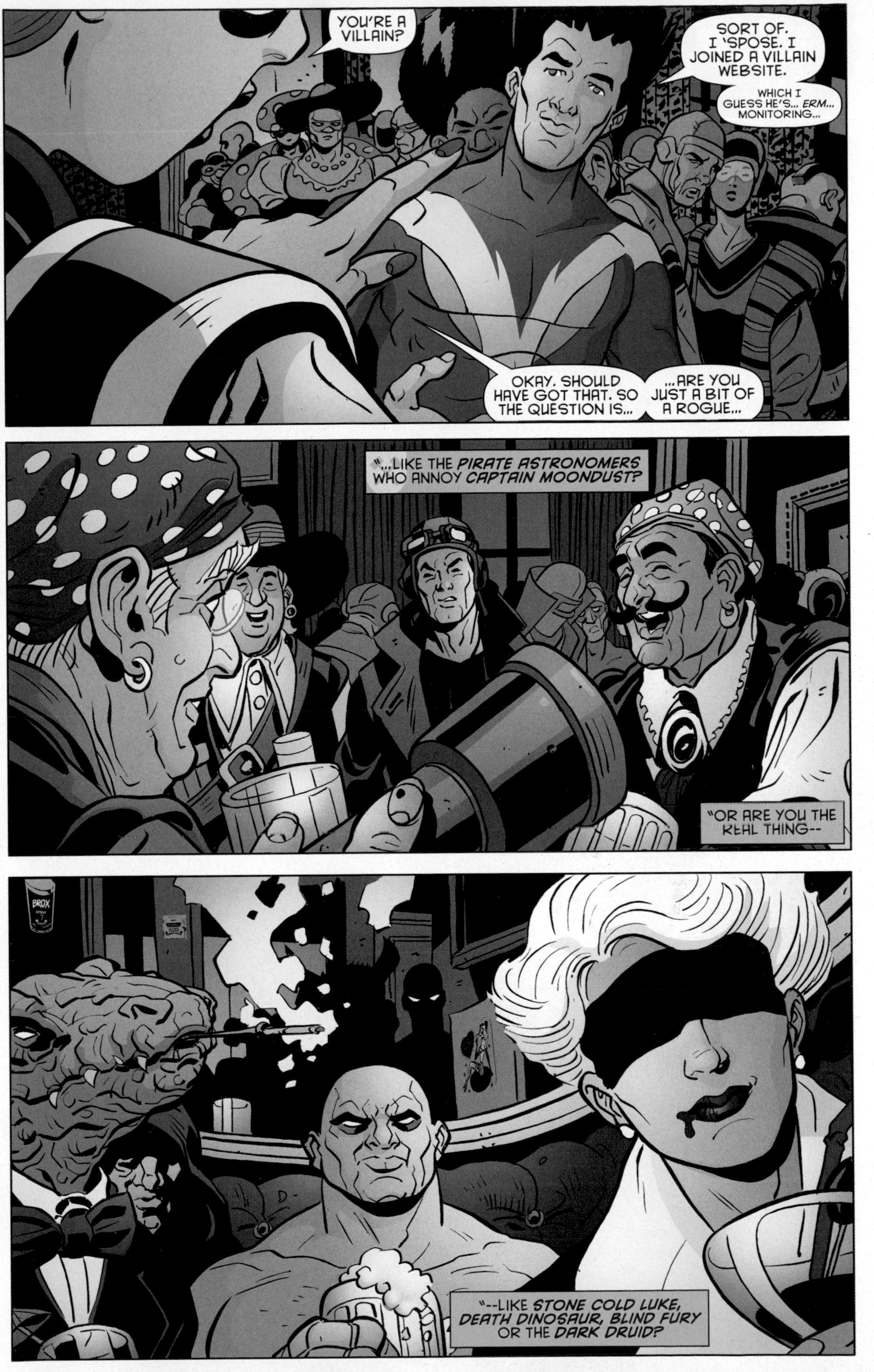
YOU'RE A VILLAIN?
SORT OF. I 'SPOSE. I JOINED A VILLAIN WEBSITE.
WHICH I GUESS HE'S... ERM... MONITORING...
OKAY. SHOULD HAVE GOT THAT. SO THE QUESTION IS...
...ARE YOU JUST A BIT OF A ROGUE...
"...LIKE THE PIRATE ASTRONOMERS WHO ANNOY CAPTAIN MOONDUST?
"OR ARE YOU THE REAL THING--
BROX STOUT
"--LIKE STONE COLD LUKE, DEATH DINOSAUR, BLIND FURY OR THE DARK DRUID?

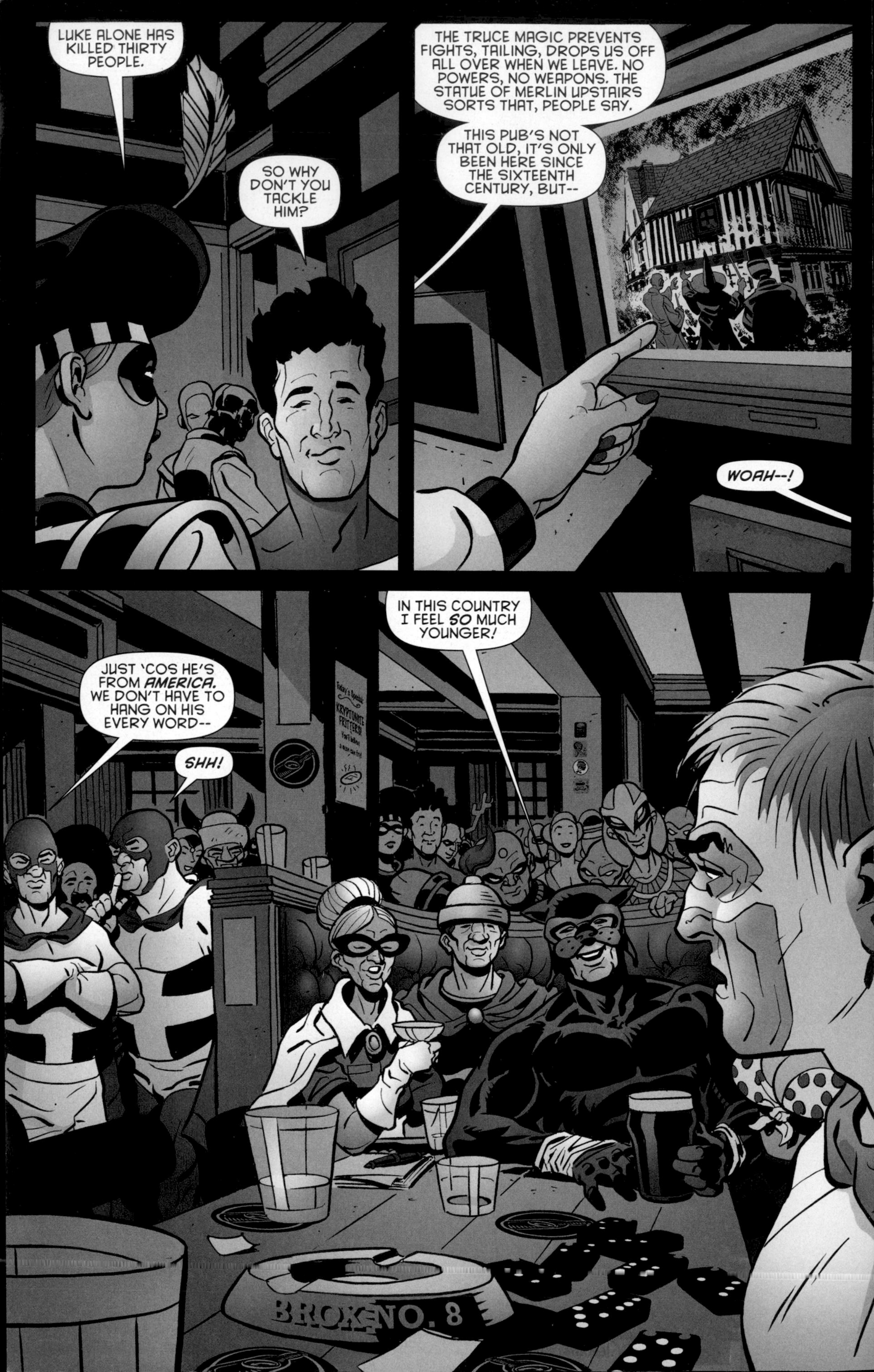
LUKE ALONE HAS KILLED THIRTY PEOPLE.
SO WHY DON'T YOU TACKLE HIM?
THE TRUCE MAGIC PREVENTS FIGHTS, TAILING, DROPS US OFF ALL OVER WHEN WE LEAVE. NO POWERS, NO WEAPONS. THE STATUE OF MERLIN UPSTAIRS SORTS THAT, PEOPLE SAY.
THIS PUB'S NOT THAT OLD, IT'S ONLY BEEN HERE SINCE THE SIXTEENTH CENTURY, BUT--
WOAH--!
JUST 'COS HE'S FROM *AMERICA*, WE DON'T HAVE TO HANG ON HIS EVERY WORD--
SHH!
IN THIS COUNTRY I FEEL *SO* MUCH YOUNGER!
Today's Special
KRYPTONITE FRITTERS!
You'll believe a man can fry!
BROK NO. 8

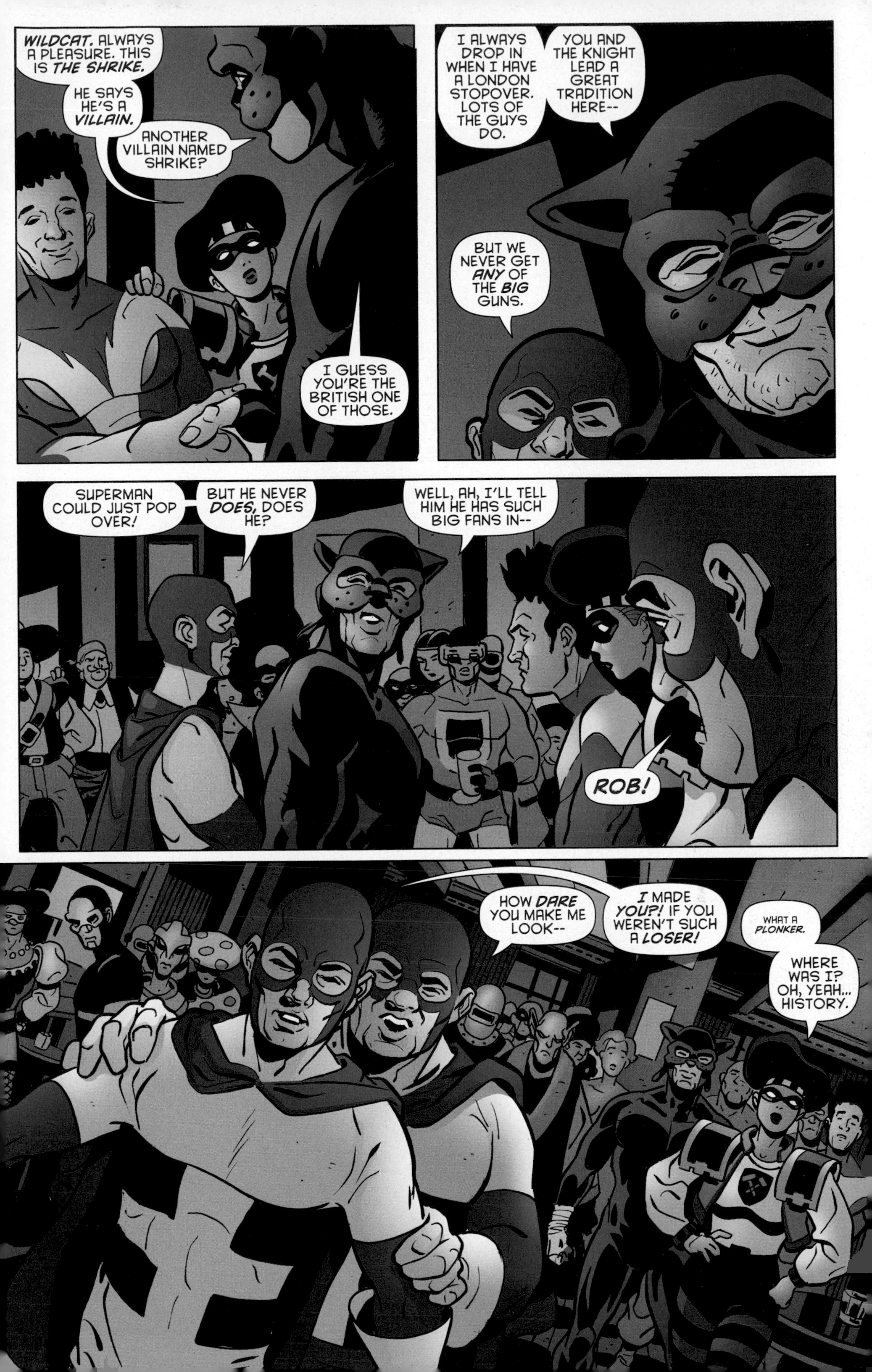
WILDCAT. ALWAYS A PLEASURE. THIS IS THE SHRIKE.
HE SAYS HE'S A VILLAIN.
ANOTHER VILLAIN NAMED SHRIKE?
I GUESS YOU'RE THE BRITISH ONE OF THOSE.
I ALWAYS DROP IN WHEN I HAVE A LONDON STOPOVER. LOTS OF THE GUYS DO.
YOU AND THE KNIGHT LEAD A GREAT TRADITION HERE--
BUT WE NEVER GET ANY OF THE BIG GUNS.
SUPERMAN COULD JUST POP OVER!
BUT HE NEVER DOES, DOES HE?
WELL, AH, I'LL TELL HIM HE HAS SUCH BIG FANS IN--
ROB!
HOW DARE YOU MAKE ME LOOK--
I MADE YOU?! IF YOU WEREN'T SUCH A LOSER!
WHAT A PLONKER.
WHERE WAS I? OH, YEAH... HISTORY.

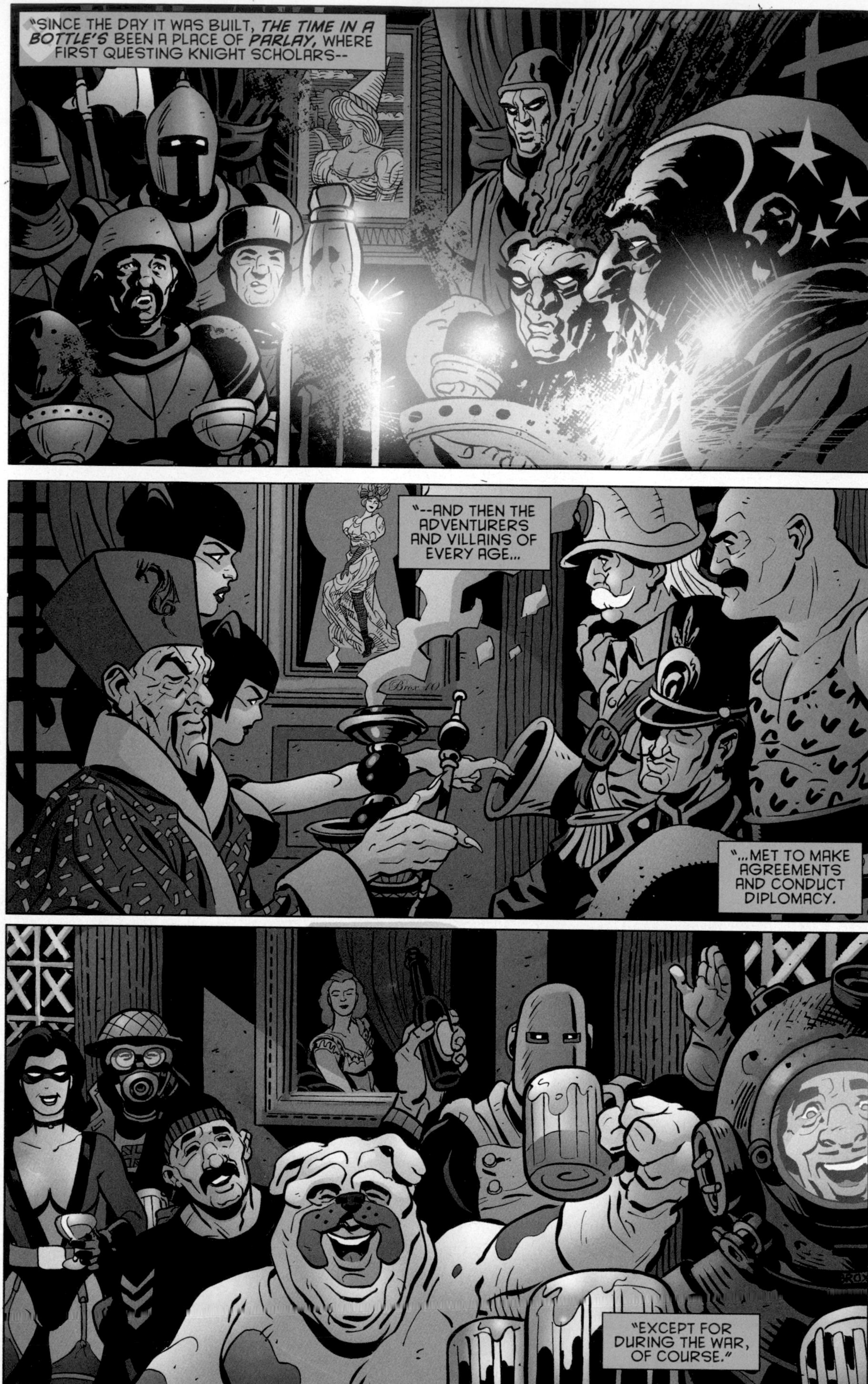
"SINCE THE DAY IT WAS BUILT, THE TIME IN A BOTTLE'S BEEN A PLACE OF PARLAY, WHERE FIRST QUESTING KNIGHT SCHOLARS--
"--AND THEN THE ADVENTURERS AND VILLAINS OF EVERY AGE...
"...MET TO MAKE AGREEMENTS AND CONDUCT DIPLOMACY.
"EXCEPT FOR DURING THE WAR, OF COURSE."

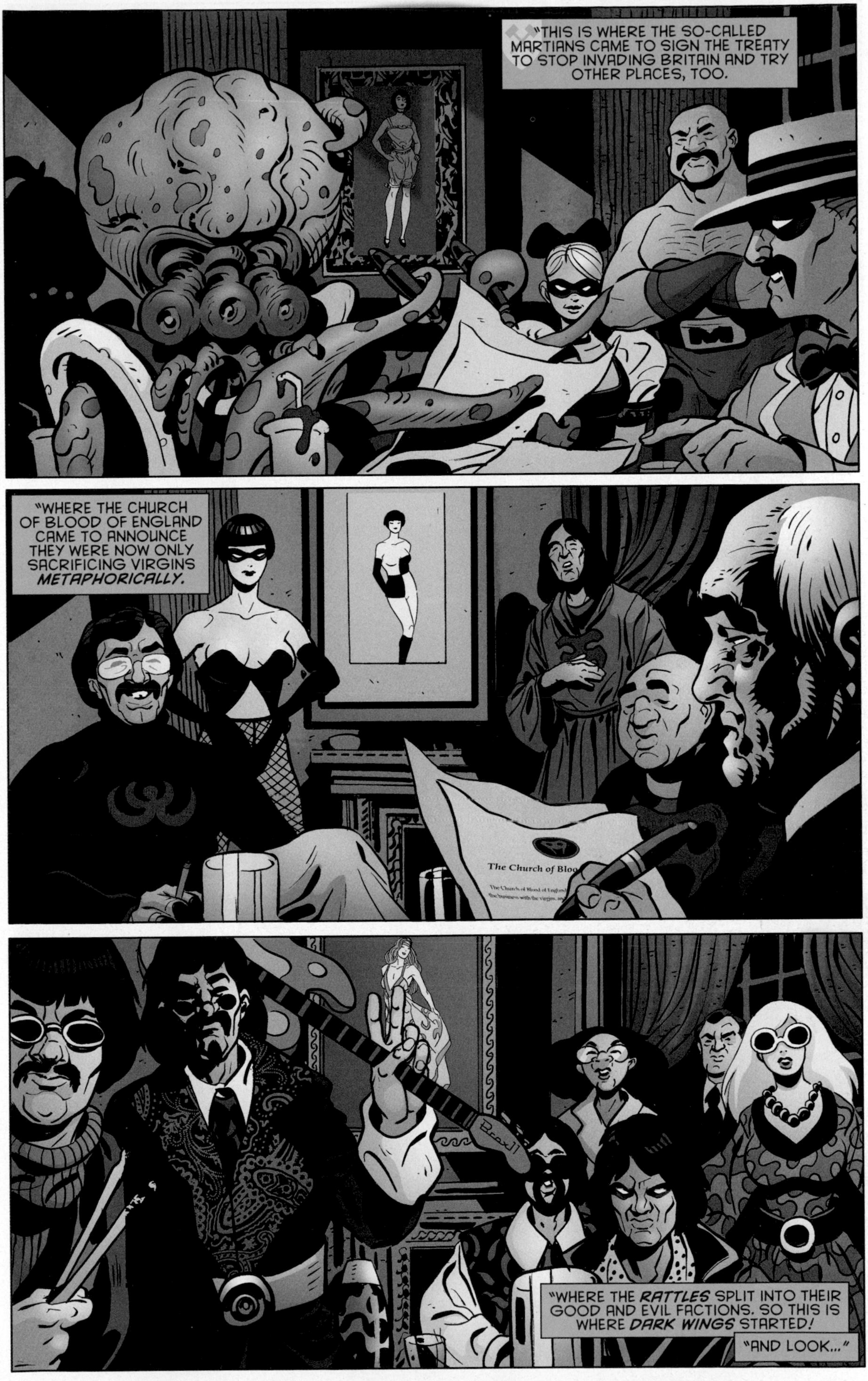
"THIS IS WHERE THE SO-CALLED MARTIANS CAME TO SIGN THE TREATY TO STOP INVADING BRITAIN AND TRY OTHER PLACES, TOO.
"WHERE THE CHURCH OF BLOOD OF ENGLAND CAME TO ANNOUNCE THEY WERE NOW ONLY SACRIFICING VIRGINS *METAPHORICALLY*.
The Church of Bloo
"WHERE THE *RATTLES* SPLIT INTO THEIR GOOD AND EVIL FACTIONS. SO THIS IS WHERE *DARK WINGS* STARTED!
"AND LOOK..."

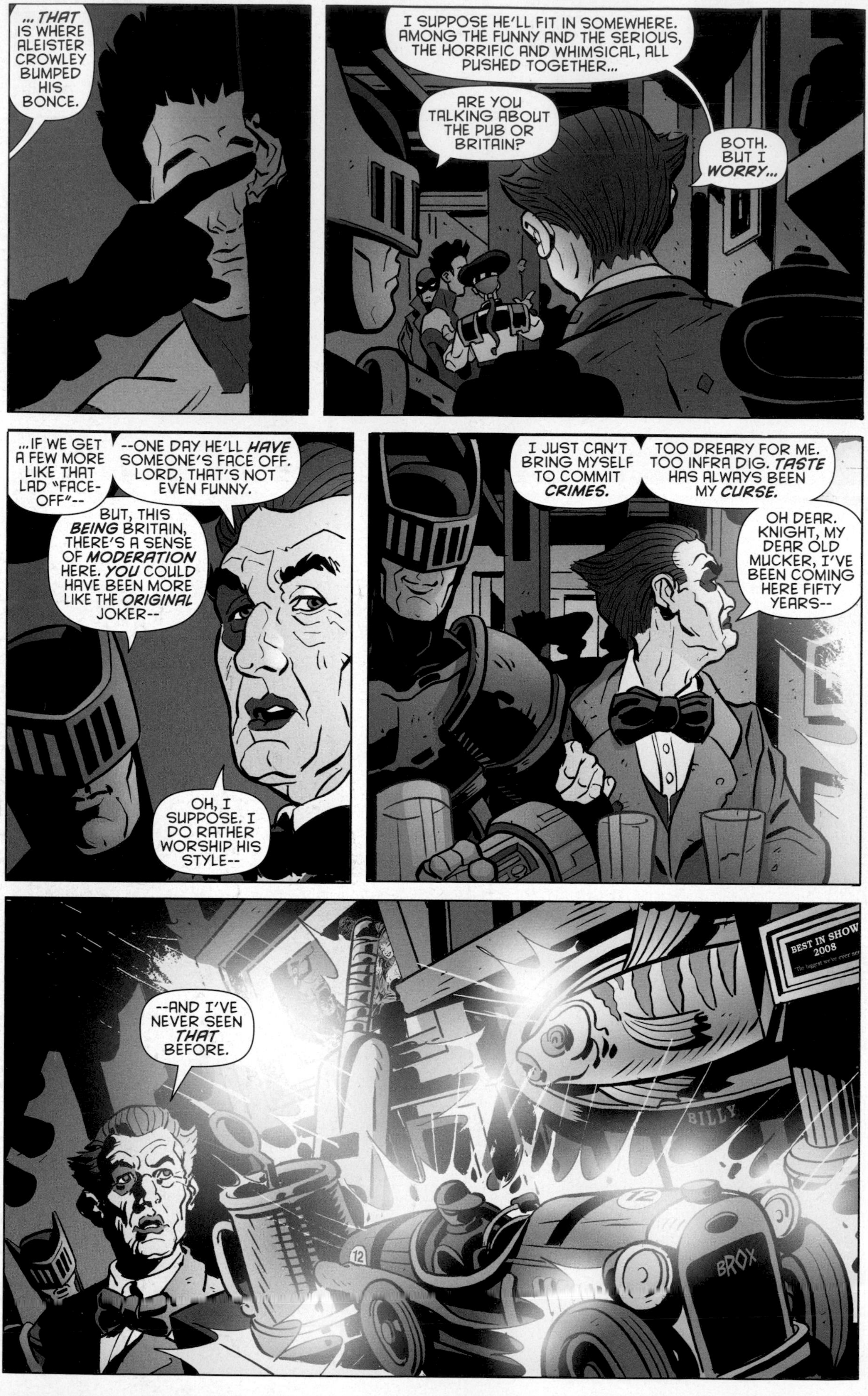
...THAT IS WHERE ALEISTER CROWLEY BUMPED HIS BONCE.
I SUPPOSE HE'LL FIT IN SOMEWHERE. AMONG THE FUNNY AND THE SERIOUS, THE HORRIFIC AND WHIMSICAL, ALL PUSHED TOGETHER...
ARE YOU TALKING ABOUT THE PUB OR BRITAIN?
BOTH. BUT I WORRY...
...IF WE GET A FEW MORE LIKE THAT LAD "FACE-OFF"--
--ONE DAY HE'LL HAVE SOMEONE'S FACE OFF. LORD, THAT'S NOT EVEN FUNNY.
BUT, THIS BEING BRITAIN, THERE'S A SENSE OF MODERATION HERE. YOU COULD HAVE BEEN MORE LIKE THE ORIGINAL JOKER--
OH, I SUPPOSE. I DO RATHER WORSHIP HIS STYLE--
I JUST CAN'T BRING MYSELF TO COMMIT CRIMES.
TOO DREARY FOR ME. TOO INFRA DIG. TASTE HAS ALWAYS BEEN MY CURSE.
OH DEAR. KNIGHT, MY DEAR OLD MUCKER, I'VE BEEN COMING HERE FIFTY YEARS--
--AND I'VE NEVER SEEN THAT BEFORE.
BEST IN SHOW 2008
BILLY
12
BROX

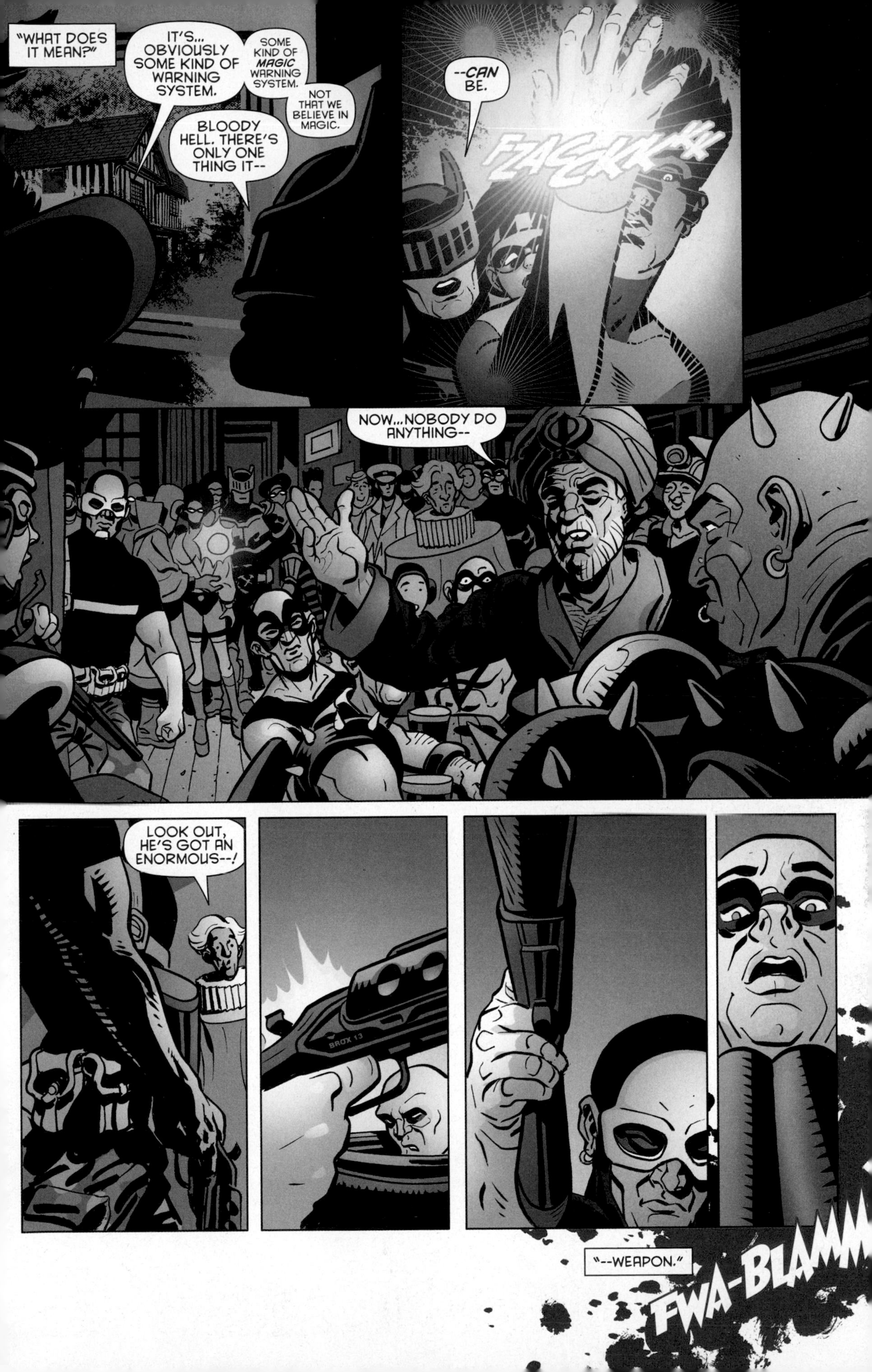
"WHAT DOES IT MEAN?"
IT'S... OBVIOUSLY SOME KIND OF WARNING SYSTEM.
SOME KIND OF MAGIC WARNING SYSTEM.
NOT THAT WE BELIEVE IN MAGIC.
BLOODY HELL. THERE'S ONLY ONE THING IT--
--CAN BE.
FZASKK
NOW... NOBODY DO ANYTHING--
LOOK OUT, HE'S GOT AN ENORMOUS--!
BROX 13
"--WEAPON."
FWA-BLAMM

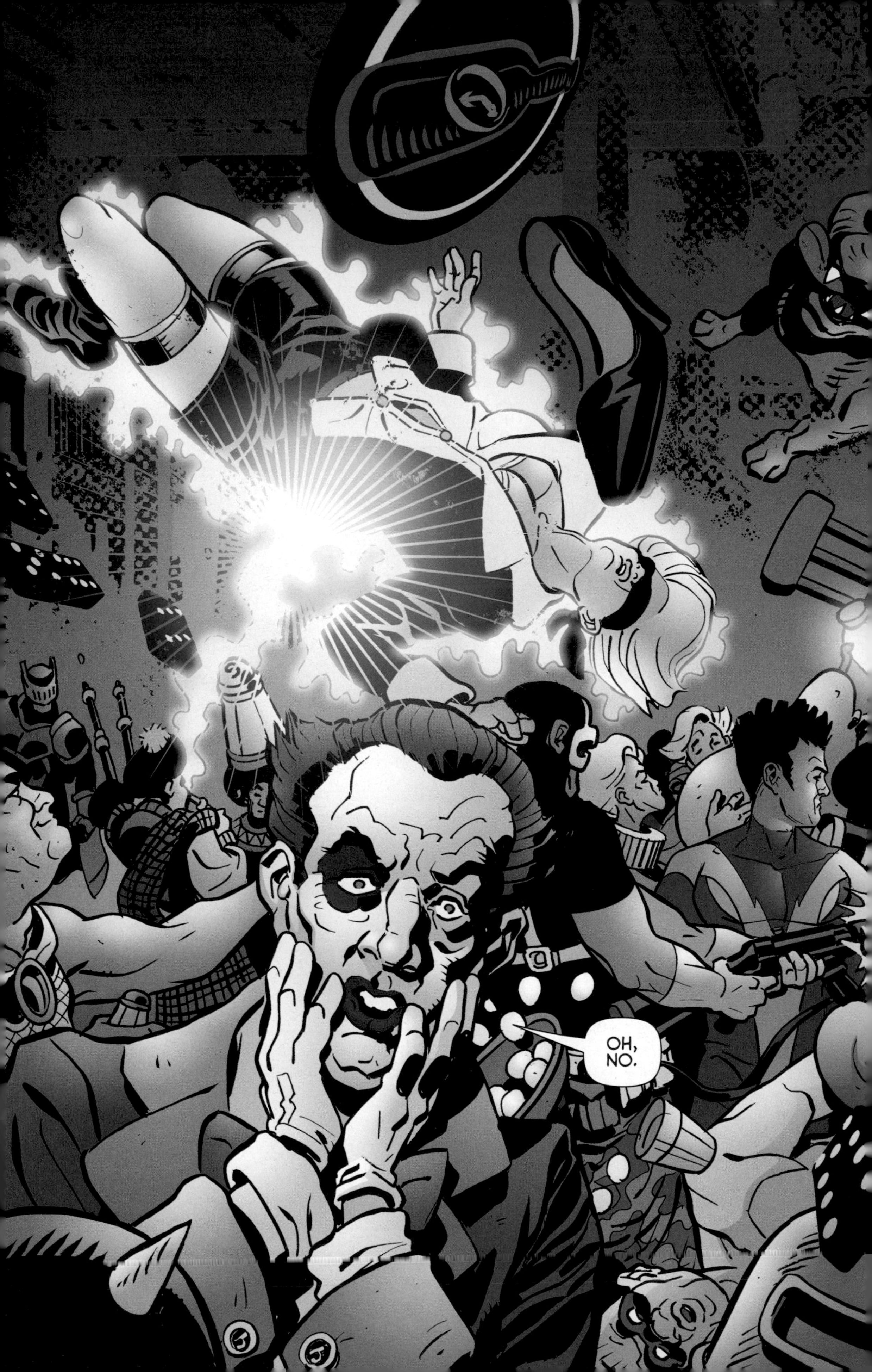
OH, NO.

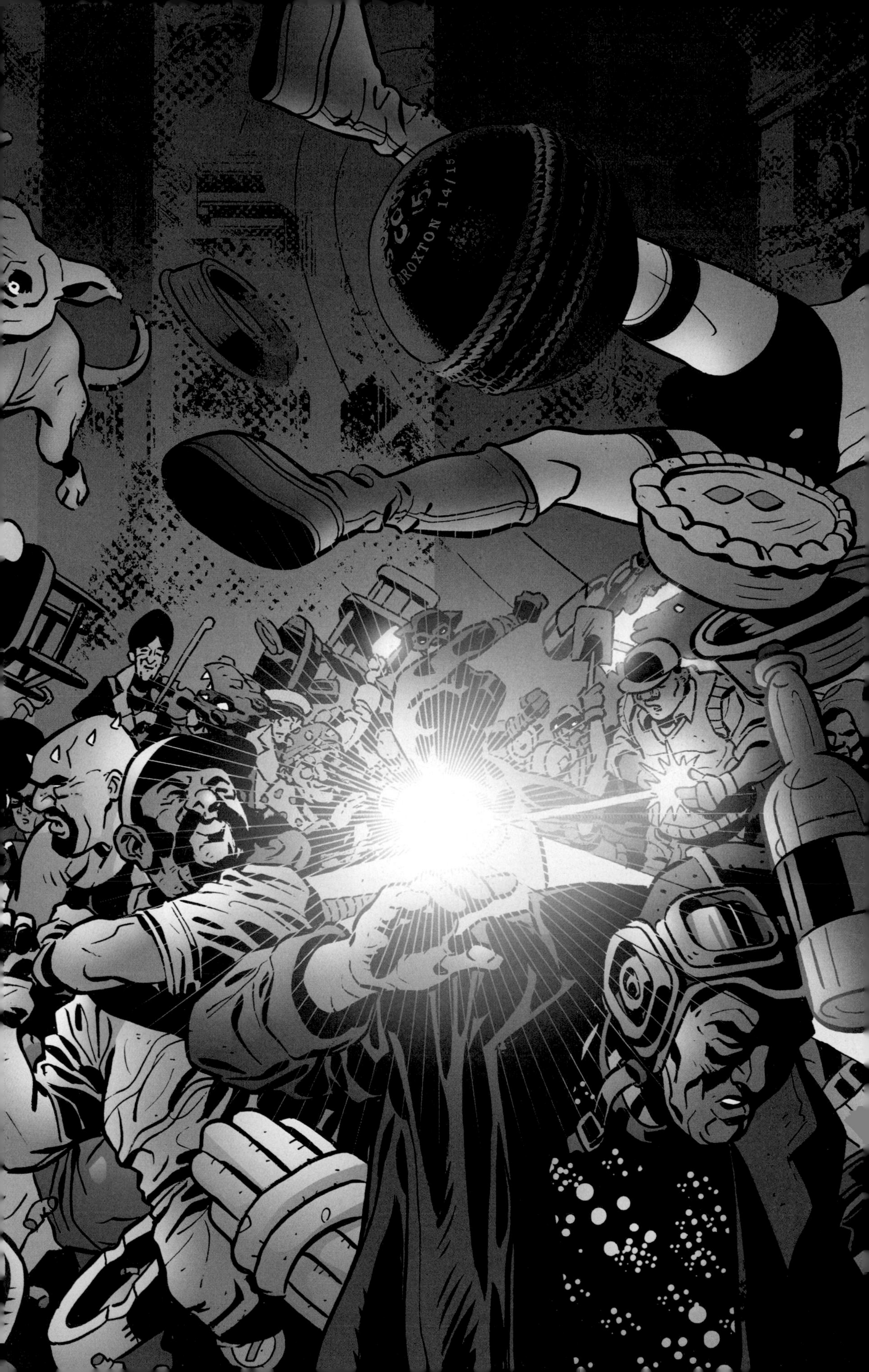
BROXTON 14/15

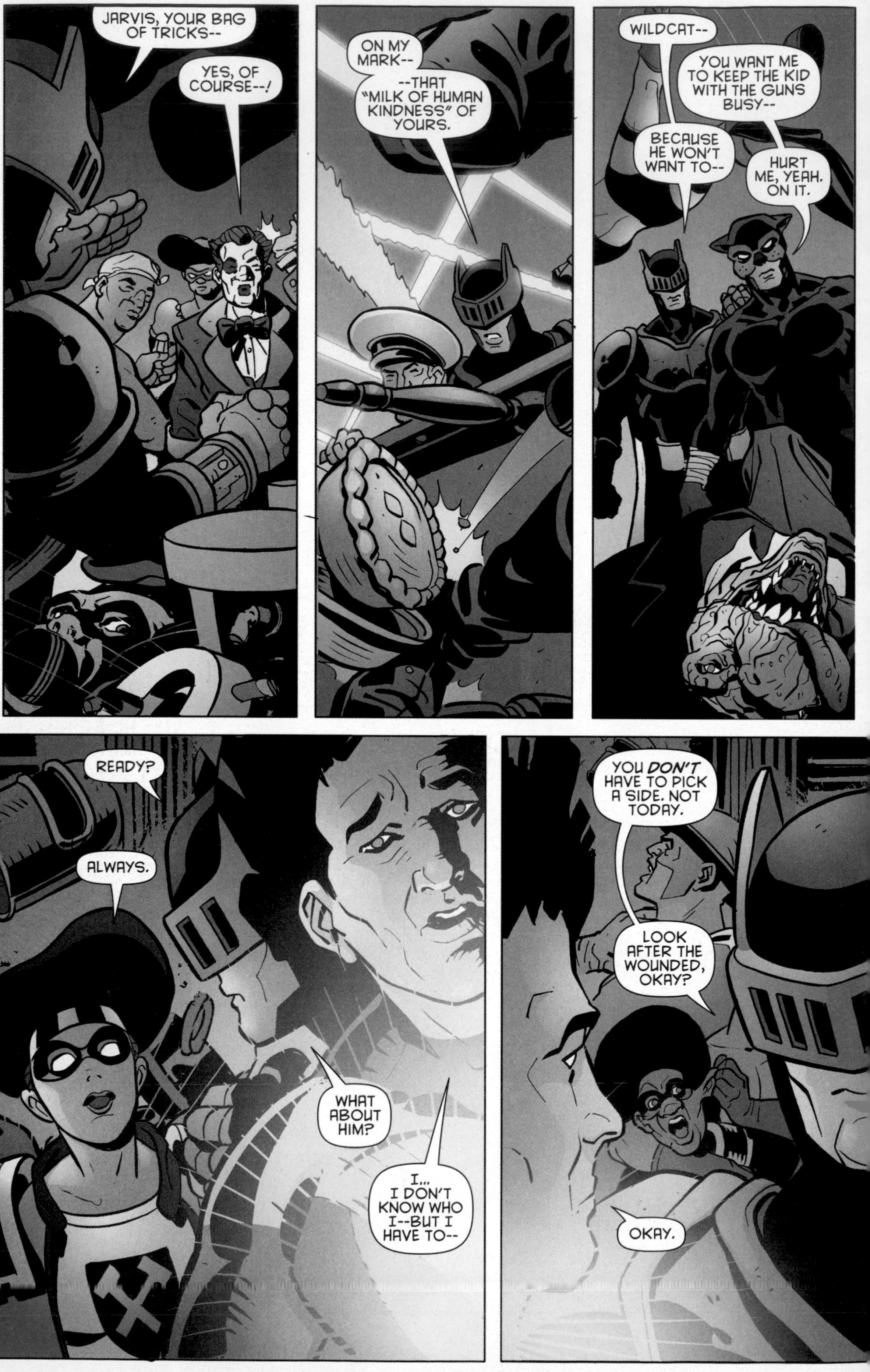
JARVIS, YOUR BAG OF TRICKS--
YES, OF COURSE--!
ON MY MARK--
--THAT "MILK OF HUMAN KINDNESS" OF YOURS.
WILDCAT--
YOU WANT ME TO KEEP THE KID WITH THE GUNS BUSY--
BECAUSE HE WON'T WANT TO--
HURT ME, YEAH. ON IT.
READY?
ALWAYS.
WHAT ABOUT HIM?
I... I DON'T KNOW WHO I--BUT I HAVE TO--
YOU *DON'T* HAVE TO PICK A SIDE. NOT TODAY.
LOOK AFTER THE WOUNDED, OKAY?
OKAY.

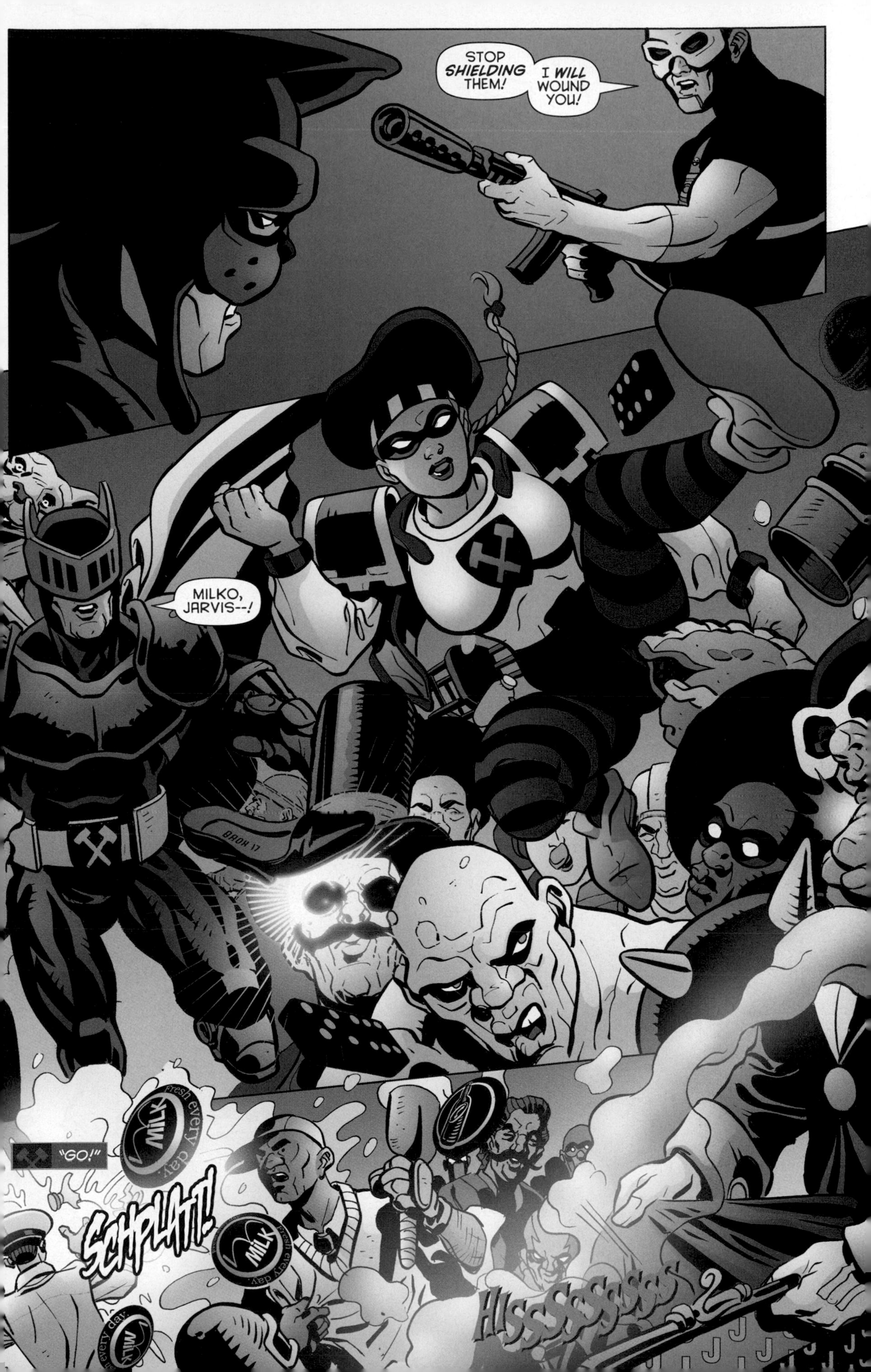
STOP SHIELDING THEM!
I WILL WOUND YOU!
MILKO, JARVIS--!
"GO!"
SCHPLATT!
HISSSSSSSSS

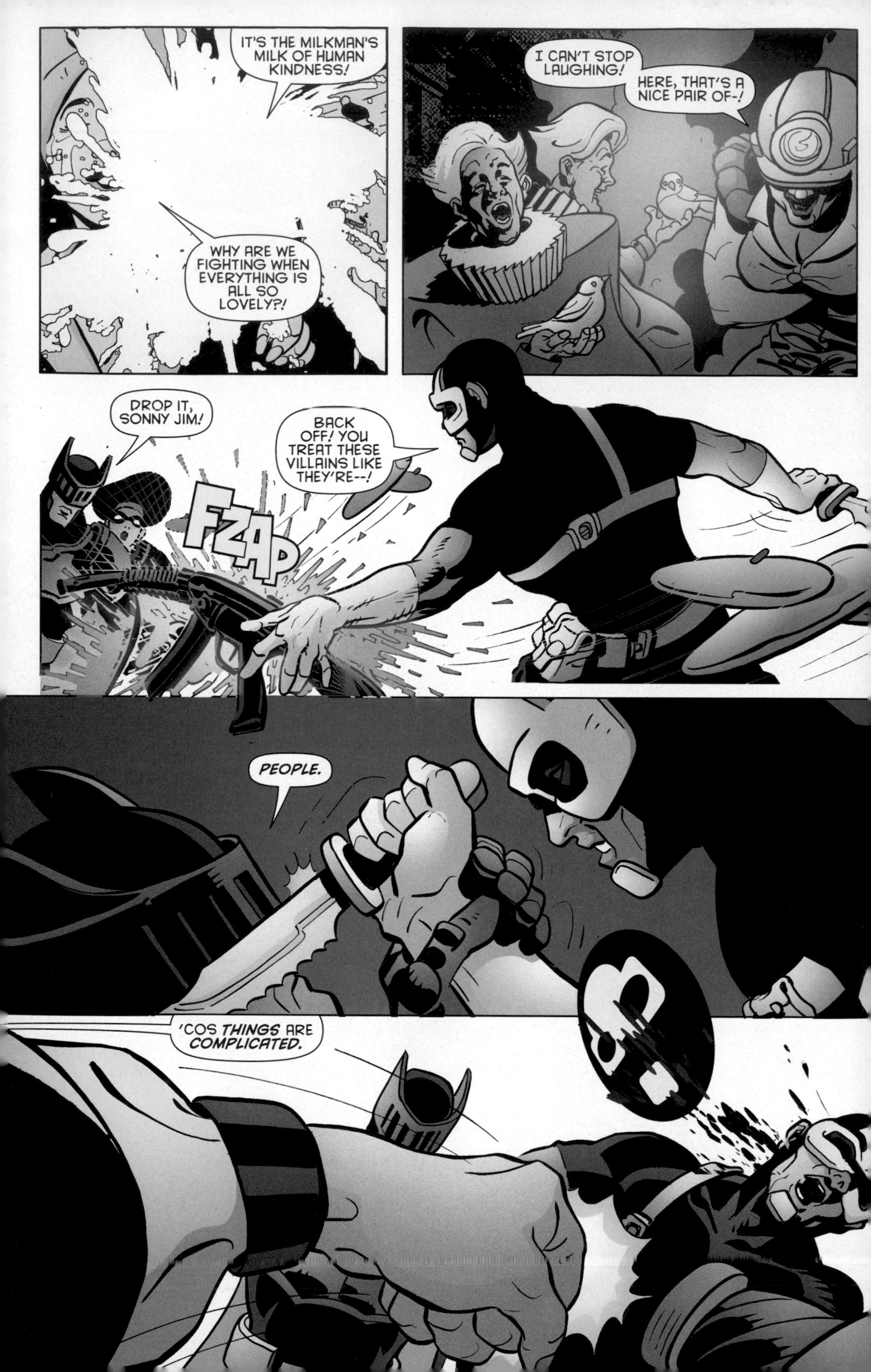
IT'S THE MILKMAN'S MILK OF HUMAN KINDNESS!
WHY ARE WE FIGHTING WHEN EVERYTHING IS ALL SO LOVELY?!
I CAN'T STOP LAUGHING!
HERE, THAT'S A NICE PAIR OF-!
DROP IT, SONNY JIM!
BACK OFF! YOU TREAT THESE VILLAINS LIKE THEY'RE--!
FZAP
PEOPLE.
'COS THINGS ARE COMPLICATED.

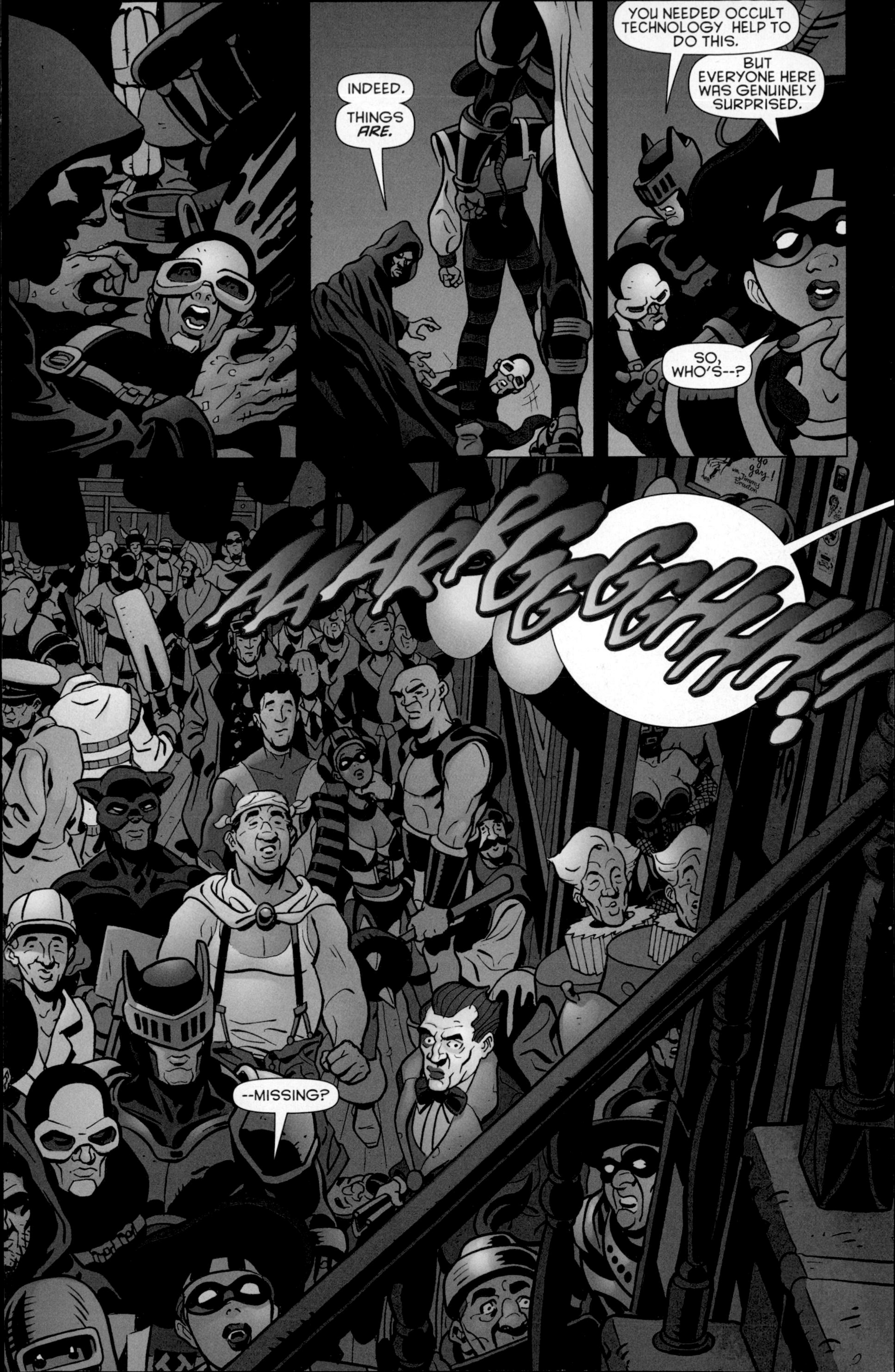
INDEED.
THINGS *ARE.*
YOU NEEDED OCCULT TECHNOLOGY HELP TO DO THIS.
BUT EVERYONE HERE WAS GENUINELY SURPRISED.
SO, WHO'S--?
AAARRGGGHHH!!
--MISSING?

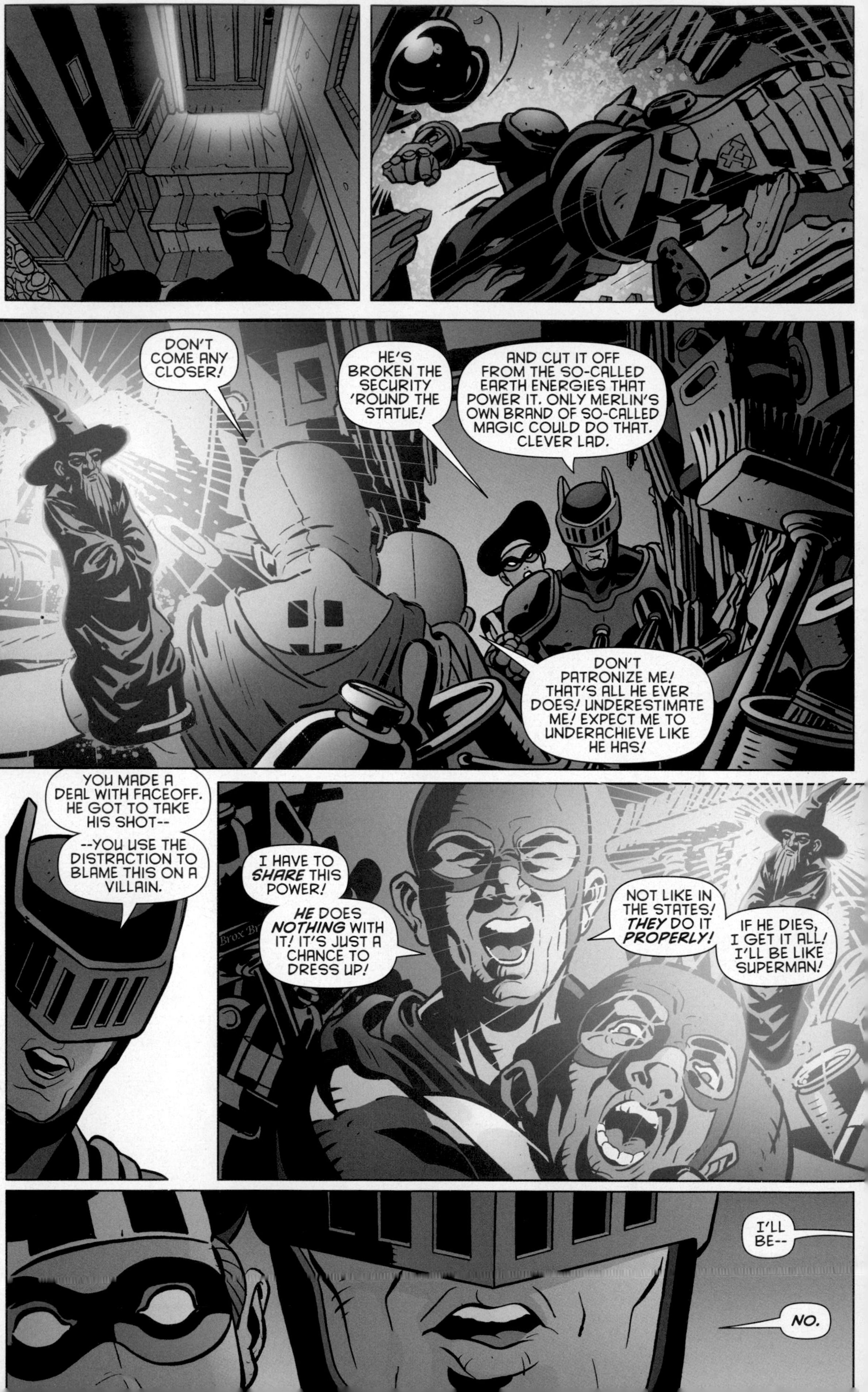
DON'T COME ANY CLOSER!
HE'S BROKEN THE SECURITY 'ROUND THE STATUE!
AND CUT IT OFF FROM THE SO-CALLED EARTH ENERGIES THAT POWER IT. ONLY MERLIN'S OWN BRAND OF SO-CALLED MAGIC COULD DO THAT. CLEVER LAD.
DON'T PATRONIZE ME! THAT'S ALL HE EVER DOES! UNDERESTIMATE ME! EXPECT ME TO UNDERACHIEVE LIKE HE HAS!
YOU MADE A DEAL WITH FACEOFF. HE GOT TO TAKE HIS SHOT--
--YOU USE THE DISTRACTION TO BLAME THIS ON A VILLAIN.
I HAVE TO SHARE THIS POWER!
HE DOES NOTHING WITH IT! IT'S JUST A CHANCE TO DRESS UP!
NOT LIKE IN THE STATES! THEY DO IT PROPERLY!
IF HE DIES, I GET IT ALL! I'LL BE LIKE SUPERMAN!
I'LL BE--
NO.

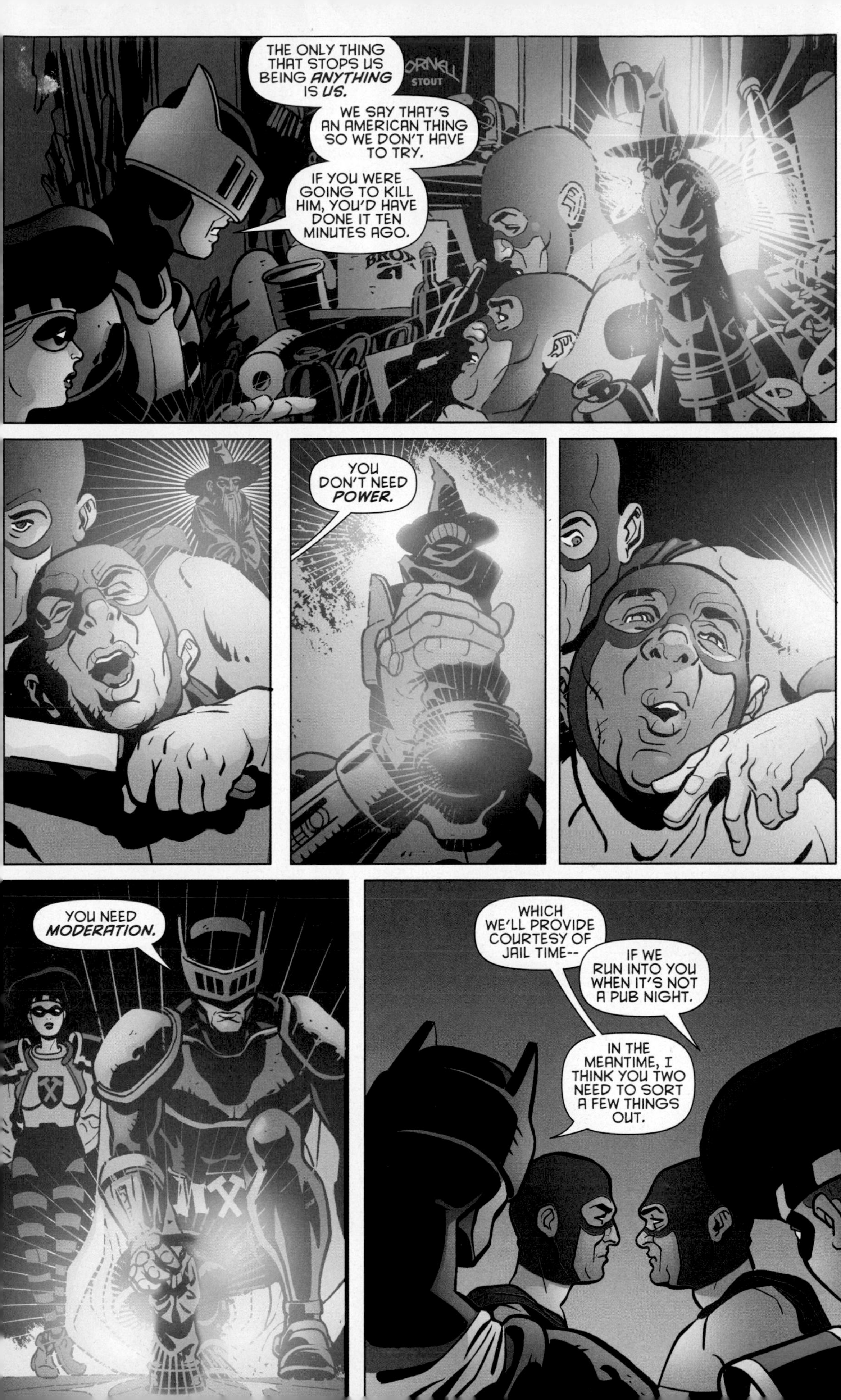
THE ONLY THING THAT STOPS US BEING *ANYTHING* IS *US.*
WE SAY THAT'S AN AMERICAN THING SO WE DON'T HAVE TO TRY.
IF YOU WERE GOING TO KILL HIM, YOU'D HAVE DONE IT TEN MINUTES AGO.
STOUT
YOU DON'T NEED *POWER.*
YOU NEED *MODERATION.*
WHICH WE'LL PROVIDE COURTESY OF JAIL TIME--
IF WE RUN INTO YOU WHEN IT'S NOT A PUB NIGHT.
IN THE MEANTIME, I THINK YOU TWO NEED TO SORT A FEW THINGS OUT.

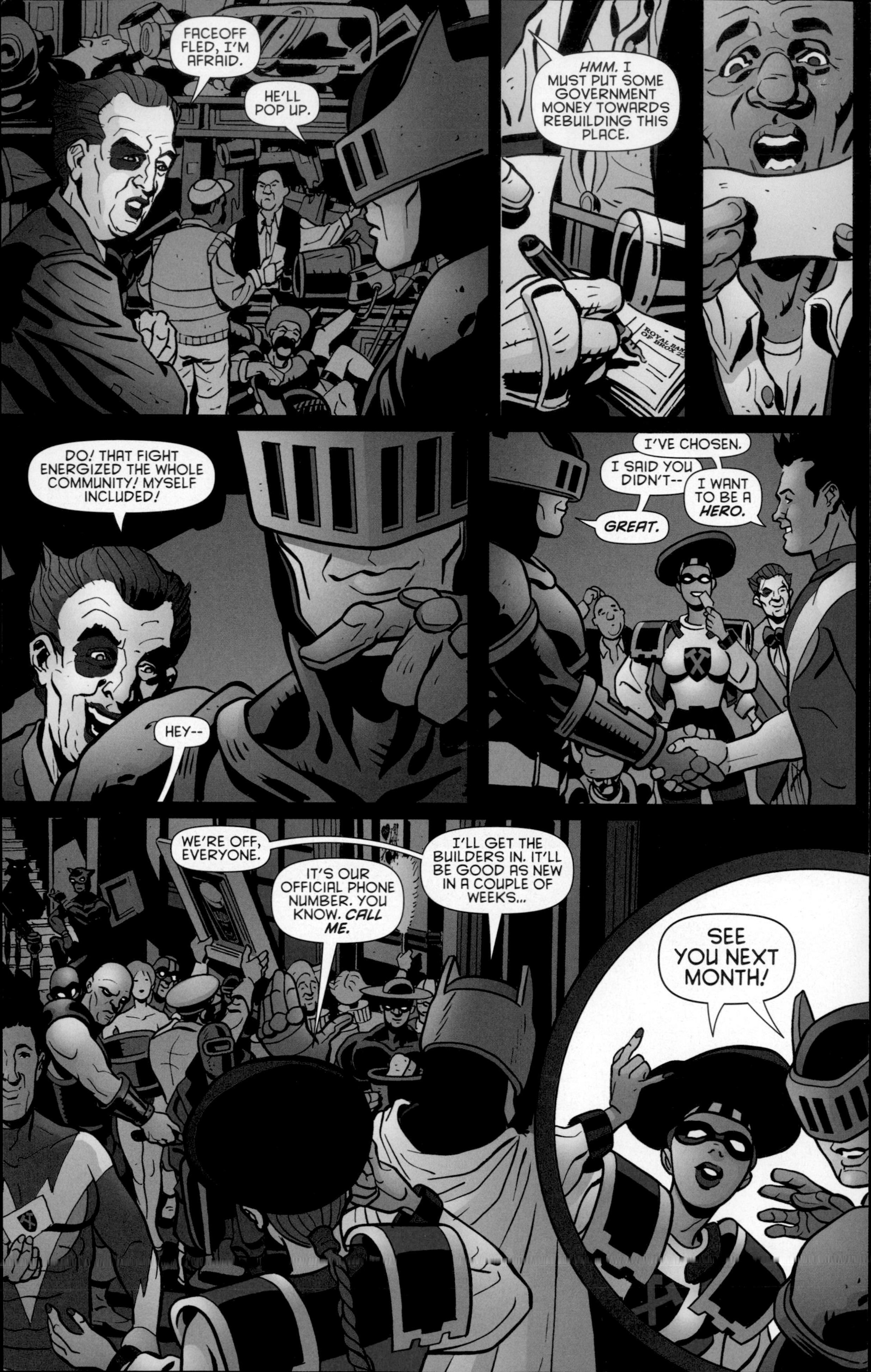
FACEOFF FLED, I'M AFRAID.
HE'LL POP UP.
HMM. I MUST PUT SOME GOVERNMENT MONEY TOWARDS REBUILDING THIS PLACE.
DO! THAT FIGHT ENERGIZED THE WHOLE COMMUNITY! MYSELF INCLUDED!
HEY--
I'VE CHOSEN.
I SAID YOU DIDN'T--
I WANT TO BE A ***HERO.***
GREAT.
WE'RE OFF, EVERYONE.
IT'S OUR OFFICIAL PHONE NUMBER. YOU KNOW. ***CALL ME.***
I'LL GET THE BUILDERS IN. IT'LL BE GOOD AS NEW IN A COUPLE OF WEEKS...
SEE YOU NEXT MONTH!

What You Missed If You're A Non-Brit
(not that there's anything wrong with that).

WE'RE AWARE THAT, THROUGH NO FAULT OF THEIR OWN, MANY (MOST EVEN, IF WE'RE LUCKY) OF OUR READERS ARE FROM THE COLONIES. SO WE THOUGHT THAT A QUICK GUIDE TO SOME OF THE CULTURAL REFERENCES MIGHT GIVE YOU A BETTER APPRECIATION OF THIS ISSUE'S CONTENTS.

- "A BEAR OF VERY LITTLE BRAIN" IS HOW WINNIE-THE-POOH THOUGHT OF HIMSELF.
- JARVIS POKER FOLLOWS THE BRITISH COMIC TRADITION OF HAVING ONE'S JOB DESCRIPTION RHYME WITH ONE'S NAME, REVIVED MORE RECENTLY BY VIZ.
- SALT OF THE EARTH IS A SEASIDE POSTCARD IMAGE OF THE BRITISH WORKING MAN ON HOLIDAY, LATER TAKEN UP BY MONTY PYTHON AND THE SEX PISTOLS.
- THE BLACK AND WHITE MINSTRELS: NAMED AFTER AN UNFORTUNATE BRITISH TV BLACKED-UP "MINSTREL SHOW" WHICH RAN UNTIL 1978 (!)
- TWO TON TED FROM TEDDINGTON: FAMILIAR TO THOSE WHO SENT BENNY HILL'S 'ERNIE: THE FASTEST MILKMAN IN THE WEST' SINGLE TO NUMBER ONE IN 1971.
- THE LEADER OF THE PIRATE ASTRONOMERS, WITH HIS MONOCLE, LOOKS A BIT LIKE BRITISH TV ASTRONOMY LEGEND PATRICK MOORE.
- DEATH DINOSAUR IS REMINISCENT OF A STRANGELY WELL-DRESSED MONSTER FROM A 1970s TOP TRUMPS "HORROR" CARD GAME PACK.

WE TRUST THE REFERENCES TO MERLIN (WHO'S IN HERE SOMEWHERE, IN A FAMILIAR GUISE), ALEISTER CROWLEY, PAUL McCARTNEY AND THE CHURCH OF ENGLAND WON'T PASS BY THOSE OF EVEN SLIGHTLY ANGLOPHILE BENT. MUCH OF THE SLANG REMAINS UNTRANSLATED TO SPARE YOUR BLUSHES (AND THOSE OF OUR LADY EDITOR).

UNTIL NEXT ISSUE,
CHEERIO!
- PAUL CORNELL

brought to you by

KNIGHT AND SQUIRE

HEXO
Magic Seasoning!

ADD A LITTLE MAGIC TO MEALTIMES

After a hard day's crime fighting, giving some evil bugger a punch up the bracket. I like nothing better, than to come home to a nice bit of supper, lovingly prepared by her indoors.
Especially seeing as though, she'll have sprinkled in a bit of something special, just the way I like it. Hexo makes any dish... delish, in just a couple of shakes!
Don't give it the dog though, I made that mistake last month, bloody article, the rug in the front room will never be the same again.
Or the dog for that matter. Blimey"

Salt of the Earth says:
"Hexo makes any dish... delish, with only a couple of shakes!

HEXO *Magic Seasoning!*

Avoid contact with sore or broken skin, do not get into the eyes, if this occurs: rinse with cold water immediately and seek medical advice. Not suitable for children or staffordshire bull terriers.

All purpose* seasoning for: chops, pies, soups, gravy, puddings and more!

ad by Jimmy Broxton

*not for crime fighting use

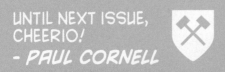

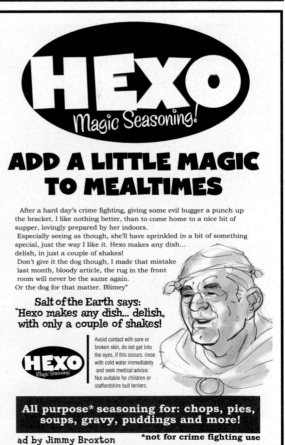

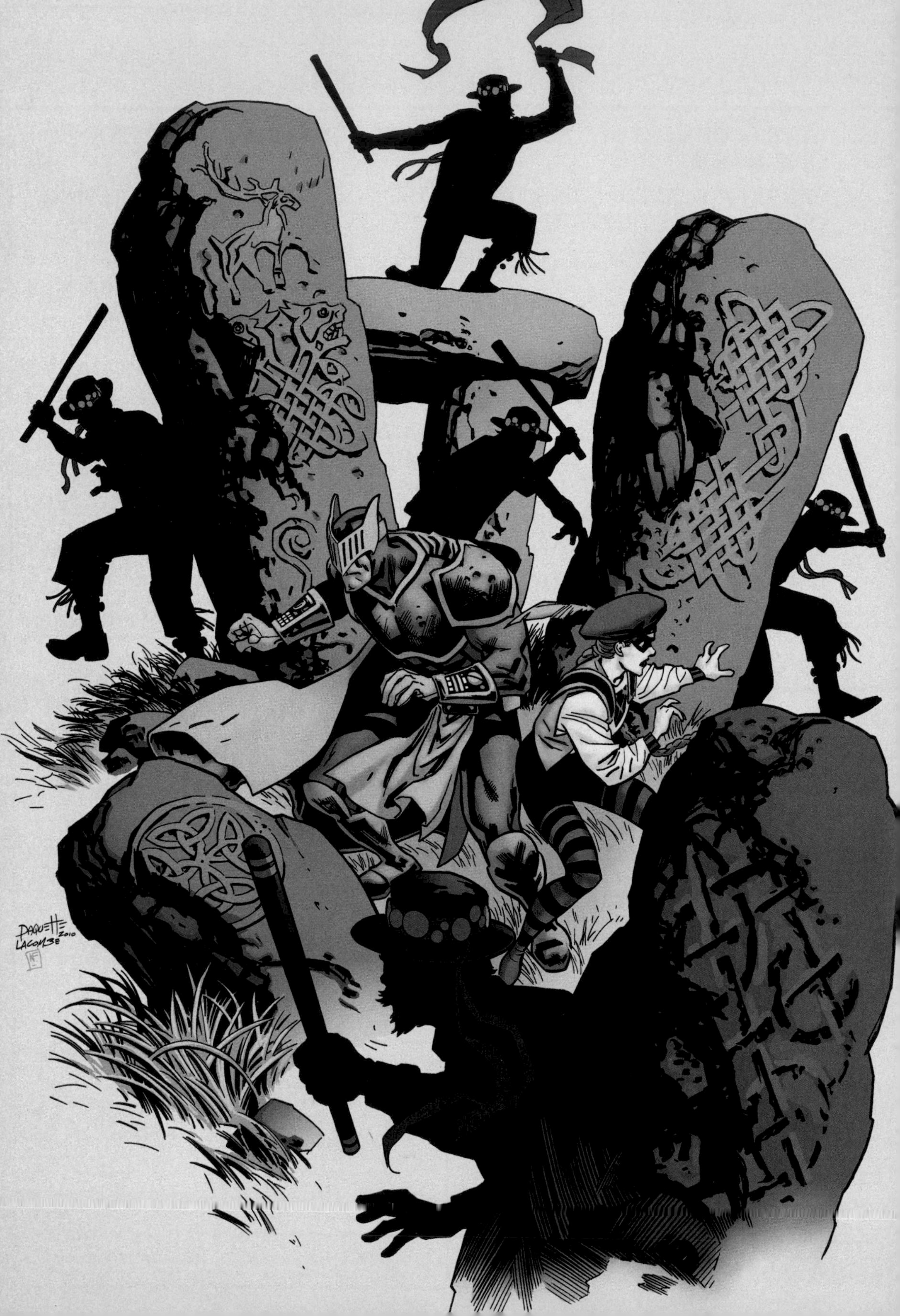
PAQUETTE
LACOMBE 2010

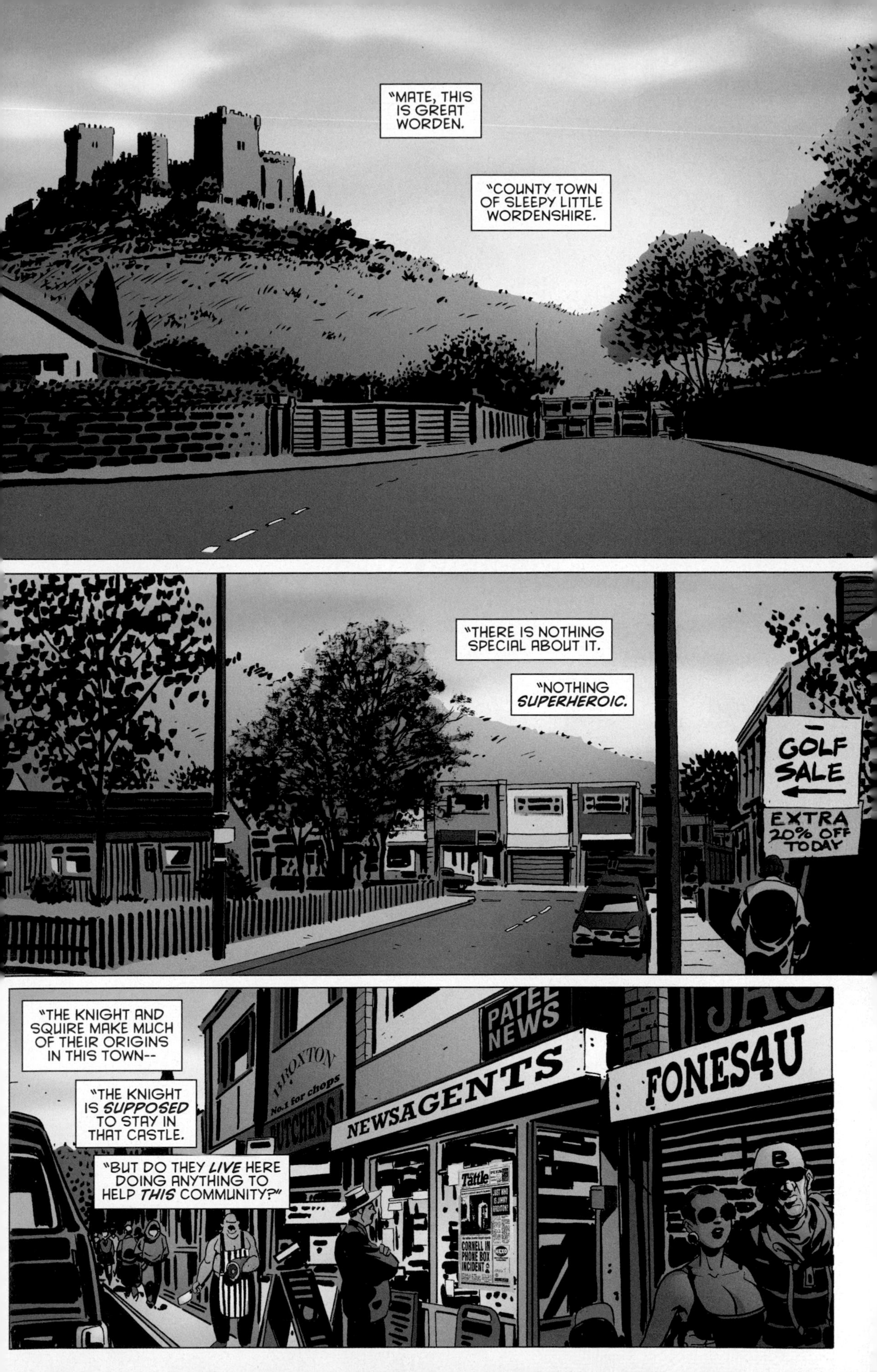

"MATE, THIS IS GREAT WORDEN.
"COUNTY TOWN OF SLEEPY LITTLE WORDENSHIRE.
"THERE IS NOTHING SPECIAL ABOUT IT.
"NOTHING *SUPERHEROIC.*
GOLF SALE
EXTRA 20% OFF TODAY
"THE KNIGHT AND SQUIRE MAKE MUCH OF THEIR ORIGINS IN THIS TOWN--
"THE KNIGHT IS *SUPPOSED* TO STAY IN THAT CASTLE.
"BUT DO THEY *LIVE* HERE DOING ANYTHING TO HELP *THIS* COMMUNITY?"
BROXTON No.1 for chops BUTCHERS
PATEL NEWS
NEWSAGENTS
FONES4U
Tattle
CORNELL IN PHONE BOX INCIDENT

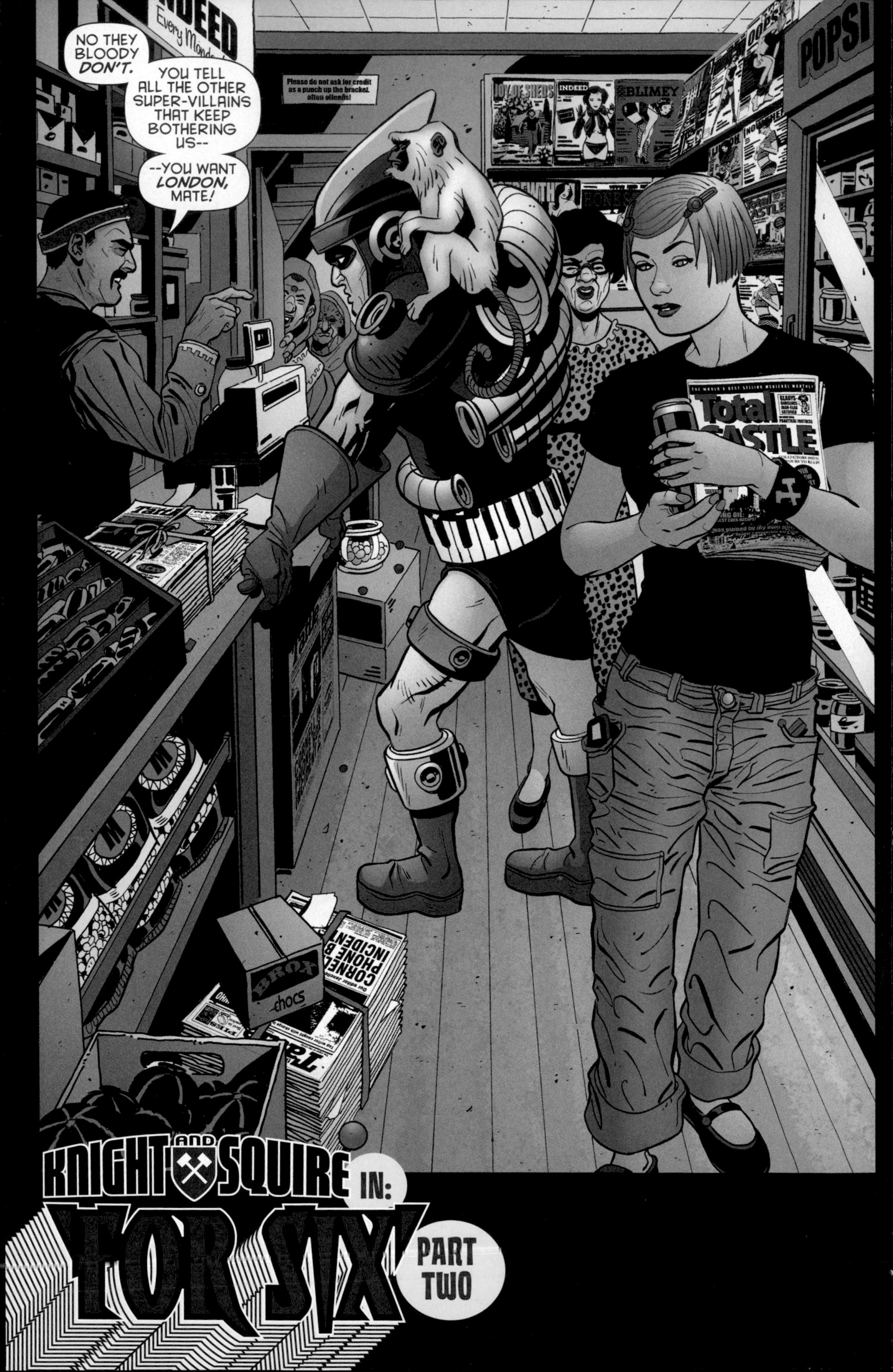
NO THEY BLOODY DON'T.
YOU TELL ALL THE OTHER SUPER-VILLAINS THAT KEEP BOTHERING US--
--YOU WANT LONDON, MATE!
Please do not ask for credit as a punch up the bracket often offends!
KNIGHT AND SQUIRE IN:
'FOR SIX' PART TWO

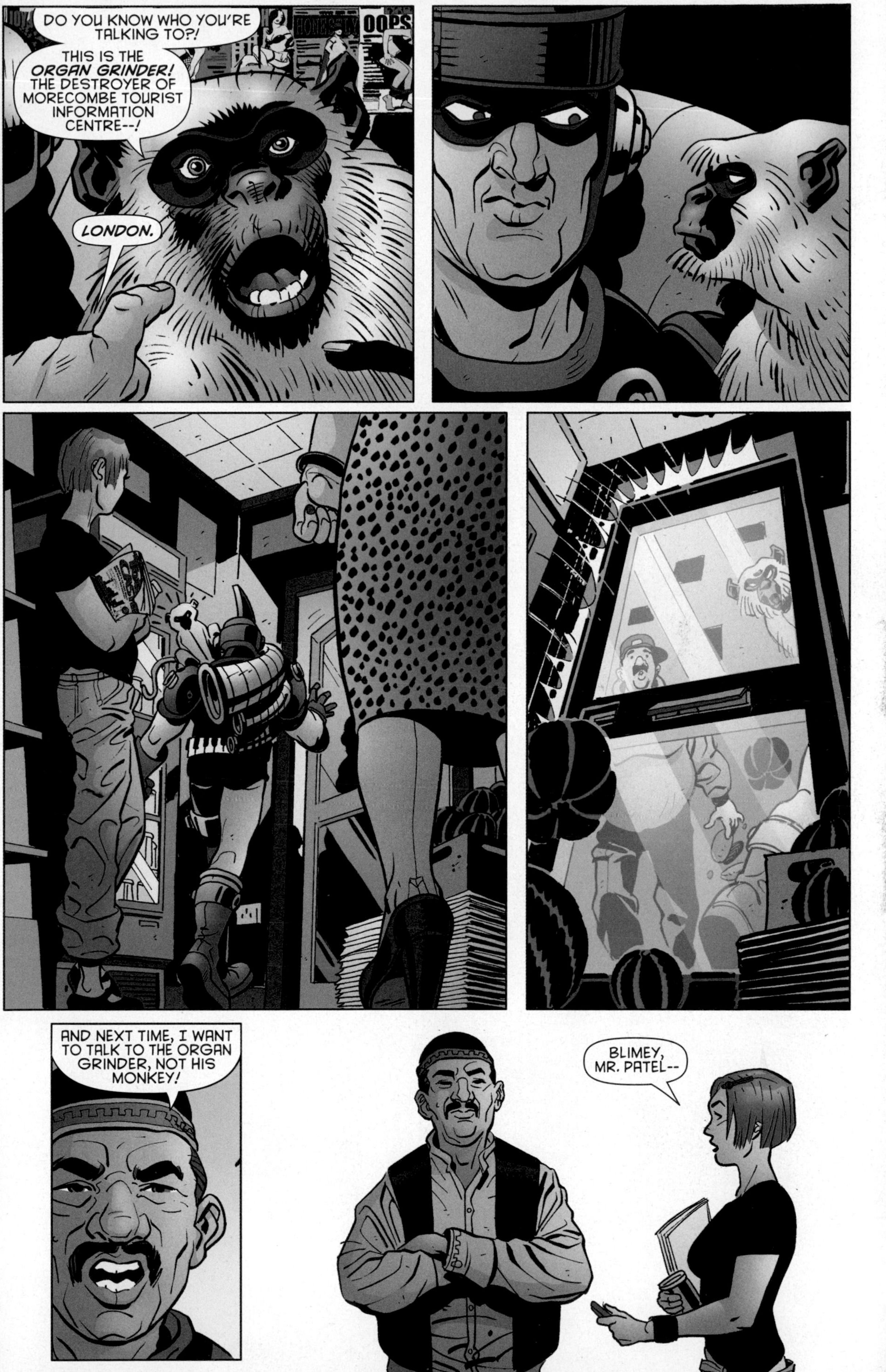
DO YOU KNOW WHO YOU'RE TALKING TO?!
THIS IS THE ORGAN GRINDER! THE DESTROYER OF MORECOMBE TOURIST INFORMATION CENTRE--!
LONDON.
AND NEXT TIME, I WANT TO TALK TO THE ORGAN GRINDER, NOT HIS MONKEY!
BLIMEY, MR. PATEL--

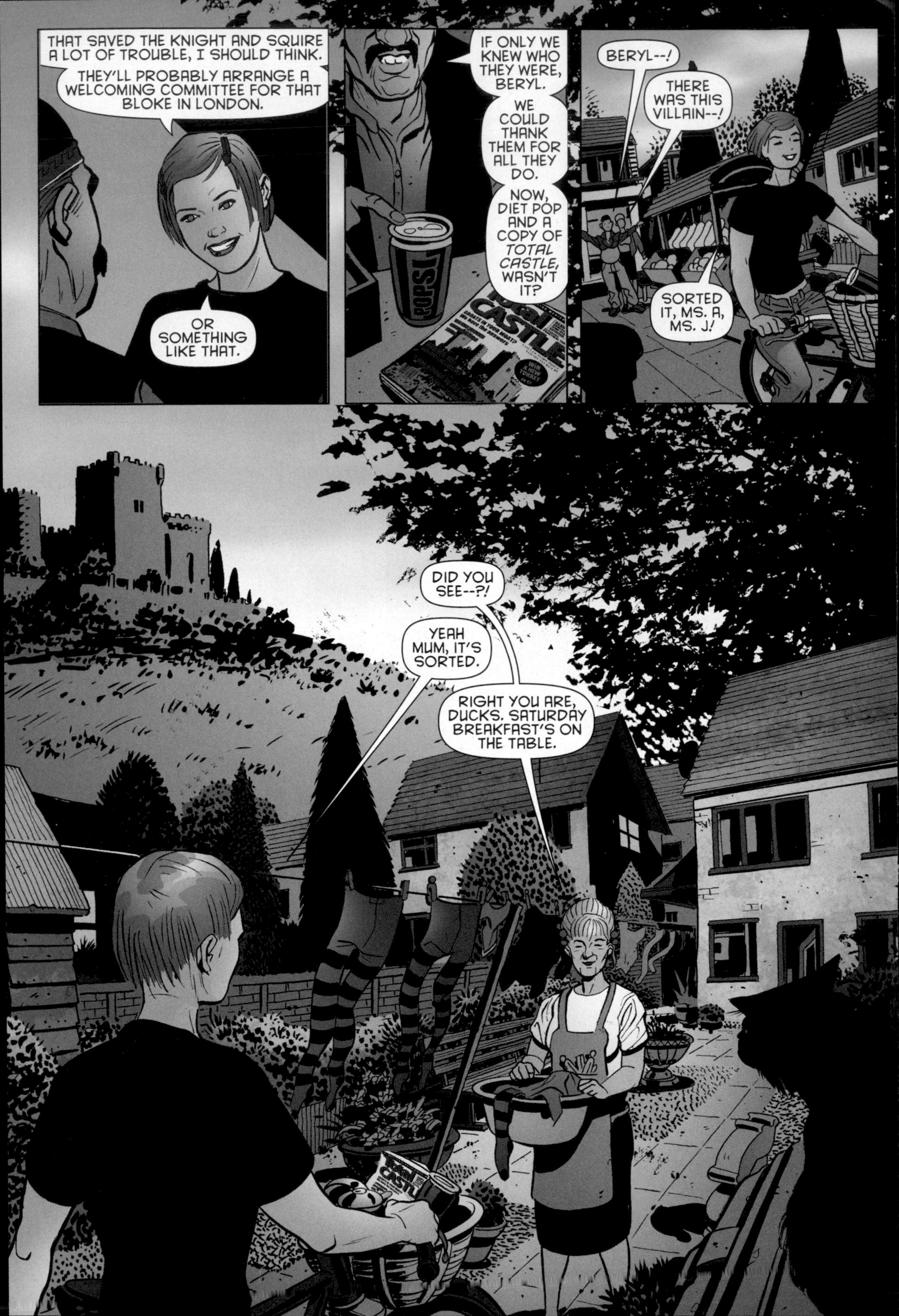
THAT SAVED THE KNIGHT AND SQUIRE A LOT OF TROUBLE, I SHOULD THINK.
THEY'LL PROBABLY ARRANGE A WELCOMING COMMITTEE FOR THAT BLOKE IN LONDON.
OR SOMETHING LIKE THAT.
IF ONLY WE KNEW WHO THEY WERE, BERYL.
WE COULD THANK THEM FOR ALL THEY DO.
NOW, DIET POP AND A COPY OF *TOTAL CASTLE*, WASN'T IT?
POPSI
TOTAL CASTLE
BERYL--!
THERE WAS THIS VILLAIN--!
SORTED IT, MS. A, MS. J!
DID YOU SEE--?!
YEAH MUM, IT'S SORTED.
RIGHT YOU ARE, DUCKS. SATURDAY BREAKFAST'S ON THE TABLE.

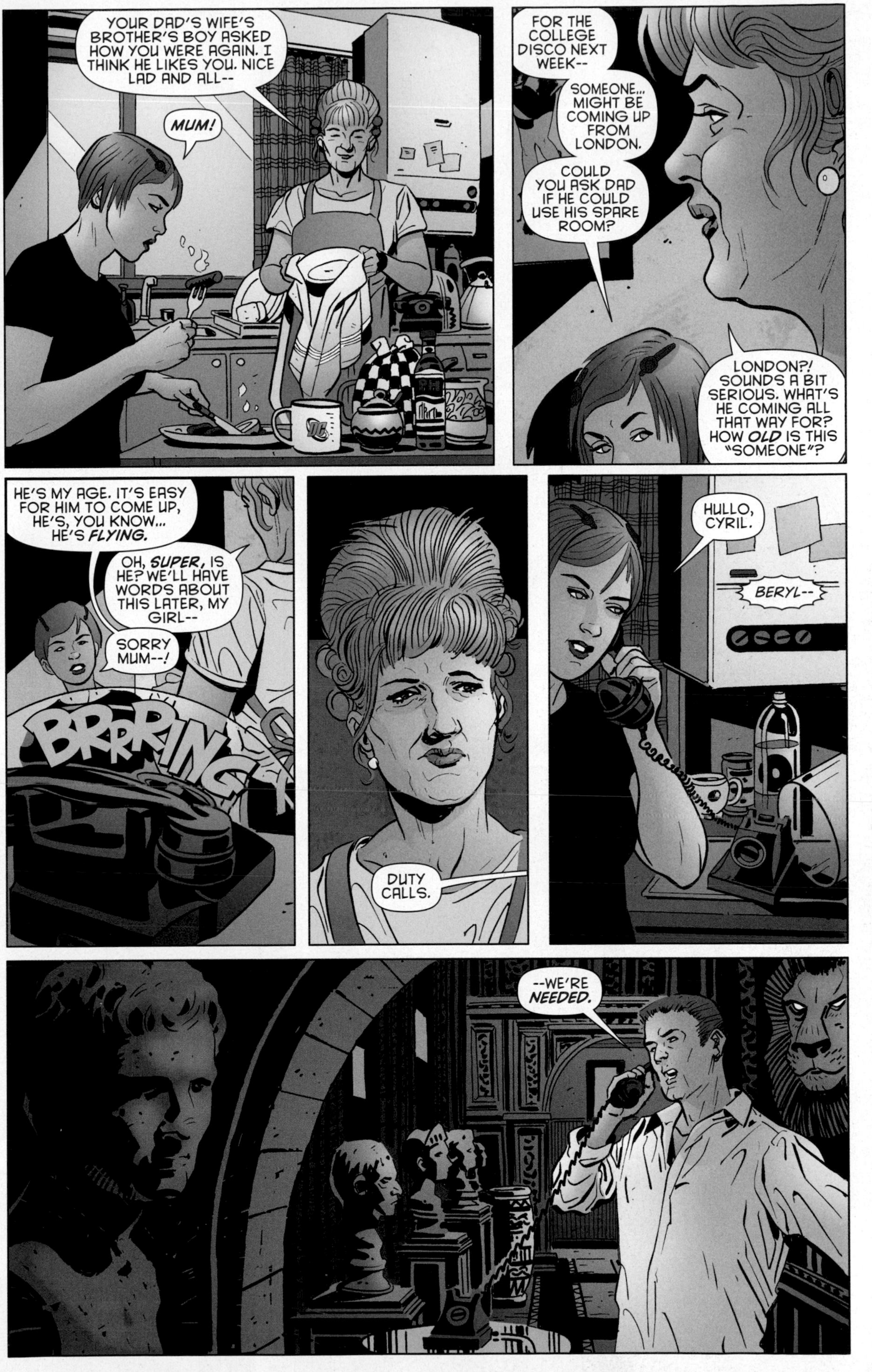
YOUR DAD'S WIFE'S BROTHER'S BOY ASKED HOW YOU WERE AGAIN. I THINK HE LIKES YOU. NICE LAD AND ALL--
MUM!
FOR THE COLLEGE DISCO NEXT WEEK--
SOMEONE... MIGHT BE COMING UP FROM LONDON.
COULD YOU ASK DAD IF HE COULD USE HIS SPARE ROOM?
LONDON?! SOUNDS A BIT SERIOUS. WHAT'S HE COMING ALL THAT WAY FOR? HOW OLD IS THIS "SOMEONE"?
HE'S MY AGE. IT'S EASY FOR HIM TO COME UP, HE'S, YOU KNOW... HE'S FLYING.
OH, SUPER, IS HE? WE'LL HAVE WORDS ABOUT THIS LATER, MY GIRL--
SORRY MUM--!
BRRRING
DUTY CALLS.
HULLO, CYRIL.
BERYL--
--WE'RE NEEDED.

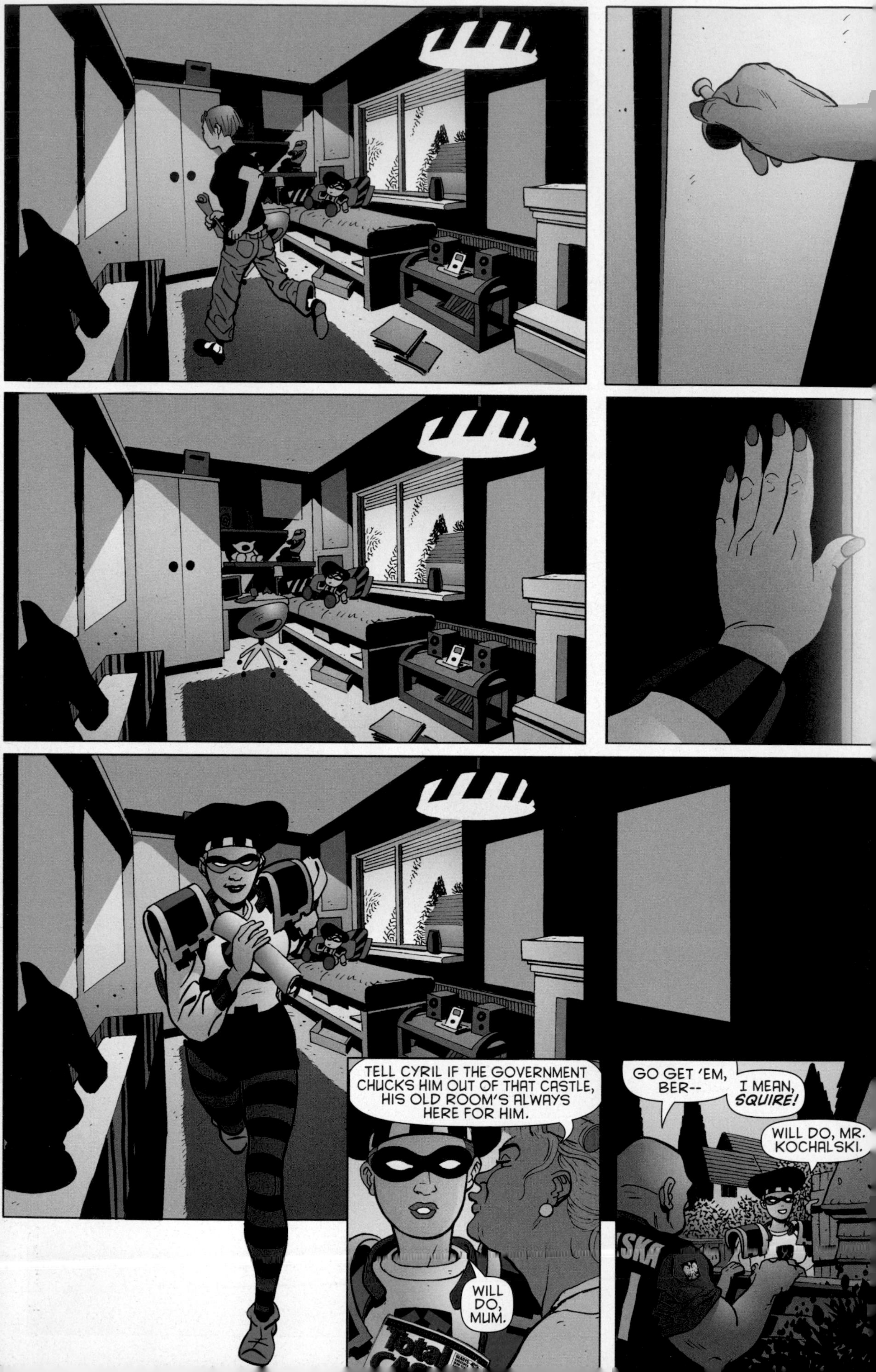
TELL CYRIL IF THE GOVERNMENT CHUCKS HIM OUT OF THAT CASTLE, HIS OLD ROOM'S ALWAYS HERE FOR HIM.
WILL DO, MUM.
GO GET 'EM, BER--
I MEAN, SQUIRE!
WILL DO, MR. KOCHALSKI.

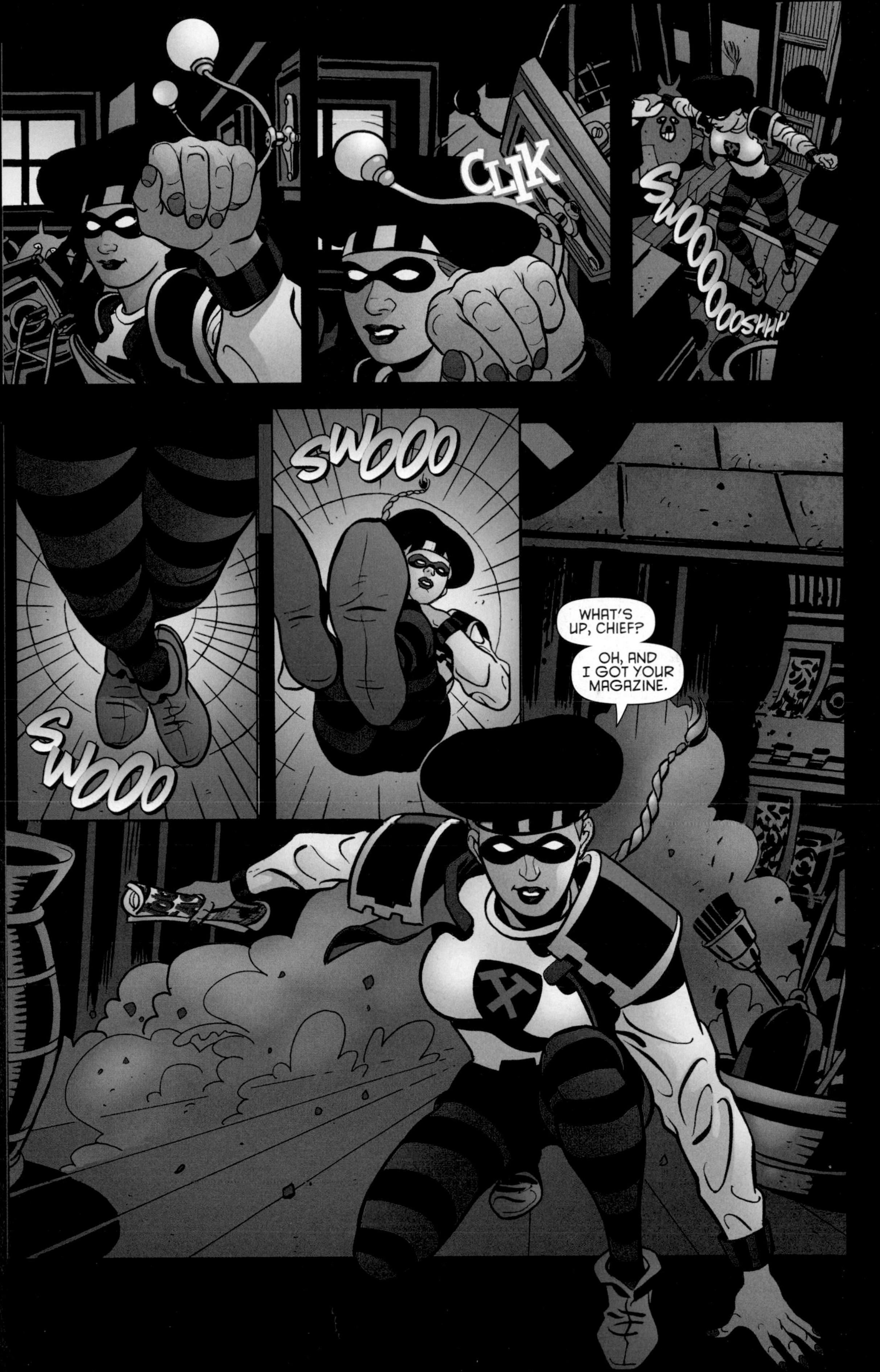
CLIK
SWOOOOOOOSHHH
SWOOO
SWOOO
WHAT'S UP, CHIEF?
OH, AND I GOT YOUR MAGAZINE.

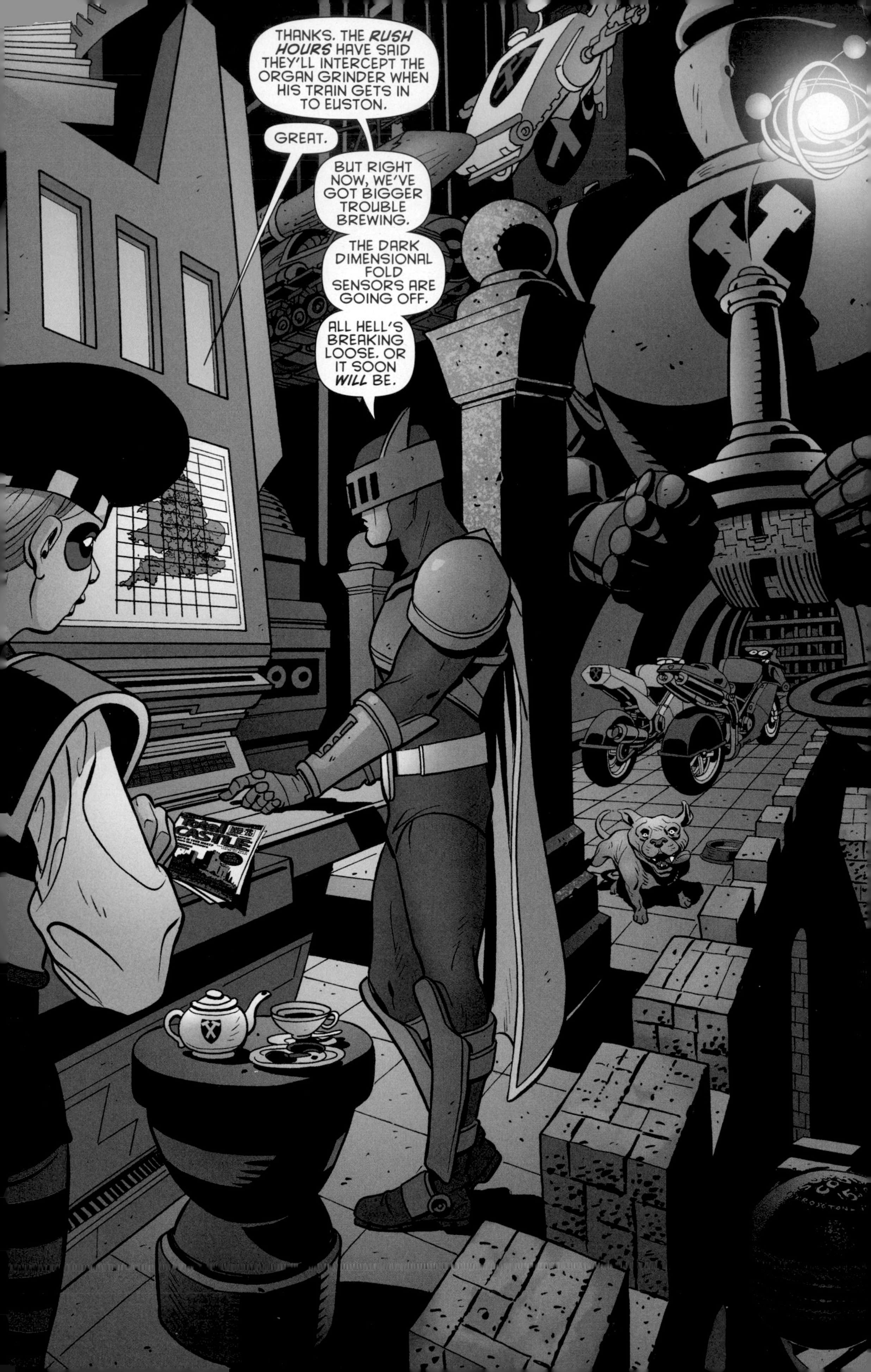
THANKS. THE RUSH HOURS HAVE SAID THEY'LL INTERCEPT THE ORGAN GRINDER WHEN HIS TRAIN GETS IN TO EUSTON.
GREAT.
BUT RIGHT NOW, WE'VE GOT BIGGER TROUBLE BREWING.
THE DARK DIMENSIONAL FOLD SENSORS ARE GOING OFF.
ALL HELL'S BREAKING LOOSE. OR IT SOON WILL BE.
CASTLE

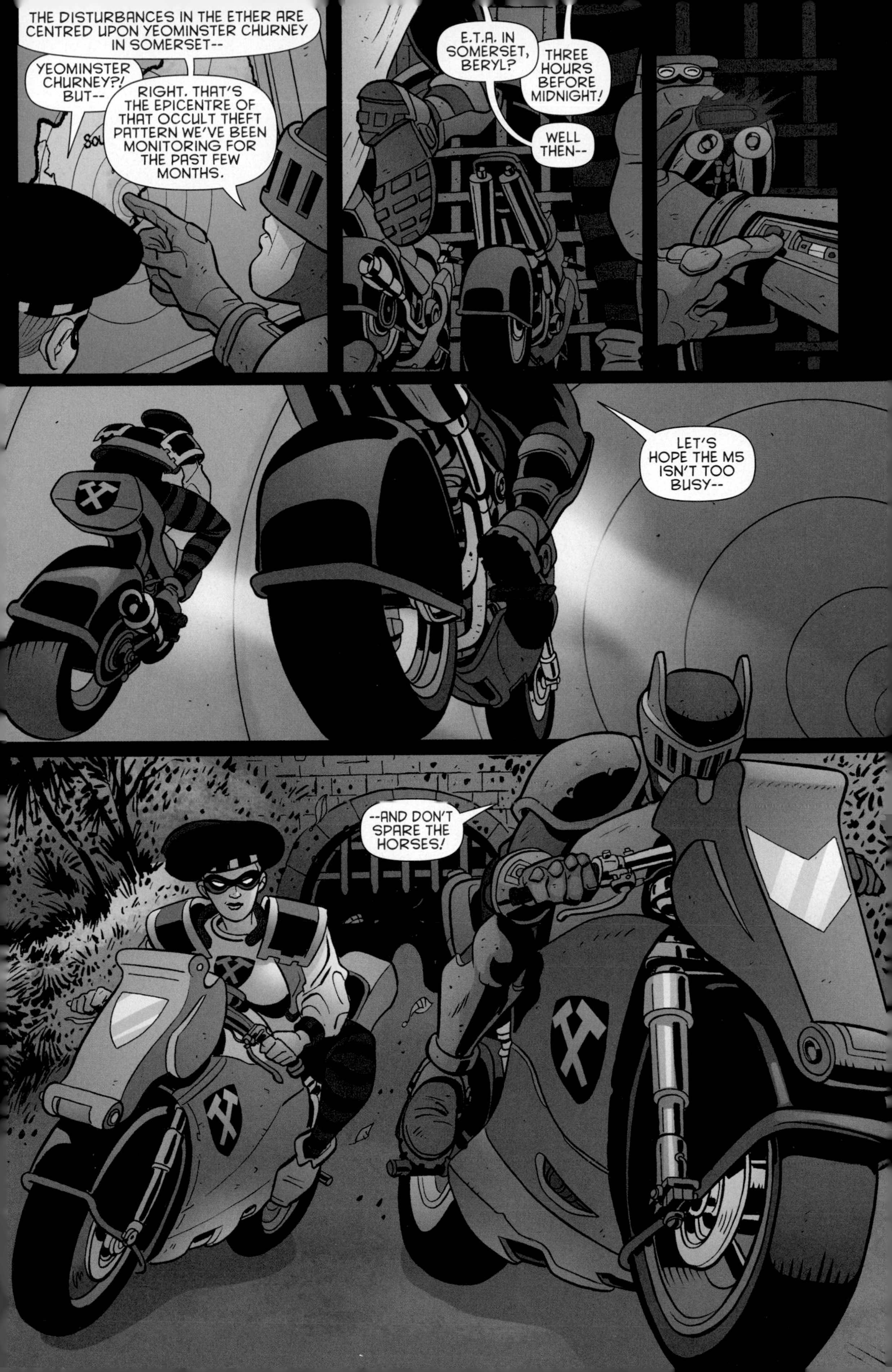
THE DISTURBANCES IN THE ETHER ARE CENTRED UPON YEOMINSTER CHURNEY IN SOMERSET--
YEOMINSTER CHURNEY?! BUT--
RIGHT. THAT'S THE EPICENTRE OF THAT OCCULT THEFT PATTERN WE'VE BEEN MONITORING FOR THE PAST FEW MONTHS.
E.T.A. IN SOMERSET, BERYL?
THREE HOURS BEFORE MIDNIGHT!
WELL THEN--
LET'S HOPE THE M5 ISN'T TOO BUSY--
--AND DON'T SPARE THE HORSES!

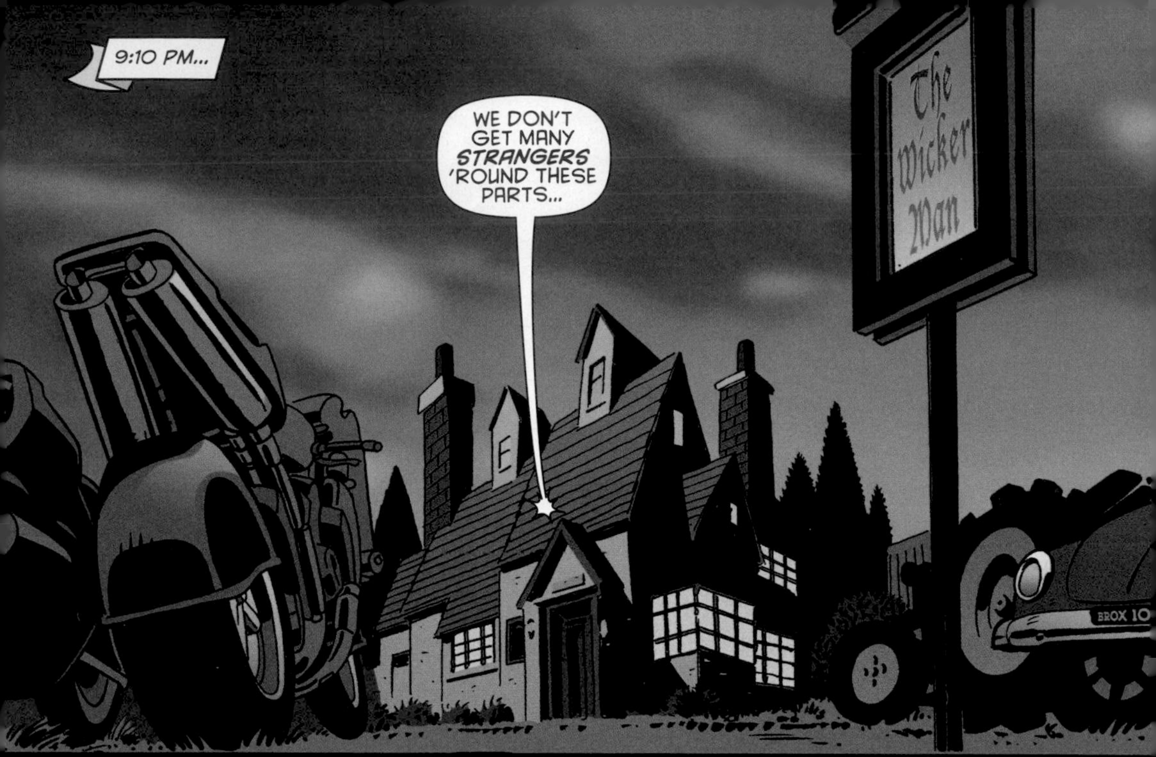
9:10 PM...
WE DON'T GET MANY STRANGERS 'ROUND THESE PARTS...
The Wicker Man
BROX 10

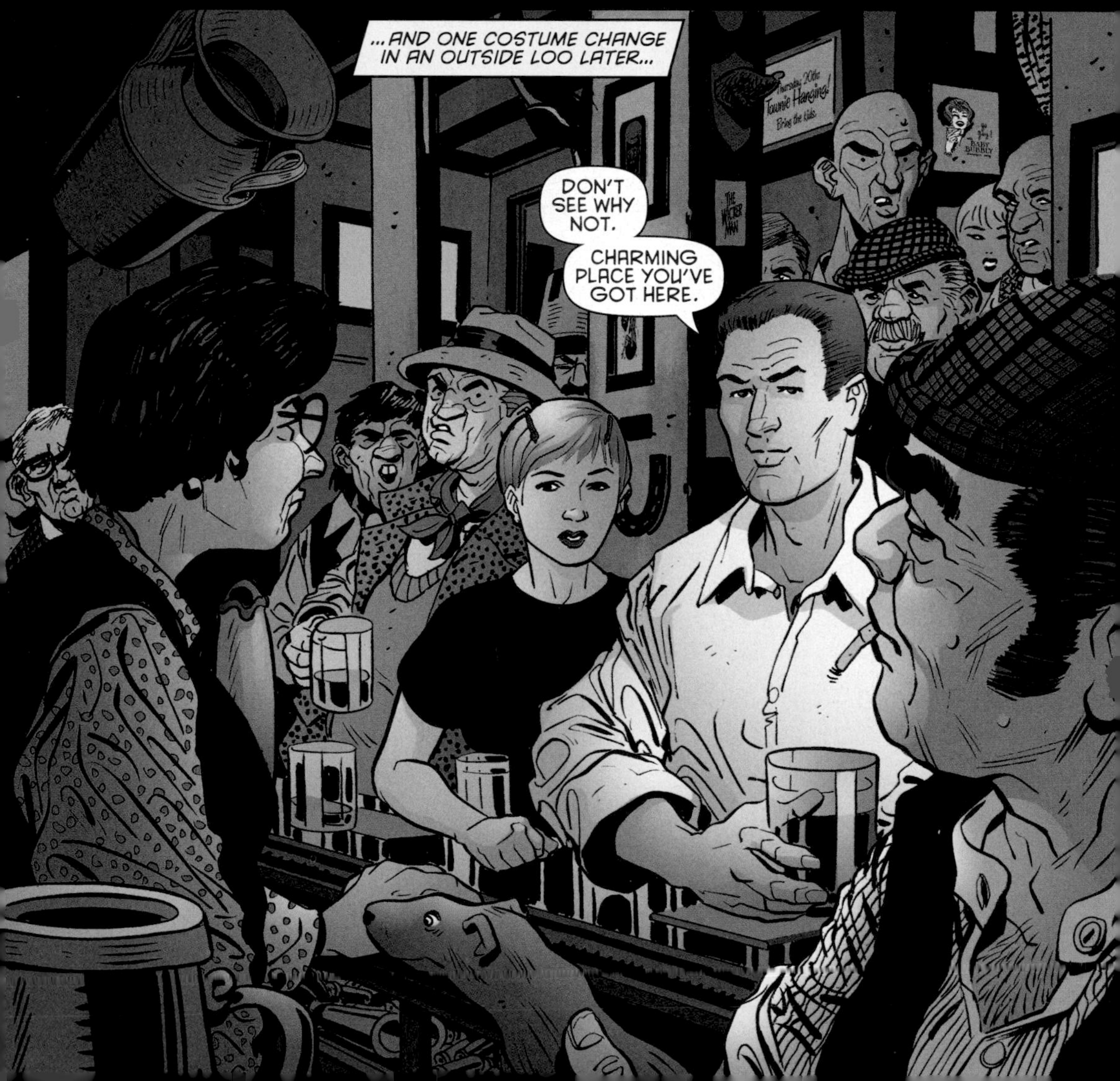
...AND ONE COSTUME CHANGE IN AN OUTSIDE LOO LATER...
Thursday 20th Townie Hanging! Bring the kids.
BABY BUBBLY
DON'T SEE WHY NOT.
CHARMING PLACE YOU'VE GOT HERE.

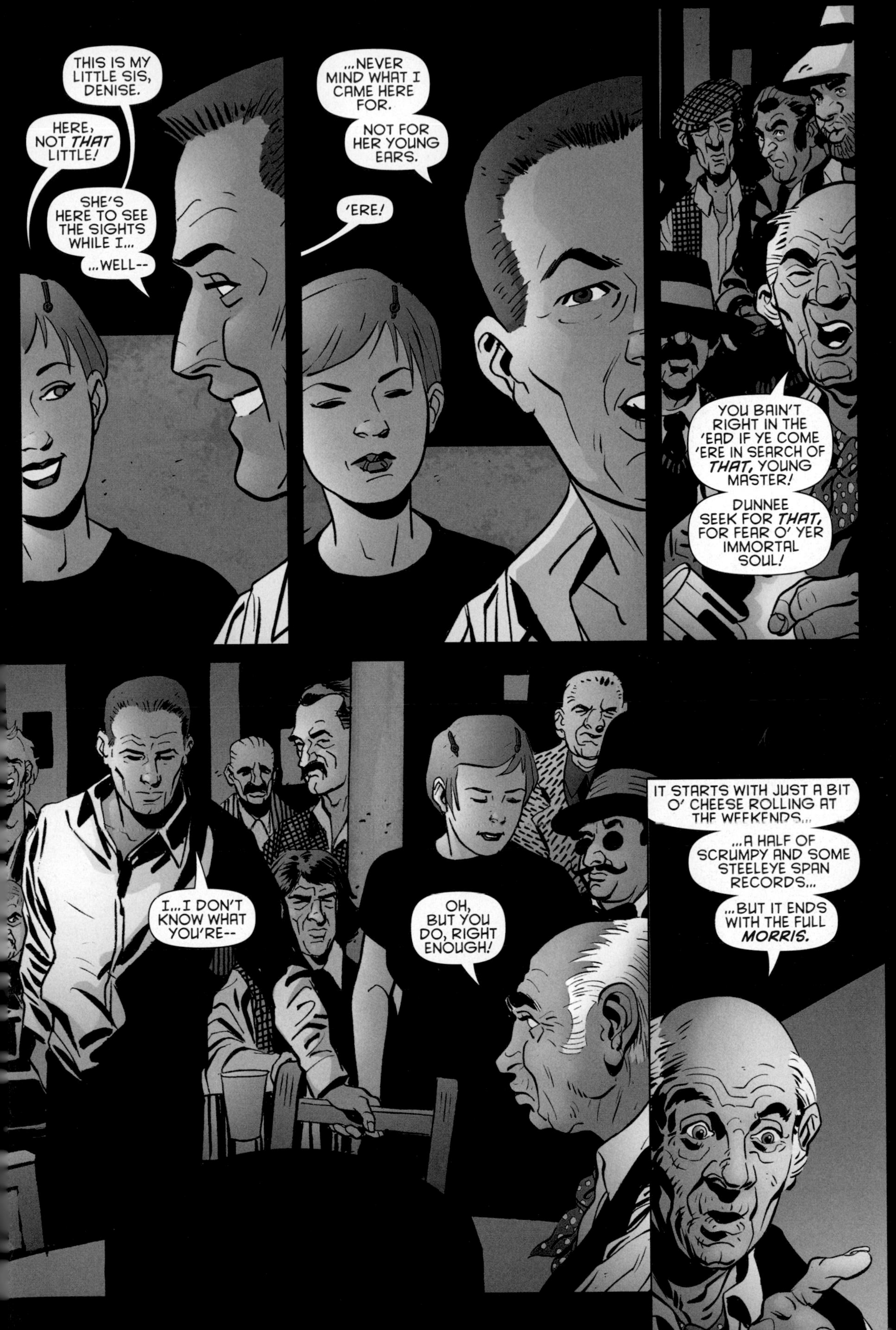
THIS IS MY LITTLE SIS, DENISE.
HERE, NOT *THAT* LITTLE!
SHE'S HERE TO SEE THE SIGHTS WHILE I...
...WELL--
...NEVER MIND WHAT I CAME HERE FOR.
NOT FOR HER YOUNG EARS.
'ERE!
YOU BAIN'T RIGHT IN THE 'EAD IF YE COME 'ERE IN SEARCH OF *THAT*, YOUNG MASTER!
DUNNEE SEEK FOR *THAT*, FOR FEAR O' YER IMMORTAL SOUL!
I...I DON'T KNOW WHAT YOU'RE--
OH, BUT YOU DO, RIGHT ENOUGH!
IT STARTS WITH JUST A BIT O' CHEESE ROLLING AT THE WEEKENDS...
...A HALF OF SCRUMPY AND SOME STEELEYE SPAN RECORDS...
...BUT IT ENDS WITH THE FULL *MORRIS.*

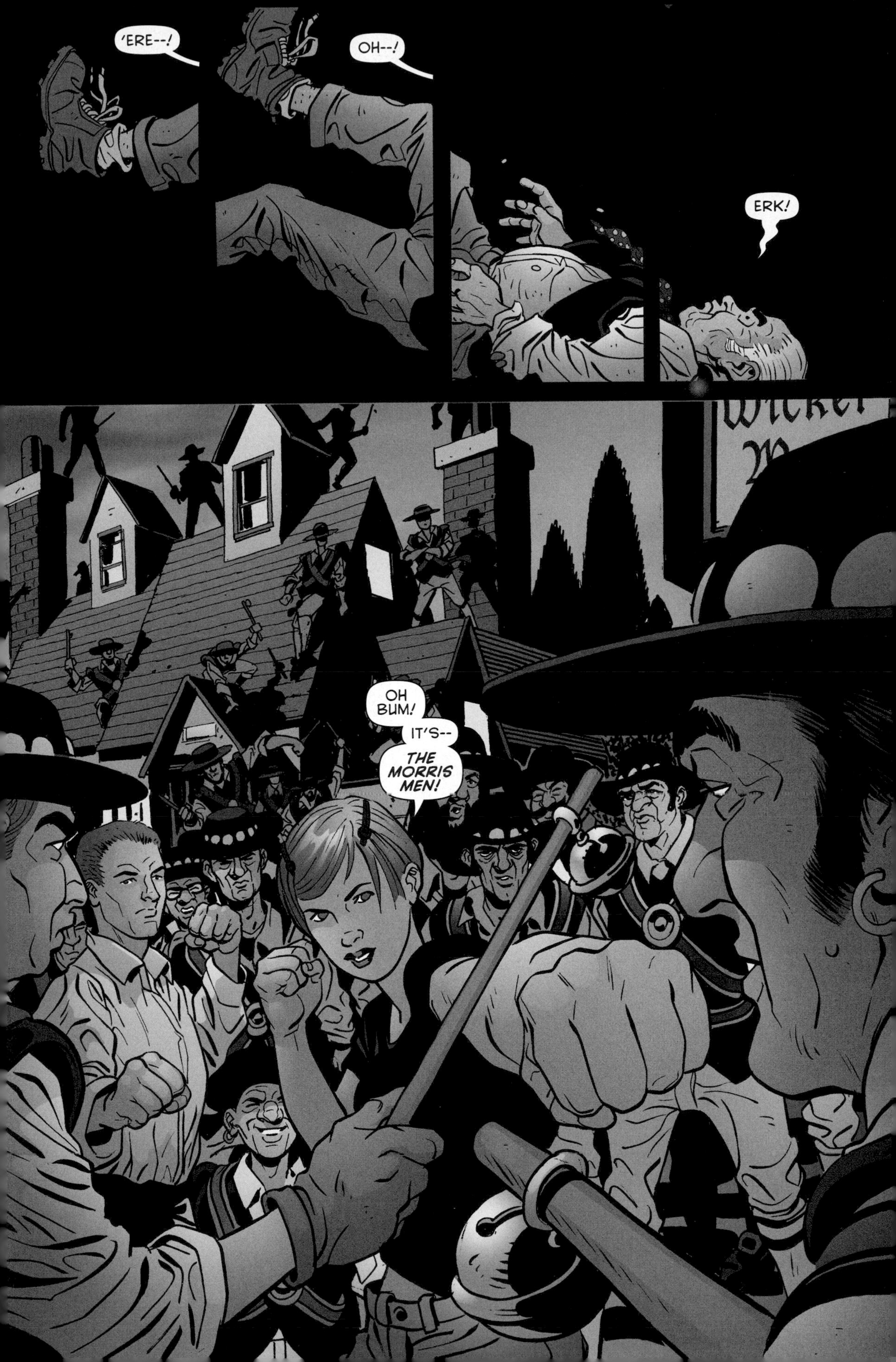
'ERE--!
OH--!
ERK!
OH BUM!
IT'S--
THE MORRIS MEN!

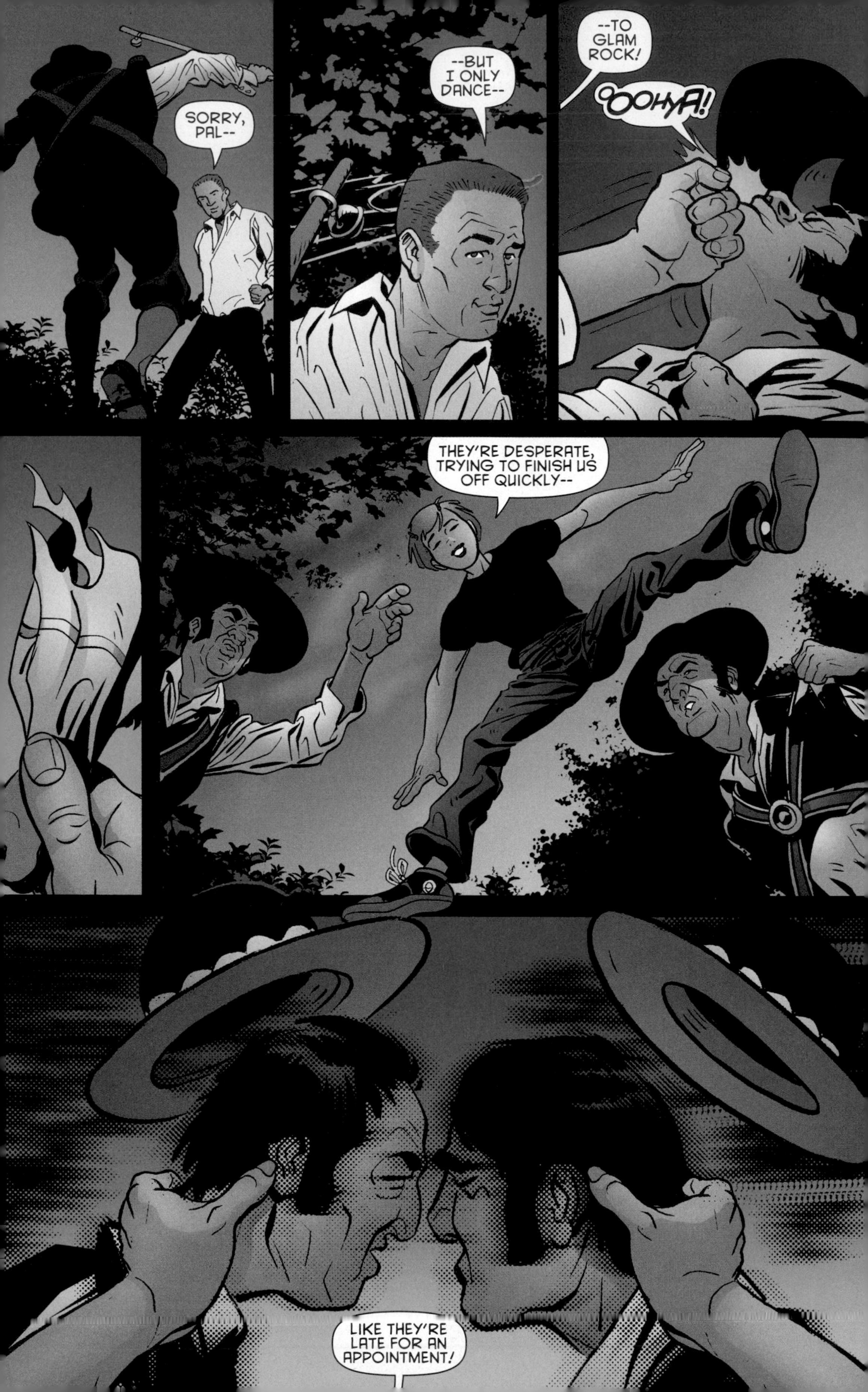
SORRY, PAL--
--BUT I ONLY DANCE--
--TO GLAM ROCK!
OOHYA!
THEY'RE DESPERATE, TRYING TO FINISH US OFF QUICKLY--
LIKE THEY'RE LATE FOR AN APPOINTMENT!

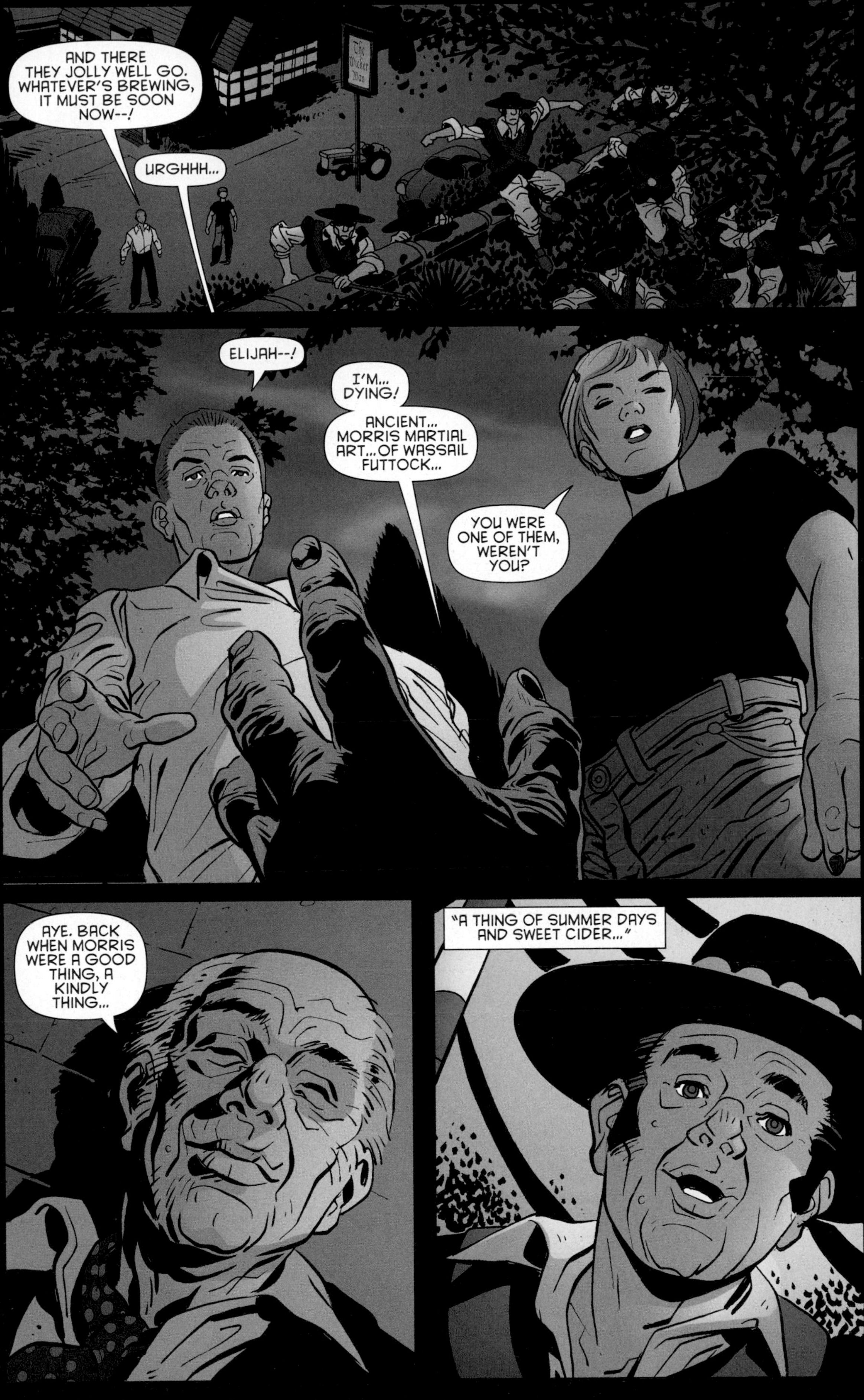
AND THERE THEY JOLLY WELL GO. WHATEVER'S BREWING, IT MUST BE SOON NOW--!
URGHHH...
ELIJAH--!
I'M... DYING!
ANCIENT... MORRIS MARTIAL ART... OF WASSAIL FUTTOCK...
YOU WERE ONE OF THEM, WEREN'T YOU?
AYE. BACK WHEN MORRIS WERE A GOOD THING, A KINDLY THING...
"A THING OF SUMMER DAYS AND SWEET CIDER..."

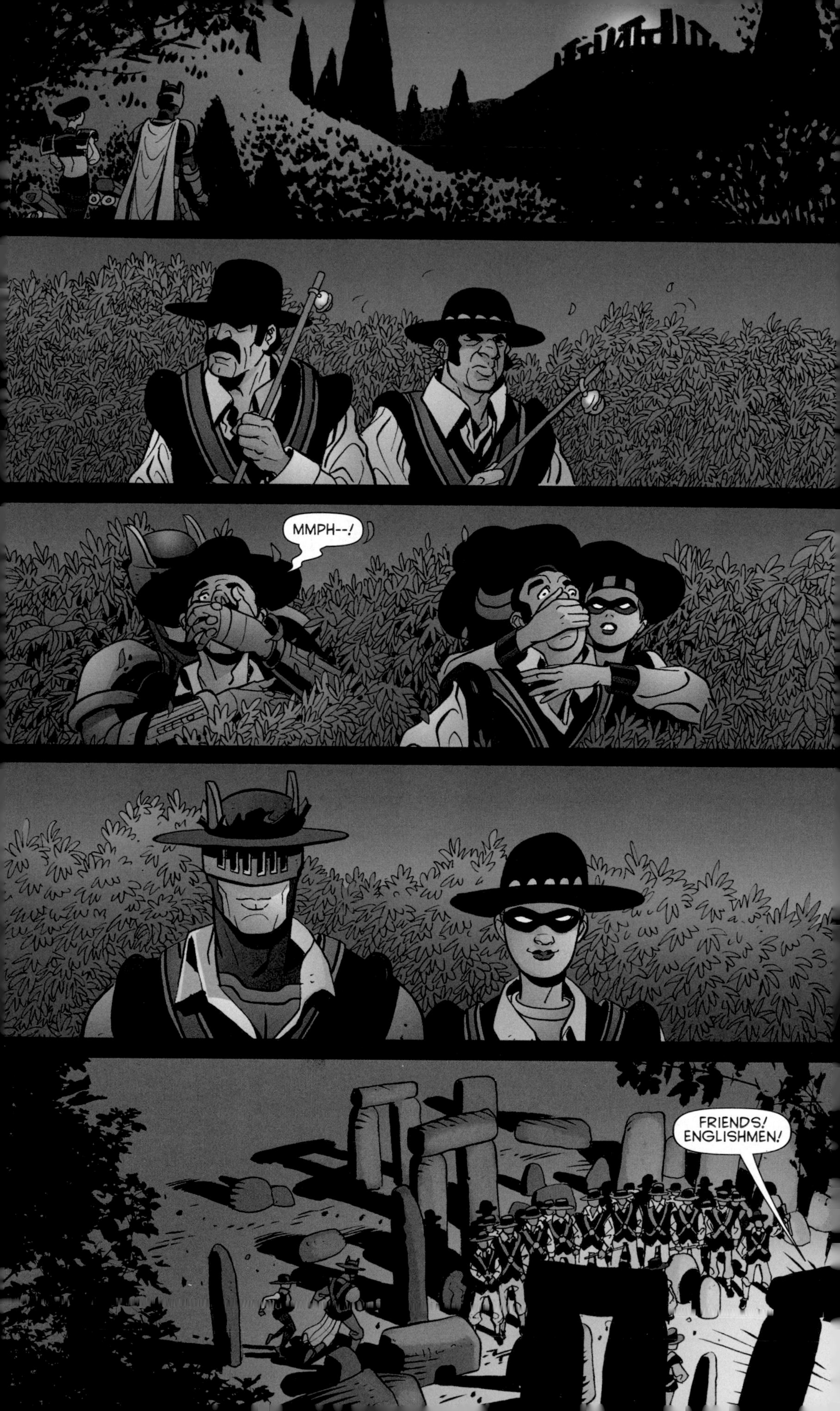
MMPH--!
FRIENDS! ENGLISHMEN!

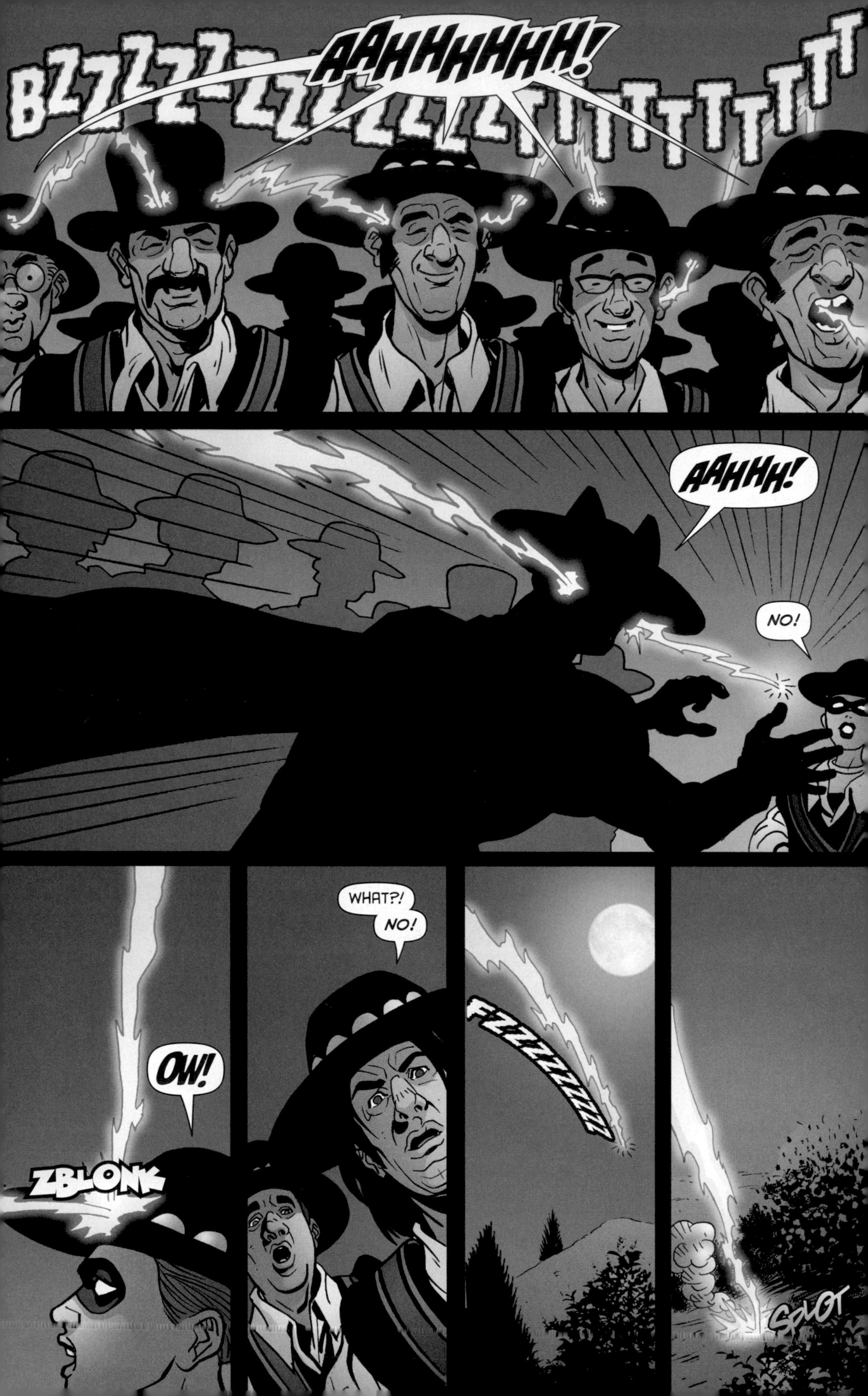
BZZZZZZZZZZZZZZTTTTTTTTTTT
AAHHHHHH!
AAHHH!
NO!
OW!
ZBLONK
WHAT?!
NO!
FZZZZZZZZ
SPLOT

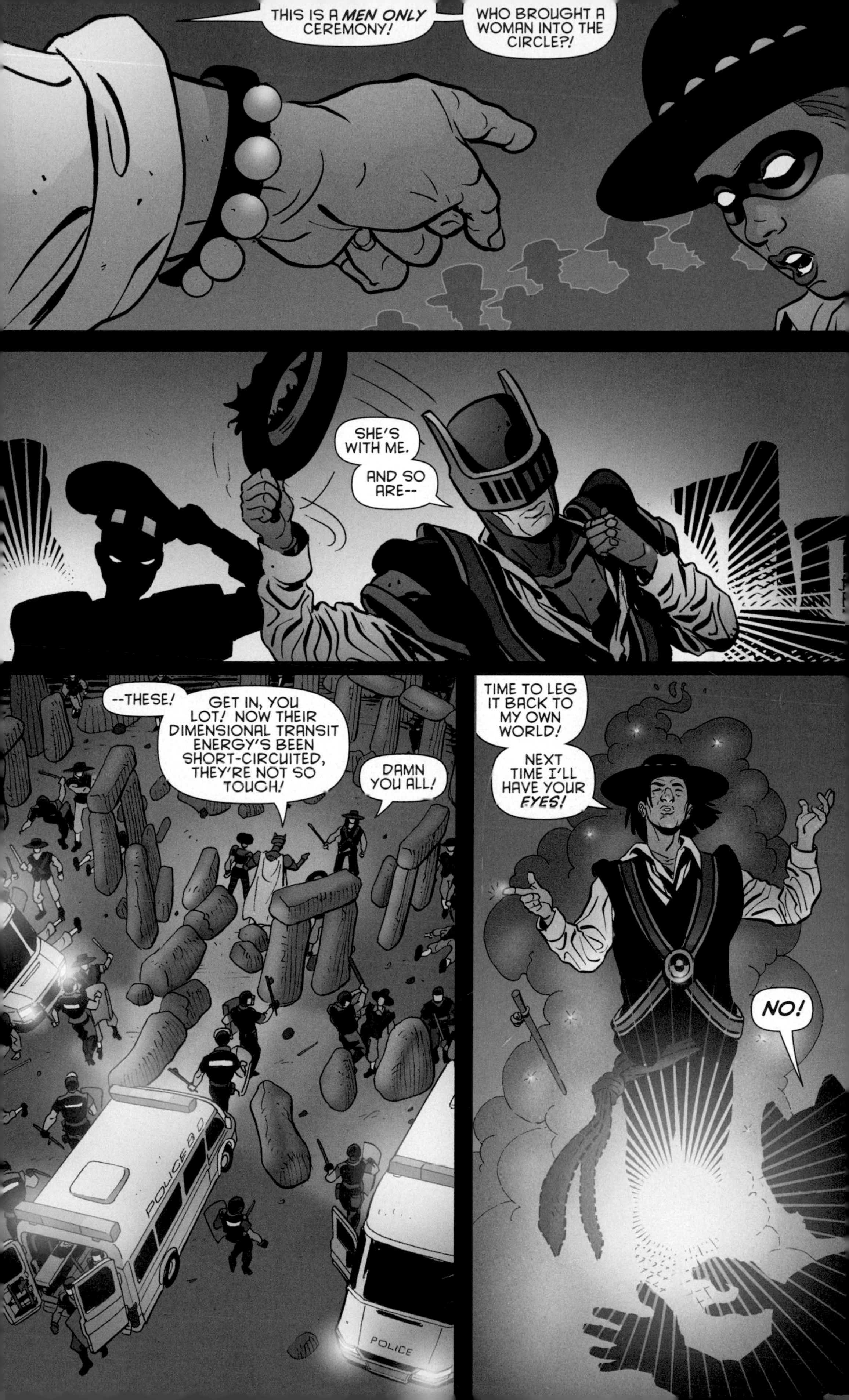
THIS IS A *MEN ONLY* CEREMONY!
WHO BROUGHT A WOMAN INTO THE CIRCLE?!
SHE'S WITH ME.
AND SO ARE--
--THESE!
GET IN, YOU LOT! NOW THEIR DIMENSIONAL TRANSIT ENERGY'S BEEN SHORT-CIRCUITED, THEY'RE NOT SO TOUGH!
DAMN YOU ALL!
POLICE
POLICE
TIME TO LEG IT BACK TO MY OWN WORLD!
NEXT TIME I'LL HAVE YOUR *EYES!*
NO!

What Morris Men are Like

WELL, LOVELY, GENERALLY. AND NOT AT ALL FASCISTIC. MORRIS DANCING IS A FOLK TRADITION INVOLVING DANCERS DRESSED IN RIBBONS AND BELLS GENTLY HITTING EACH OTHER WITH SMALL STICKS. IT HAPPENS IN MARKET SQUARES AND ON VILLAGE GREENS ON FESTIVAL DAYS. GENUINELY ANCIENT ORIGINS ARE CLAIMED, BUT IT CERTAINLY DATES BACK TO BEFORE THE ENGLISH CIVIL WAR. IT'S THOUGHT IT WAS ORIGINALLY A SWORD DANCE, CREATED IN SPAIN IN THE VICTORY CELEBRATIONS WHEN THE MOORS WERE DRIVEN OUT. HENCE, "MOORISH DANCE." IN RECENT YEARS THERE HAVE BEEN RUCTIONS IN THE TRADITIONALLY ALL-MALE MORRIS COMMUNITY ABOUT LETTING WOMEN DANCE.

THE INITIAL THOUGHT BEHIND THIS STORY WAS READING NEWS REPORTS ABOUT FOLK AGAINST FASCISM, A MOVEMENT IN BRITISH FOLK MUSIC THAT FIGHTS FAR RIGHT ORGANISATIONS CO-OPTING (OFTEN STRIDENTLY LEFT WING) FOLK GROUPS AND PERFORMANCES. I BECAME VERY WORRIED, BEFORE THE LAST GENERAL ELECTION, THAT THE EXTREMISTS MIGHT CONTROL A LONDON COUNCIL, OR EVEN GET AN MP. TO MY IMMENSE RELIEF, ELECTORAL TURNOUT WAS ENORMOUS AND THEY WERE ALL KICKED OUT.

MORRIS MAJOR'S "CRICKET ON THE VILLAGE GREEN" SPEECH MAY REMIND BRITISH READERS OF FORMER TORY PRIME MINISTER JOHN MAJOR'S NOSTALGIC YEARNINGS. MAJOR WAS A MODERATE, BUT THE SPEECH WOULD DOUBTLESS RESONATE WITH PEOPLE LIKE MORRIS, WHOSE NAME ALSO INVOKES A BRITISH CAR.

"WE'RE NEEDED" WILL BE FAMILIAR TO FANS OF THE AVENGERS. STEELEYE SPAN ARE A BRITISH FOLK BAND OF THE 1960s, CHEESE-ROLLING IS A FOLK SPORT WHERE ROUND CHEESES ARE CHASED DOWNHILL (NO, REALLY), SCRUMPY IS ANOTHER NAME FOR ALCOHOLIC CIDER (OF COURSE, ALL BRITISH CIDER IS ALCOHOLIC), "WURZEL" IS ANOTHER NAME FOR A TURNIP, A DEROGATORY TERM FOR COUNTRY FOLK AND THE NAME OF A COMEDY FOLK BAND. "WASSAIL FUTTOCK" SOUNDS A BIT LIKE WASSAILING, THAT IS, A FOLK TRADITION INVOLVING APPLES, AND THE SORT OF THING YOU MIGHT HEAR ON RADIO COMEDY "ROUND THE HORNE." ANASTASIA WAS THE NAME OF DAN DARE'S SPACESHIP. "THE RICH MAN AT HIS CASTLE, THE POOR MAN AT HIS GATE" IS FROM THE HYMN ALL THINGS BRIGHT AND BEAUTIFUL WHICH MAKES THE EXTRAORDINARY CLAIM THAT SOCIAL INEQUALITY IS HOW GOD LIKES IT.

I'M FROM WURZEL COUNTRY MYSELF, SO I'M ALLOWED TO TAKE THE MICKEY.

UNTIL NEXT ISSUE, CHEERIO!
- PAUL CORNELL

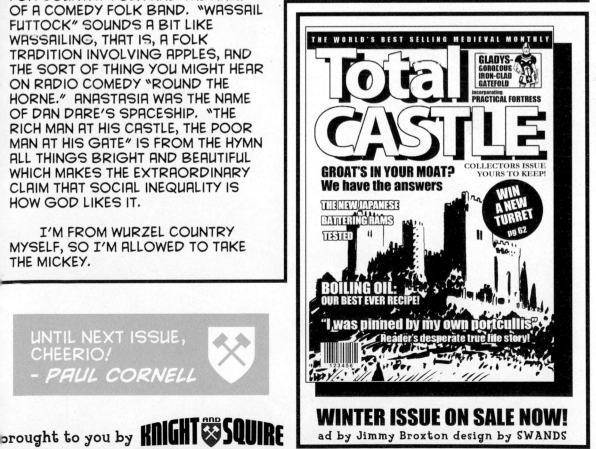

brought to you by KNIGHT AND SQUIRE

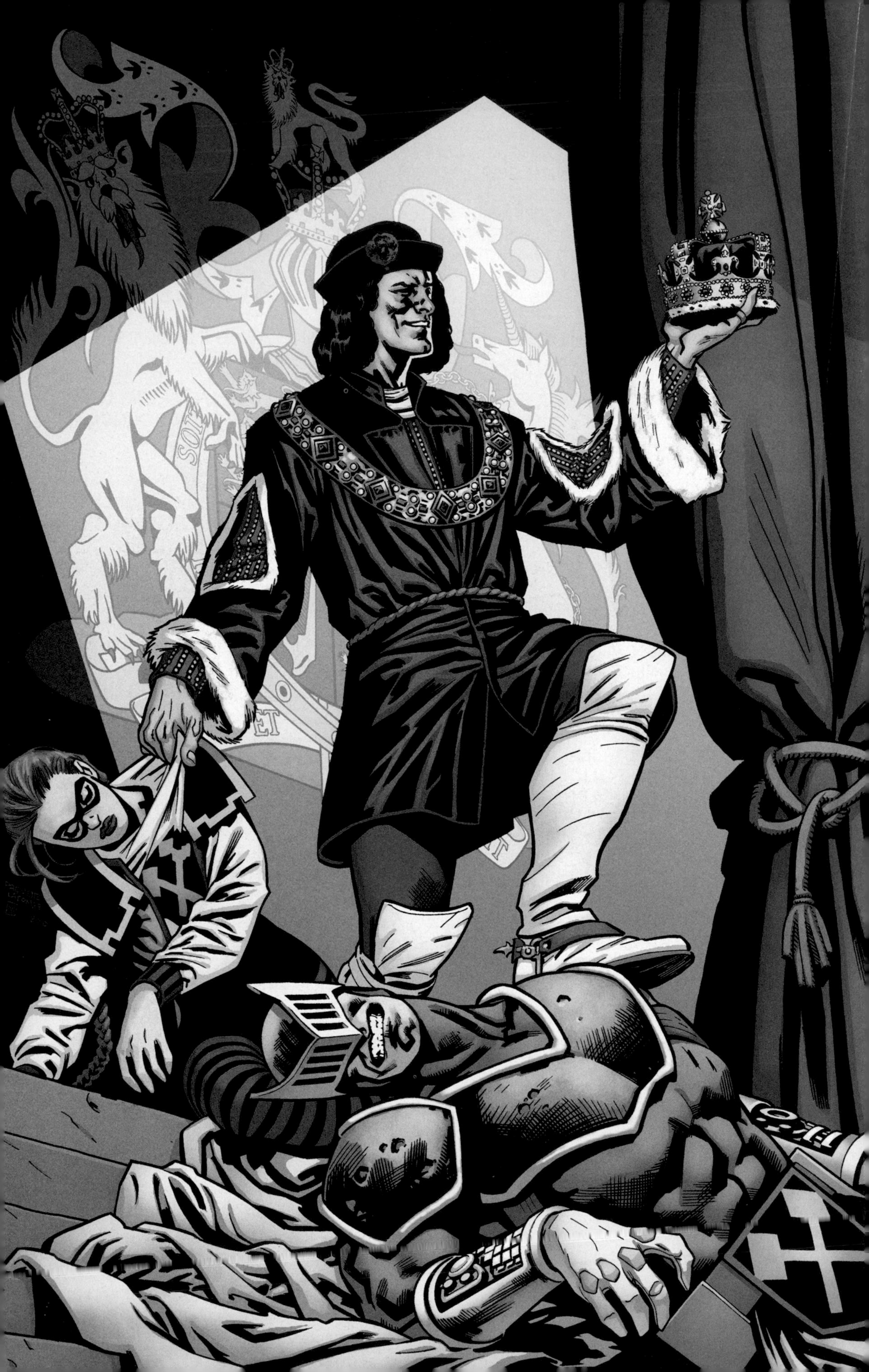

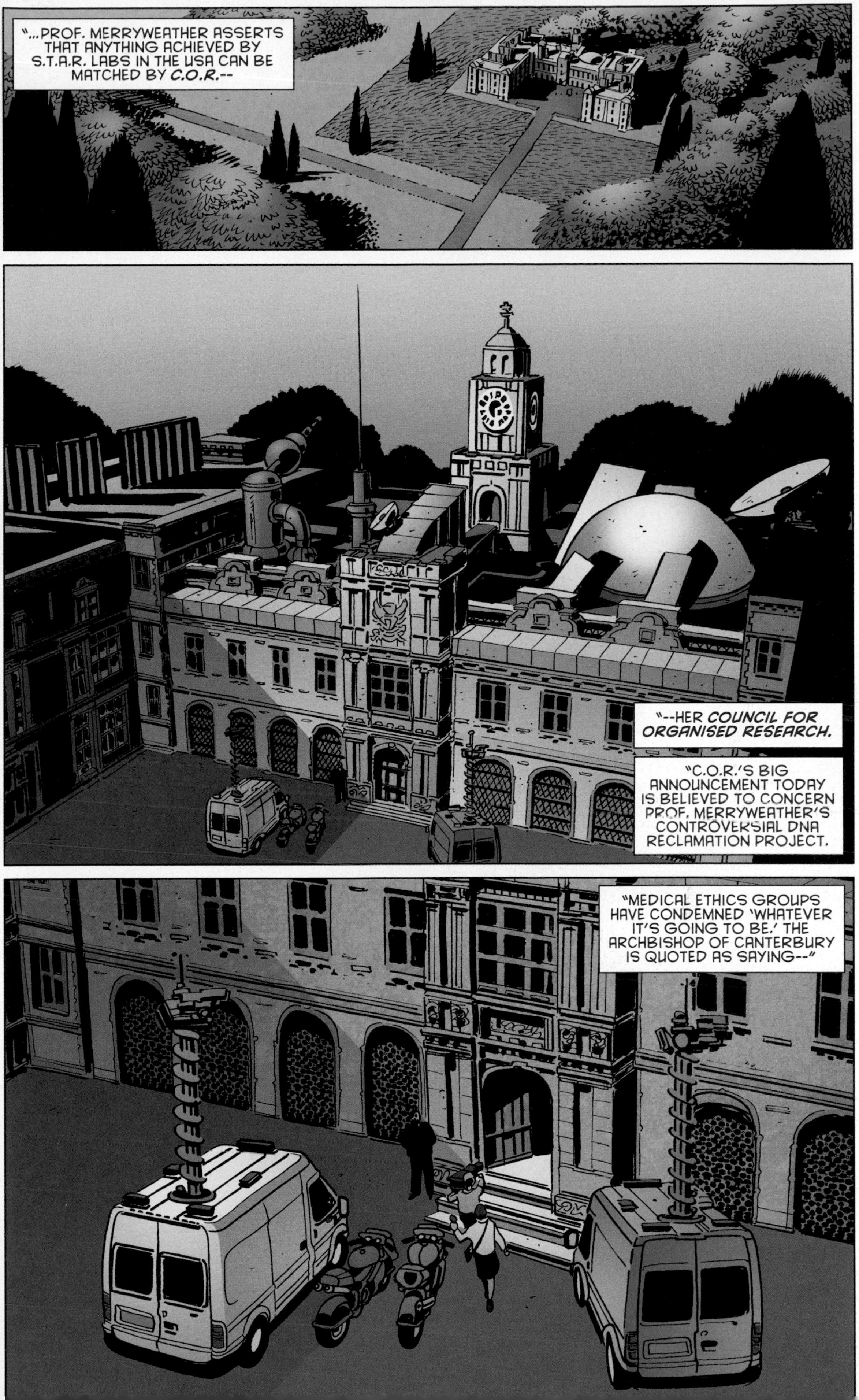
"...PROF. MERRYWEATHER ASSERTS THAT ANYTHING ACHIEVED BY S.T.A.R. LABS IN THE USA CAN BE MATCHED BY C.O.R.--
"--HER COUNCIL FOR ORGANISED RESEARCH.
"C.O.R.'S BIG ANNOUNCEMENT TODAY IS BELIEVED TO CONCERN PROF. MERRYWEATHER'S CONTROVERSIAL DNA RECLAMATION PROJECT.
"MEDICAL ETHICS GROUPS HAVE CONDEMNED 'WHATEVER IT'S GOING TO BE.' THE ARCHBISHOP OF CANTERBURY IS QUOTED AS SAYING--"

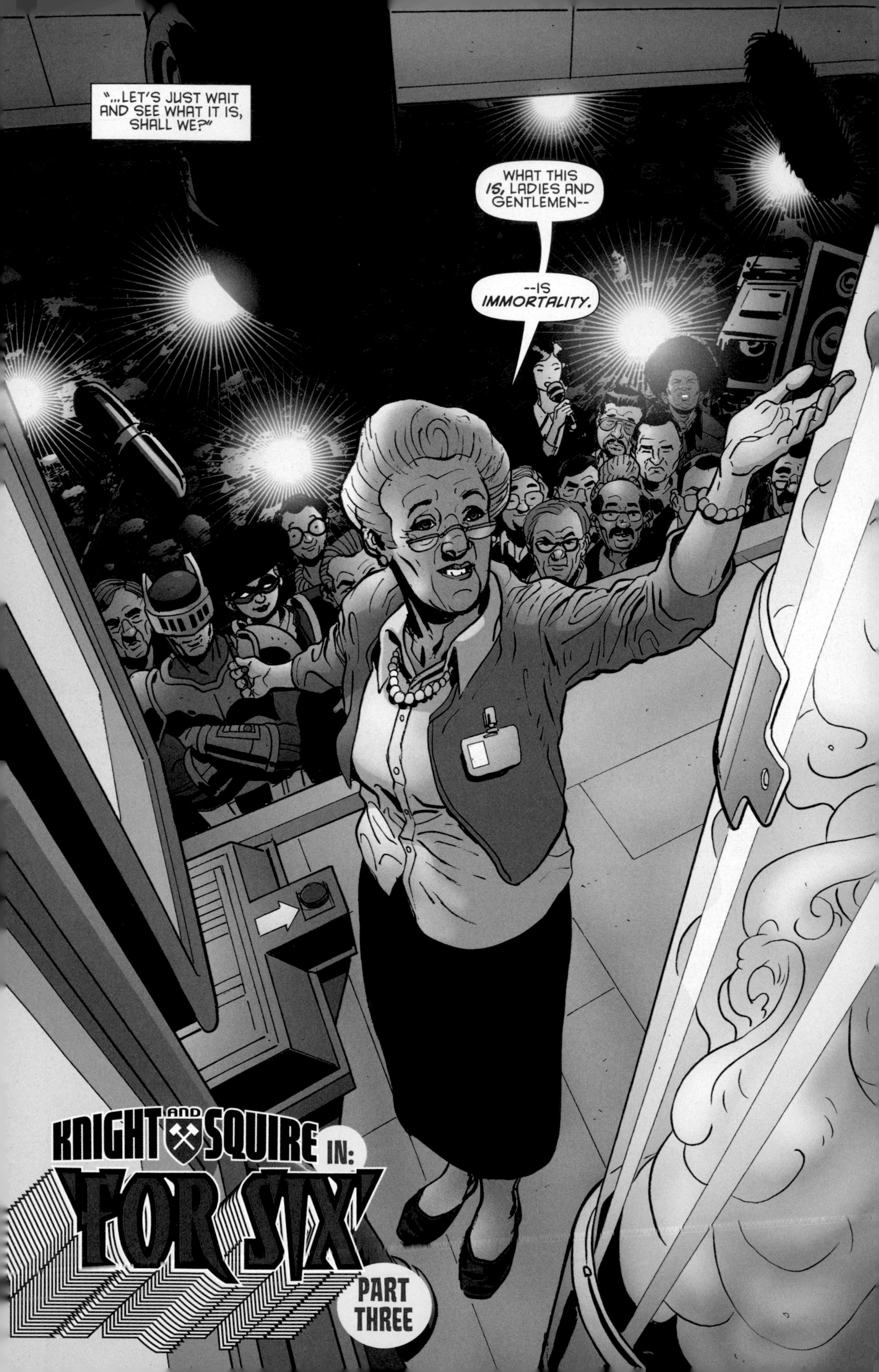
"...LET'S JUST WAIT AND SEE WHAT IT IS, SHALL WE?"
WHAT THIS IS, LADIES AND GENTLEMEN--
--IS IMMORTALITY.
KNIGHT AND SQUIRE IN:
'FOR SIX'
PART THREE

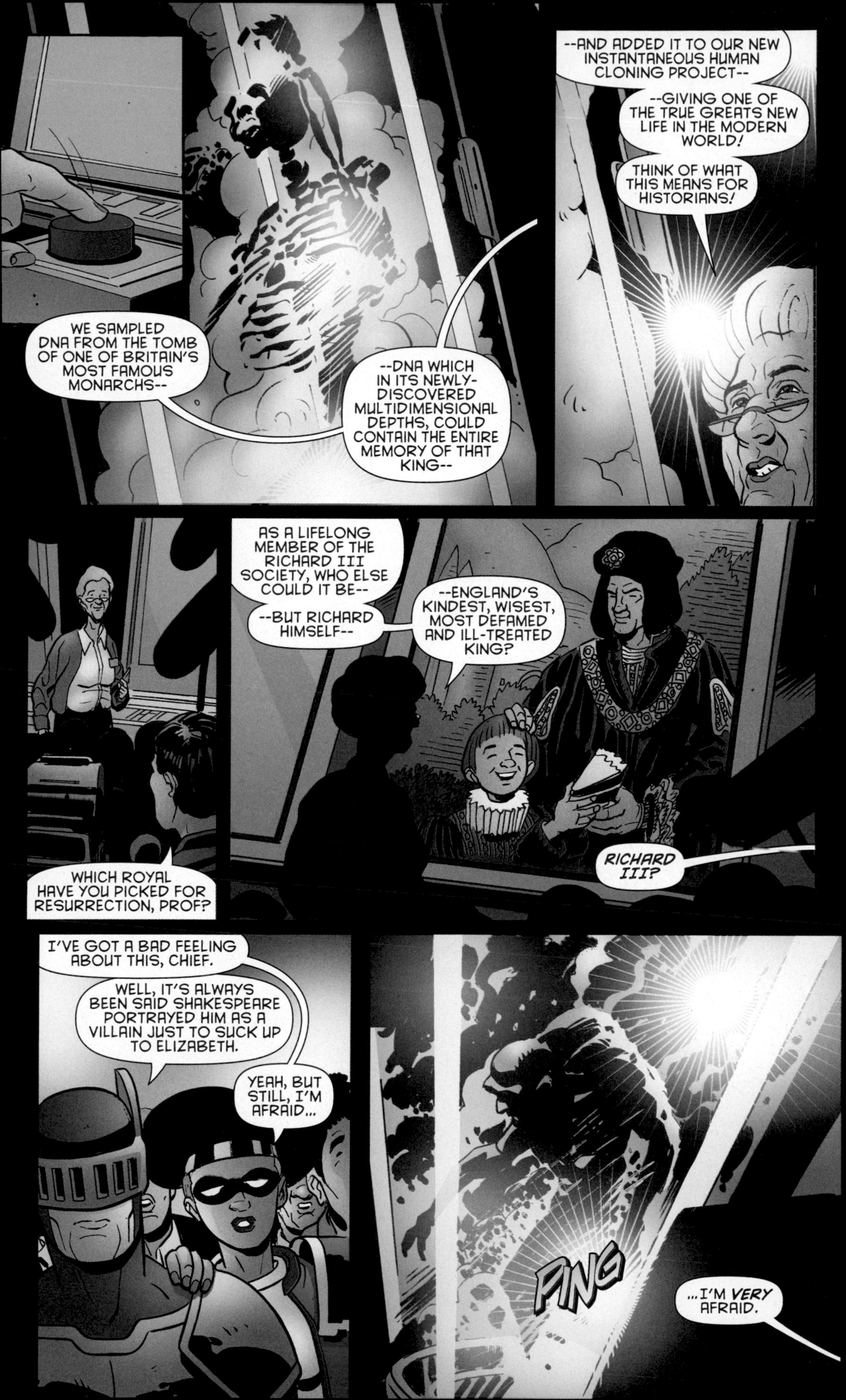
WE SAMPLED DNA FROM THE TOMB OF ONE OF BRITAIN'S MOST FAMOUS MONARCHS--
--DNA WHICH IN ITS NEWLY-DISCOVERED MULTIDIMENSIONAL DEPTHS, COULD CONTAIN THE ENTIRE MEMORY OF THAT KING--
--AND ADDED IT TO OUR NEW INSTANTANEOUS HUMAN CLONING PROJECT--
--GIVING ONE OF THE TRUE GREATS NEW LIFE IN THE MODERN WORLD!
THINK OF WHAT THIS MEANS FOR HISTORIANS!
WHICH ROYAL HAVE YOU PICKED FOR RESURRECTION, PROF?
AS A LIFELONG MEMBER OF THE RICHARD III SOCIETY, WHO ELSE COULD IT BE--
--BUT RICHARD HIMSELF--
--ENGLAND'S KINDEST, WISEST, MOST DEFAMED AND ILL-TREATED KING?
RICHARD III?
I'VE GOT A BAD FEELING ABOUT THIS, CHIEF.
WELL, IT'S ALWAYS BEEN SAID SHAKESPEARE PORTRAYED HIM AS A VILLAIN JUST TO SUCK UP TO ELIZABETH.
YEAH, BUT STILL, I'M AFRAID...
FING
...I'M VERY AFRAID.

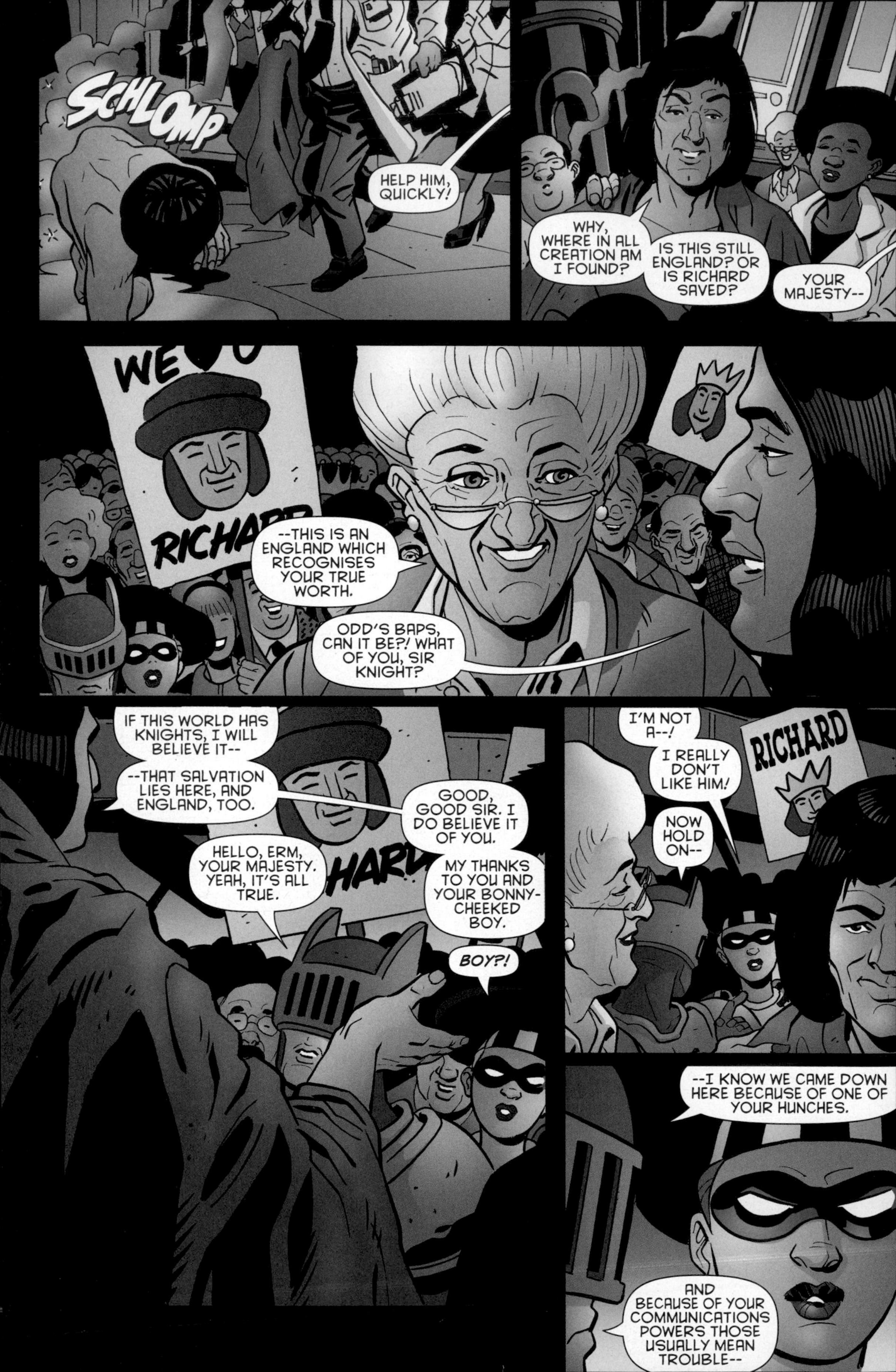
SCHLOMP
HELP HIM, QUICKLY!
WHY, WHERE IN ALL CREATION AM I FOUND?
IS THIS STILL ENGLAND? OR IS RICHARD SAVED?
YOUR MAJESTY--
WE
RICHARD
--THIS IS AN ENGLAND WHICH RECOGNISES YOUR TRUE WORTH.
ODD'S BAPS, CAN IT BE?! WHAT OF YOU, SIR KNIGHT?
IF THIS WORLD HAS KNIGHTS, I WILL BELIEVE IT--
--THAT SALVATION LIES HERE, AND ENGLAND, TOO.
GOOD, GOOD SIR. I DO BELIEVE IT OF YOU.
HELLO, ERM, YOUR MAJESTY. YEAH, IT'S ALL TRUE.
MY THANKS TO YOU AND YOUR BONNY-CHEEKED BOY.
BOY?!
I'M NOT A--!
I REALLY DON'T LIKE HIM!
NOW HOLD ON--
RICHARD
--I KNOW WE CAME DOWN HERE BECAUSE OF ONE OF YOUR HUNCHES.
AND BECAUSE OF YOUR COMMUNICATIONS POWERS THOSE USUALLY MEAN TROUBLE--

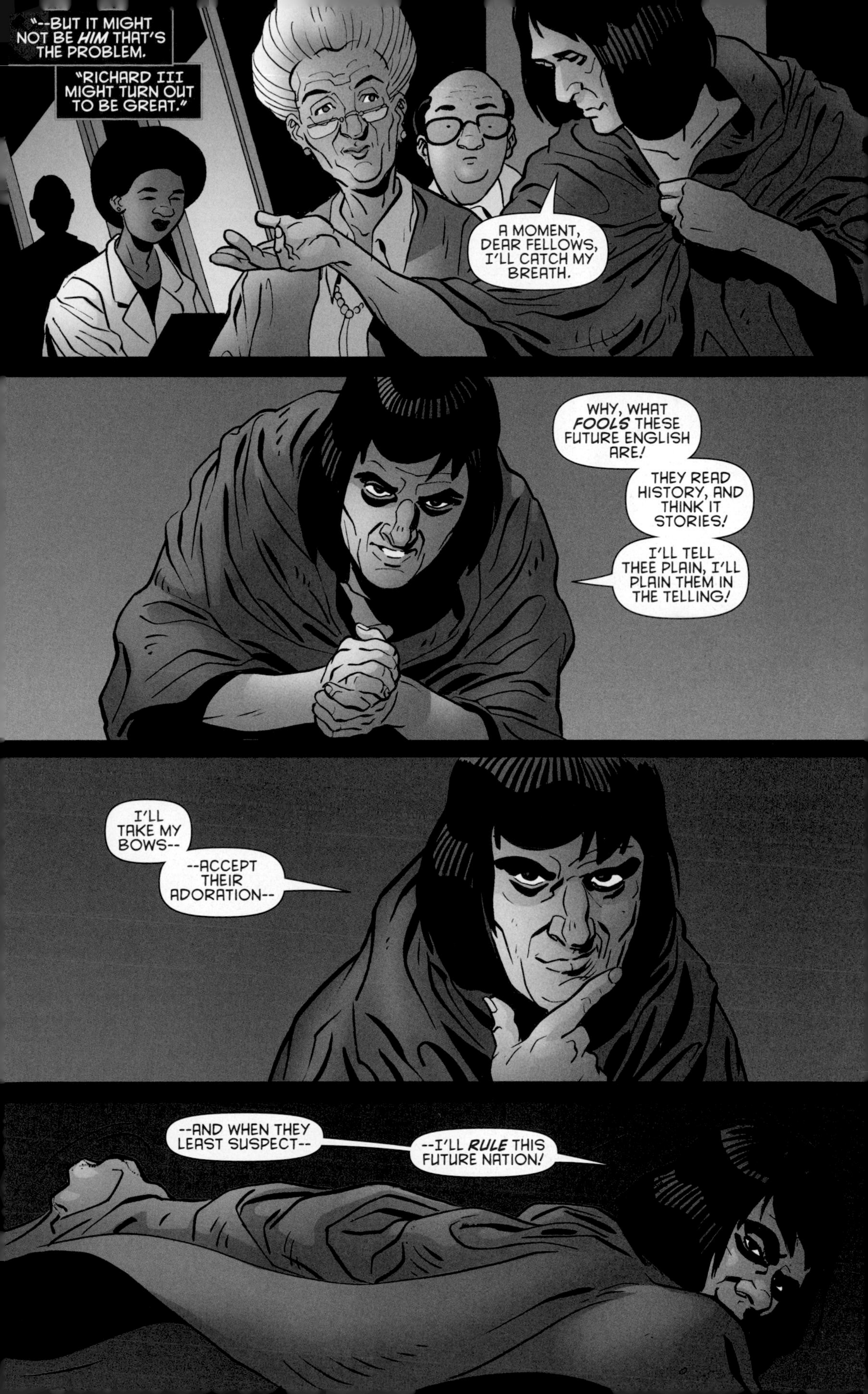
"--BUT IT MIGHT NOT BE *HIM* THAT'S THE PROBLEM.
"RICHARD III MIGHT TURN OUT TO BE GREAT."
A MOMENT, DEAR FELLOWS, I'LL CATCH MY BREATH.
WHY, WHAT *FOOLS* THESE FUTURE ENGLISH ARE!
THEY READ HISTORY, AND THINK IT STORIES!
I'LL TELL THEE PLAIN, I'LL PLAIN THEM IN THE TELLING!
I'LL TAKE MY BOWS--
--ACCEPT THEIR ADORATION--
--AND WHEN THEY LEAST SUSPECT--
--I'LL *RULE* THIS FUTURE NATION!

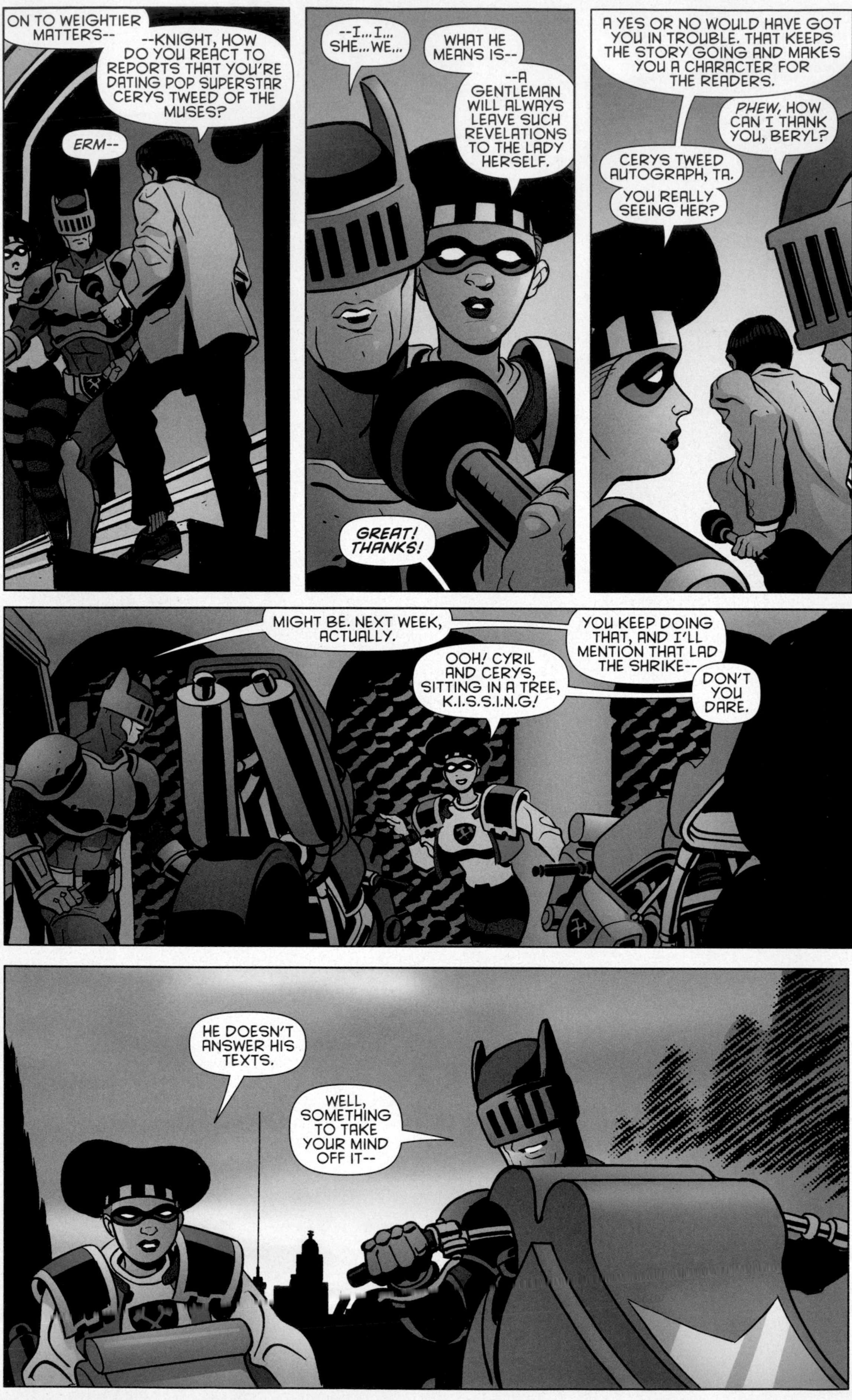
ON TO WEIGHTIER MATTERS--
--KNIGHT, HOW DO YOU REACT TO REPORTS THAT YOU'RE DATING POP SUPERSTAR CERYS TWEED OF THE MUSES?
ERM--
--I...I... SHE...WE...
WHAT HE MEANS IS--
--A GENTLEMAN WILL ALWAYS LEAVE SUCH REVELATIONS TO THE LADY HERSELF.
GREAT! THANKS!
A YES OR NO WOULD HAVE GOT YOU IN TROUBLE. THAT KEEPS THE STORY GOING AND MAKES YOU A CHARACTER FOR THE READERS.
PHEW, HOW CAN I THANK YOU, BERYL?
CERYS TWEED AUTOGRAPH, TA.
YOU REALLY SEEING HER?
MIGHT BE. NEXT WEEK, ACTUALLY.
OOH! CYRIL AND CERYS, SITTING IN A TREE, K.I.S.S.I.N.G!
YOU KEEP DOING THAT, AND I'LL MENTION THAT LAD THE SHRIKE--
DON'T YOU DARE.
HE DOESN'T ANSWER HIS TEXTS.
WELL, SOMETHING TO TAKE YOUR MIND OFF IT--

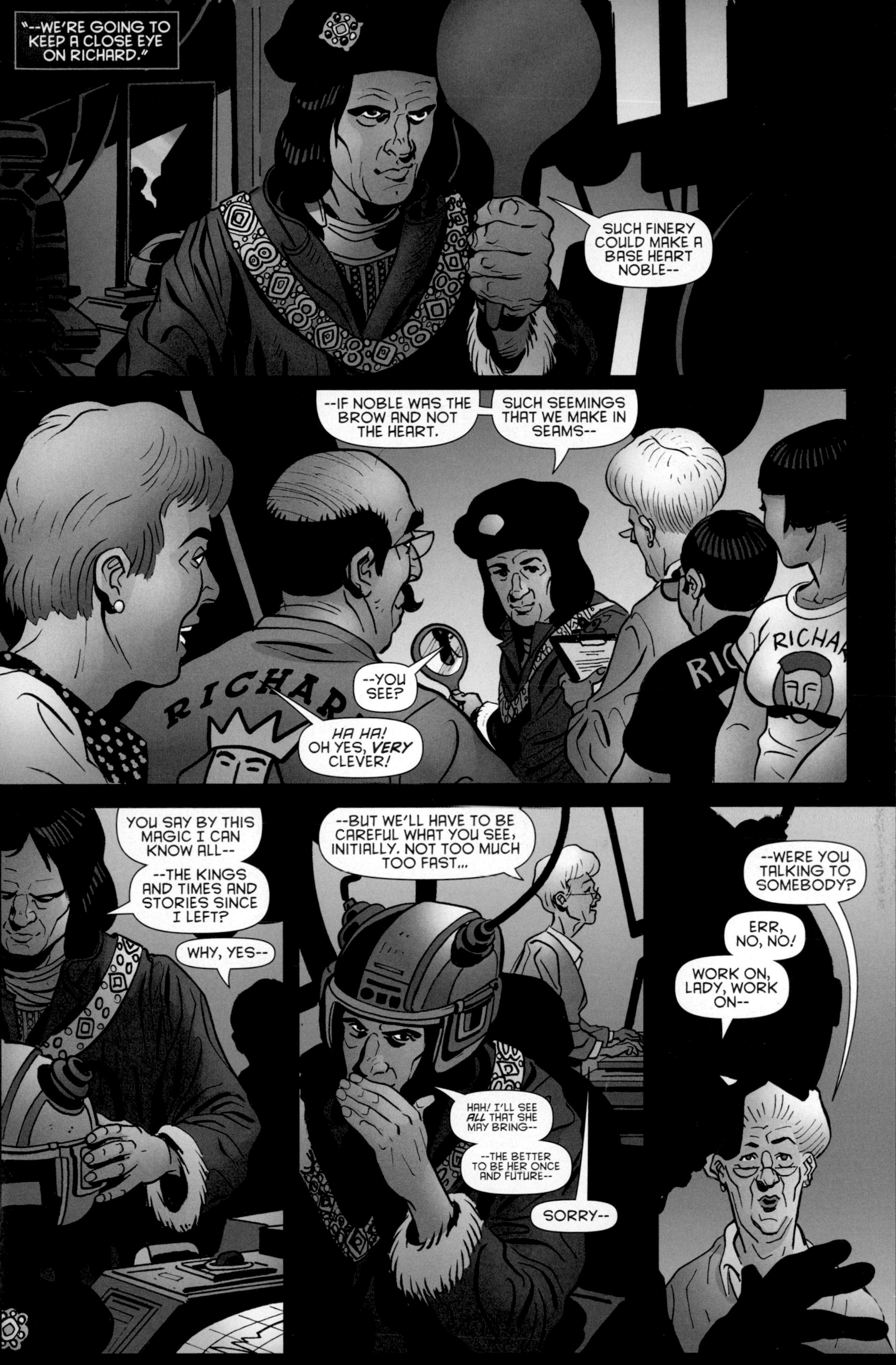
"--WE'RE GOING TO KEEP A CLOSE EYE ON RICHARD."
SUCH FINERY COULD MAKE A BASE HEART NOBLE--
--IF NOBLE WAS THE BROW AND NOT THE HEART.
SUCH SEEMINGS THAT WE MAKE IN SEAMS--
--YOU SEE?
HA HA! OH YES, VERY CLEVER!
YOU SAY BY THIS MAGIC I CAN KNOW ALL--
--THE KINGS AND TIMES AND STORIES SINCE I LEFT?
WHY, YES--
--BUT WE'LL HAVE TO BE CAREFUL WHAT YOU SEE, INITIALLY. NOT TOO MUCH TOO FAST...
HAH! I'LL SEE ALL THAT SHE MAY BRING--
--THE BETTER TO BE HER ONCE AND FUTURE--
SORRY--
--WERE YOU TALKING TO SOMEBODY?
ERR, NO, NO!
WORK ON, LADY, WORK ON--

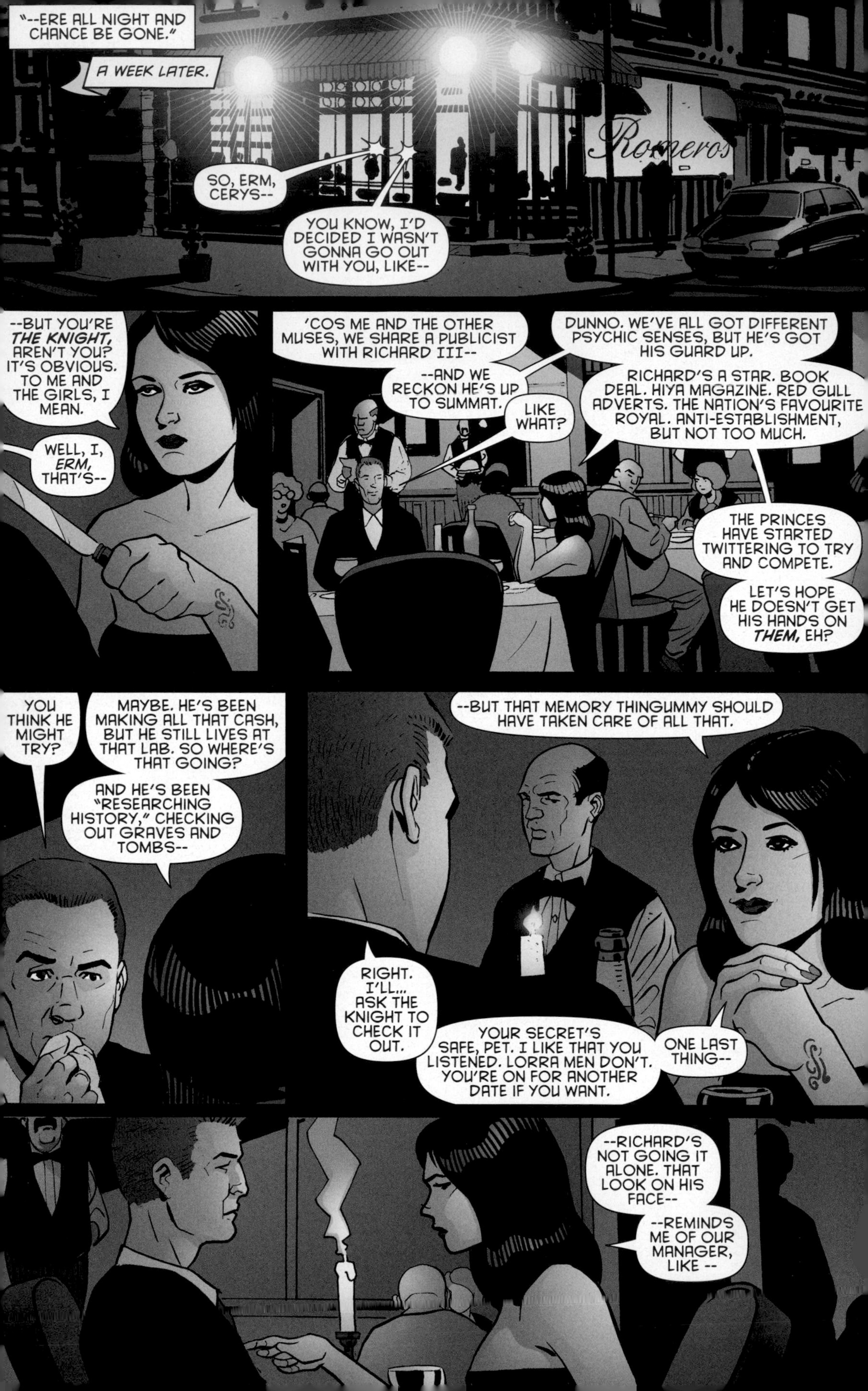
"--ERE ALL NIGHT AND CHANCE BE GONE."
A WEEK LATER.
Romeros
SO, ERM, CERYS--
YOU KNOW, I'D DECIDED I WASN'T GONNA GO OUT WITH YOU, LIKE--
--BUT YOU'RE THE KNIGHT, AREN'T YOU? IT'S OBVIOUS. TO ME AND THE GIRLS, I MEAN.
WELL, I, ERM, THAT'S--
'COS ME AND THE OTHER MUSES, WE SHARE A PUBLICIST WITH RICHARD III--
--AND WE RECKON HE'S UP TO SUMMAT.
LIKE WHAT?
DUNNO. WE'VE ALL GOT DIFFERENT PSYCHIC SENSES, BUT HE'S GOT HIS GUARD UP.
RICHARD'S A STAR. BOOK DEAL. HIYA MAGAZINE. RED GULL ADVERTS. THE NATION'S FAVOURITE ROYAL. ANTI-ESTABLISHMENT, BUT NOT TOO MUCH.
THE PRINCES HAVE STARTED TWITTERING TO TRY AND COMPETE.
LET'S HOPE HE DOESN'T GET HIS HANDS ON THEM, EH?
YOU THINK HE MIGHT TRY?
MAYBE. HE'S BEEN MAKING ALL THAT CASH, BUT HE STILL LIVES AT THAT LAB. SO WHERE'S THAT GOING?
AND HE'S BEEN "RESEARCHING HISTORY," CHECKING OUT GRAVES AND TOMBS--
--BUT THAT MEMORY THINGUMMY SHOULD HAVE TAKEN CARE OF ALL THAT.
RIGHT. I'LL... ASK THE KNIGHT TO CHECK IT OUT.
YOUR SECRET'S SAFE, PET. I LIKE THAT YOU LISTENED. LORRA MEN DON'T. YOU'RE ON FOR ANOTHER DATE IF YOU WANT.
ONE LAST THING--
--RICHARD'S NOT GOING IT ALONE. THAT LOOK ON HIS FACE--
--REMINDS ME OF OUR MANAGER, LIKE --

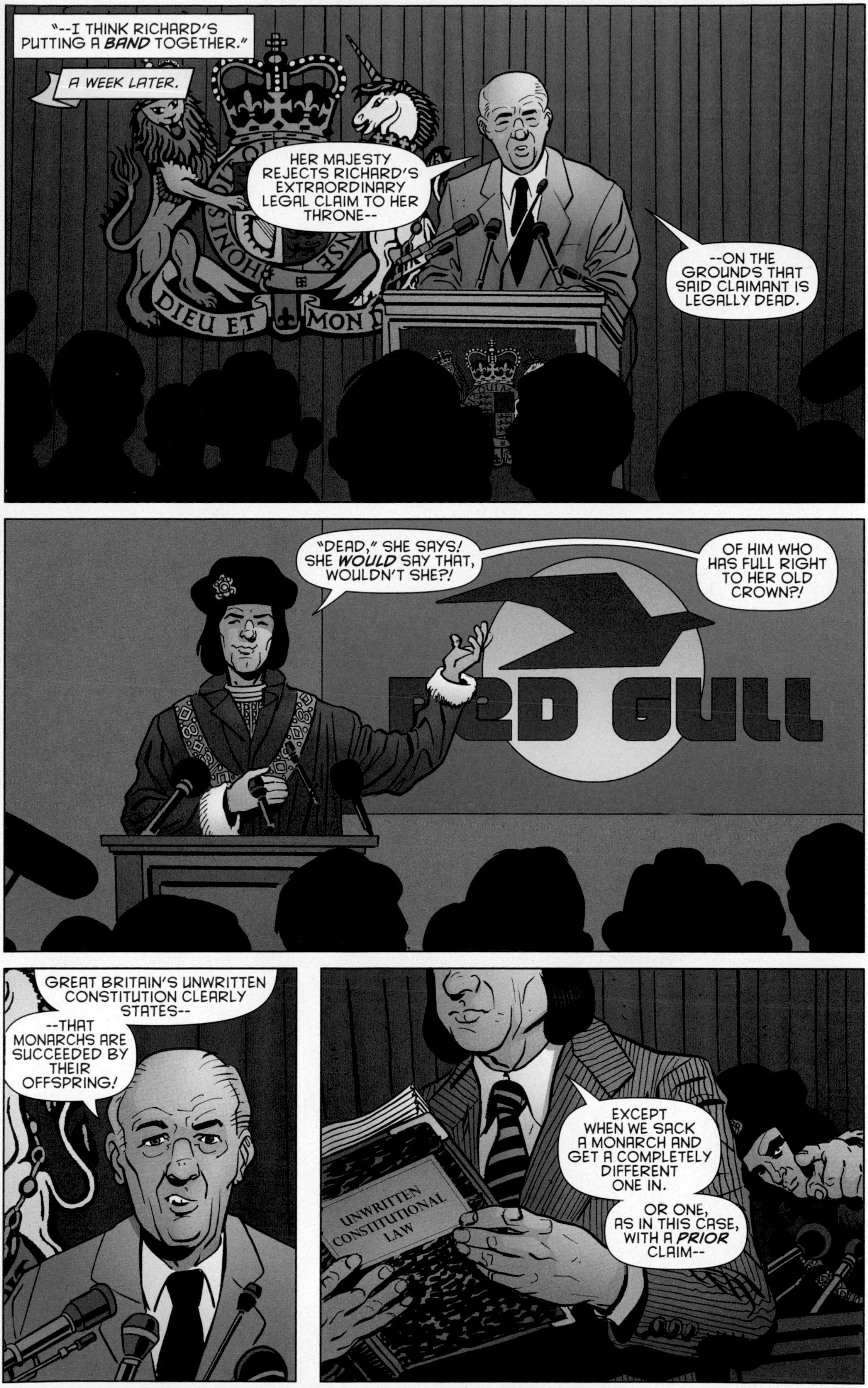
"--I THINK RICHARD'S PUTTING A *BAND* TOGETHER."
A WEEK LATER.
HER MAJESTY REJECTS RICHARD'S EXTRAORDINARY LEGAL CLAIM TO HER THRONE--
--ON THE GROUNDS THAT SAID CLAIMANT IS LEGALLY DEAD.
"DEAD," SHE SAYS! SHE *WOULD* SAY THAT, WOULDN'T SHE?!
OF HIM WHO HAS FULL RIGHT TO HER OLD CROWN?!
GREAT BRITAIN'S UNWRITTEN CONSTITUTION CLEARLY STATES--
--THAT MONARCHS ARE SUCCEEDED BY THEIR OFFSPRING!
UNWRITTEN CONSTITUTIONAL LAW
EXCEPT WHEN WE SACK A MONARCH AND GET A COMPLETELY DIFFERENT ONE IN.
OR ONE, AS IN THIS CASE, WITH A *PRIOR* CLAIM--

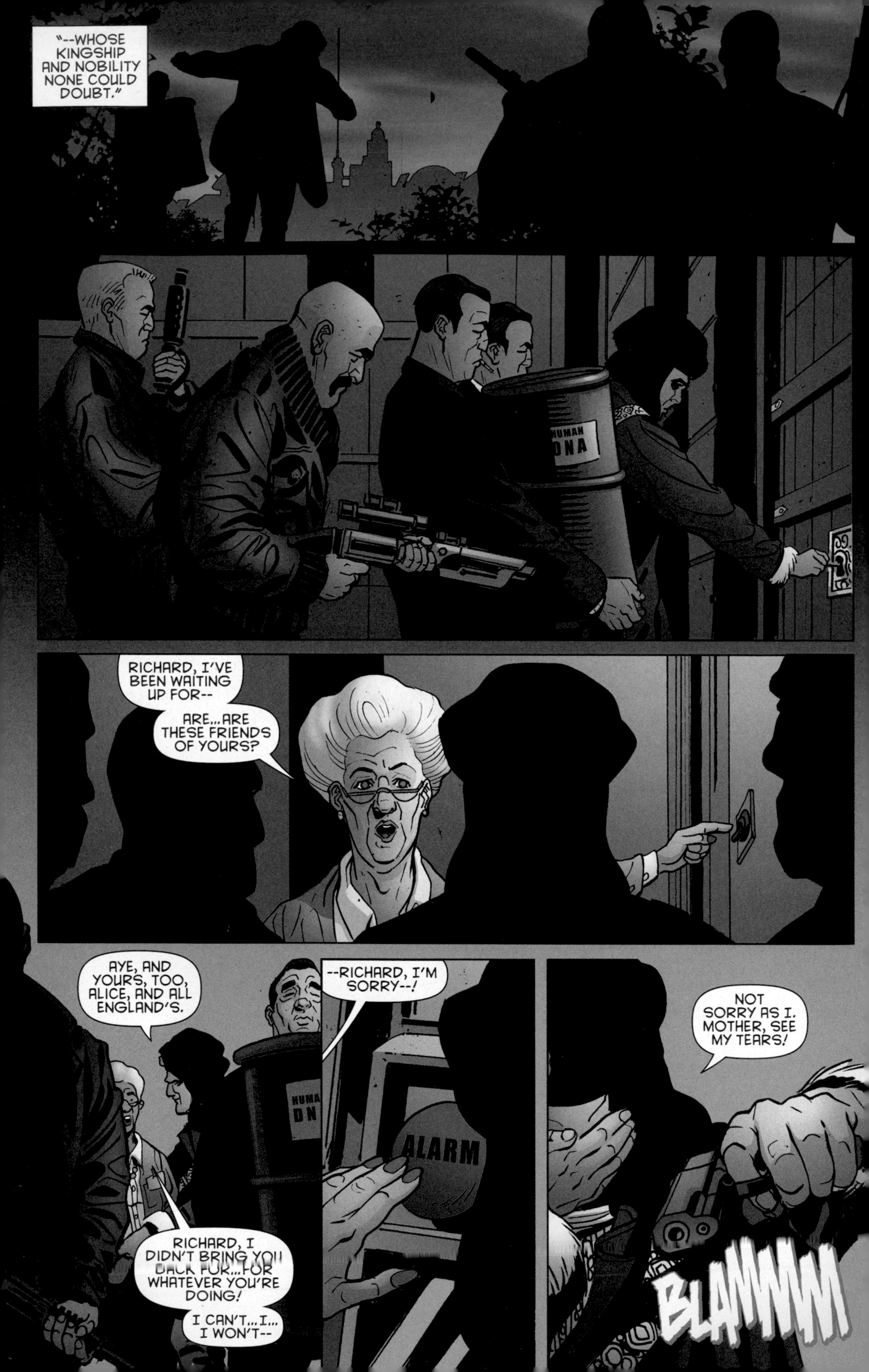
"--WHOSE KINGSHIP AND NOBILITY NONE COULD DOUBT."
HUMAN DNA
RICHARD, I'VE BEEN WAITING UP FOR--
ARE...ARE THESE FRIENDS OF YOURS?
AYE, AND YOURS, TOO, ALICE, AND ALL ENGLAND'S.
HUMAN DNA
RICHARD, I DIDN'T BRING YOU BACK FOR...FOR WHATEVER YOU'RE DOING!
I CAN'T...I... I WON'T--
--RICHARD, I'M SORRY--!
ALARM
NOT SORRY AS I. MOTHER, SEE MY TEARS!
BLAMMM

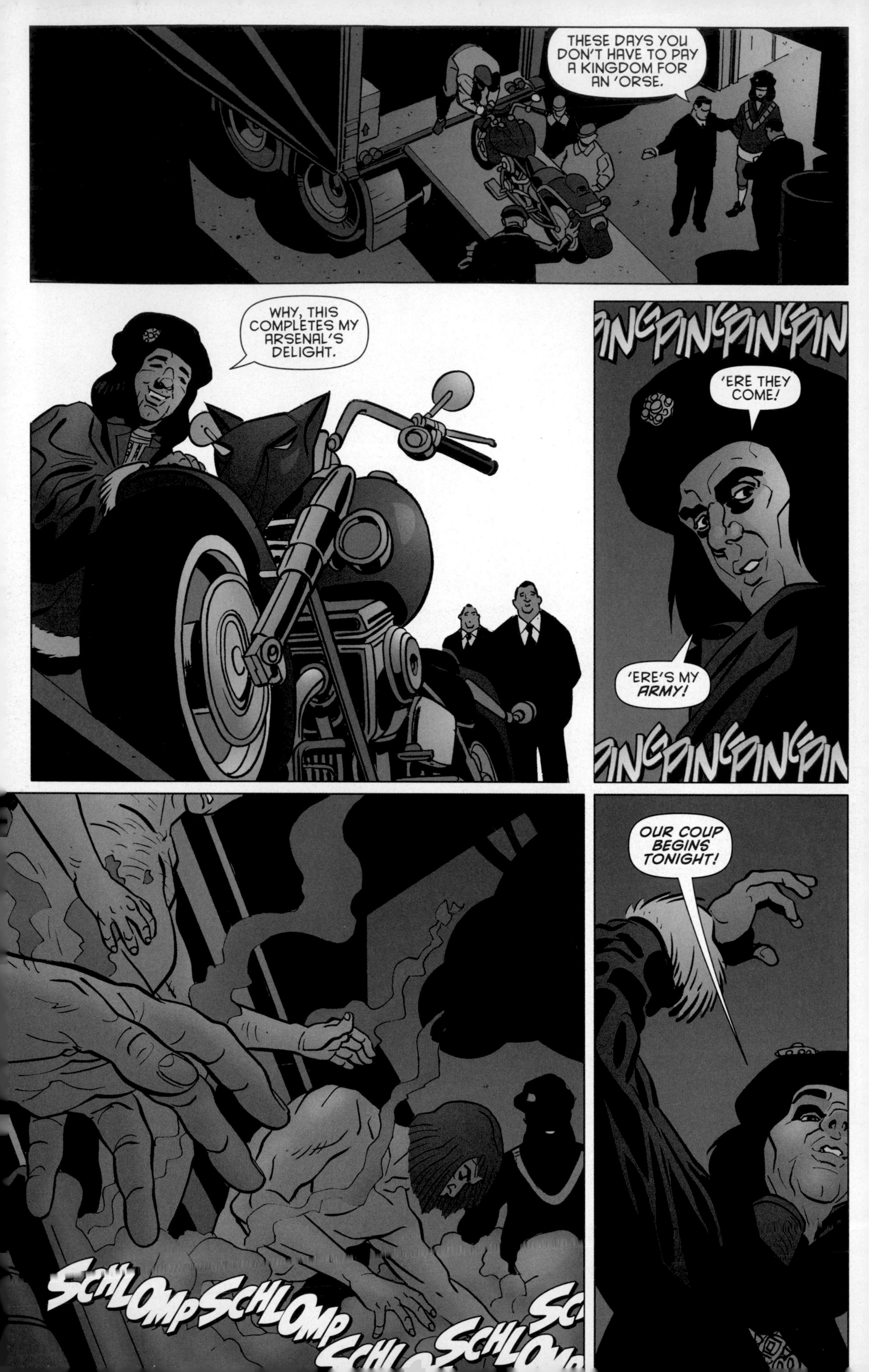
THESE DAYS YOU DON'T HAVE TO PAY A KINGDOM FOR AN 'ORSE.
WHY, THIS COMPLETES MY ARSENAL'S DELIGHT.
PINGPINGPINGPIN
'ERE THEY COME!
'ERE'S MY ARMY!
PINGPINGPINGPIN
SCHLOMP SCHLOMP SCHLOMP SCHLOMP
OUR COUP BEGINS TONIGHT!

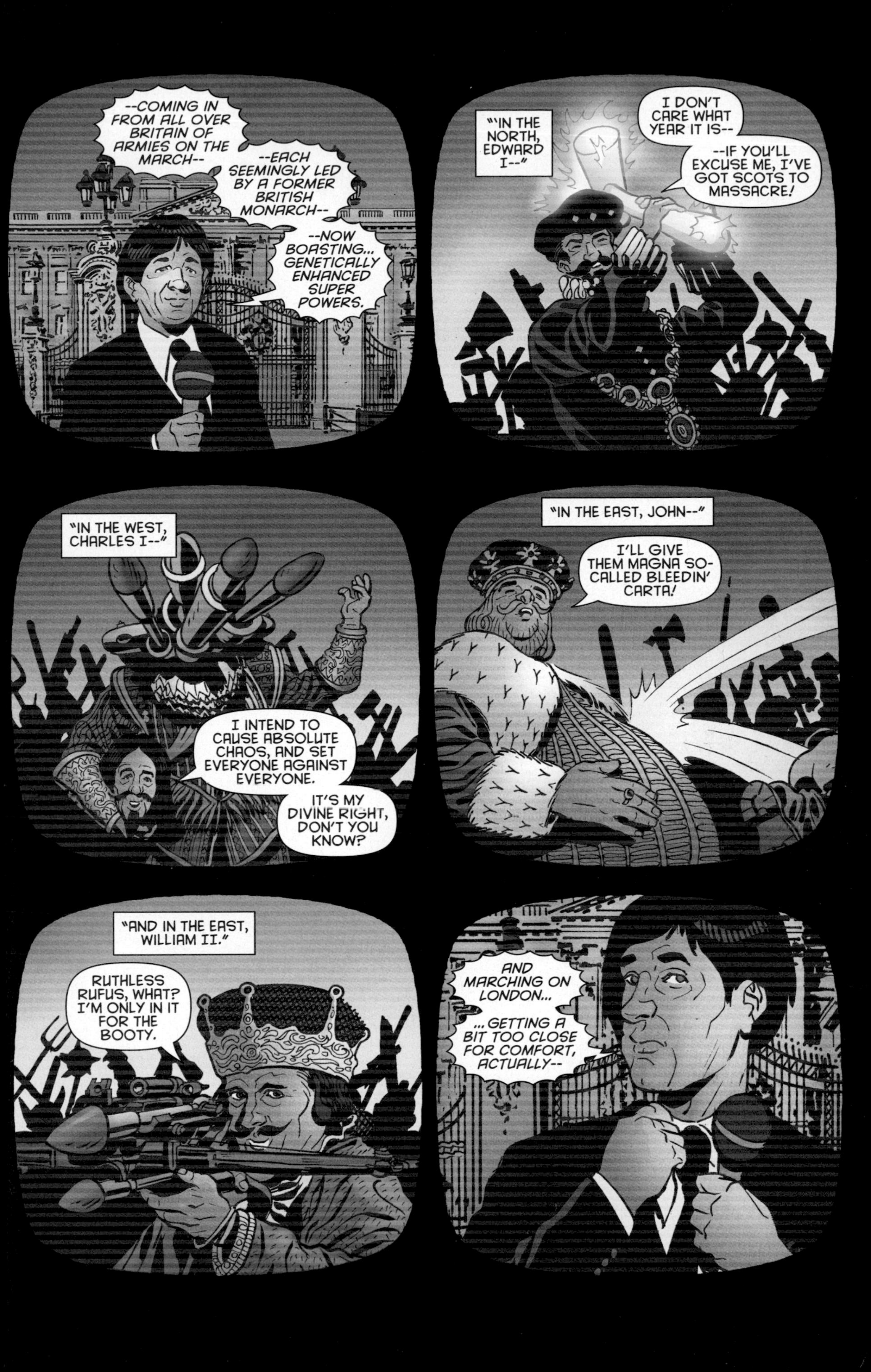
--COMING IN FROM ALL OVER BRITAIN OF ARMIES ON THE MARCH--
--EACH SEEMINGLY LED BY A FORMER BRITISH MONARCH--
--NOW BOASTING... GENETICALLY ENHANCED SUPER POWERS.
"'IN THE NORTH, EDWARD I--"
I DON'T CARE WHAT YEAR IT IS--
--IF YOU'LL EXCUSE ME, I'VE GOT SCOTS TO MASSACRE!
"IN THE WEST, CHARLES I--"
I INTEND TO CAUSE ABSOLUTE CHAOS, AND SET EVERYONE AGAINST EVERYONE.
IT'S MY DIVINE RIGHT, DON'T YOU KNOW?
"IN THE EAST, JOHN--"
I'LL GIVE THEM MAGNA SO-CALLED BLEEDIN' CARTA!
"AND IN THE EAST, WILLIAM II."
RUTHLESS RUFUS, WHAT? I'M ONLY IN IT FOR THE BOOTY.
AND MARCHING ON LONDON...
...GETTING A BIT TOO CLOSE FOR COMFORT, ACTUALLY--

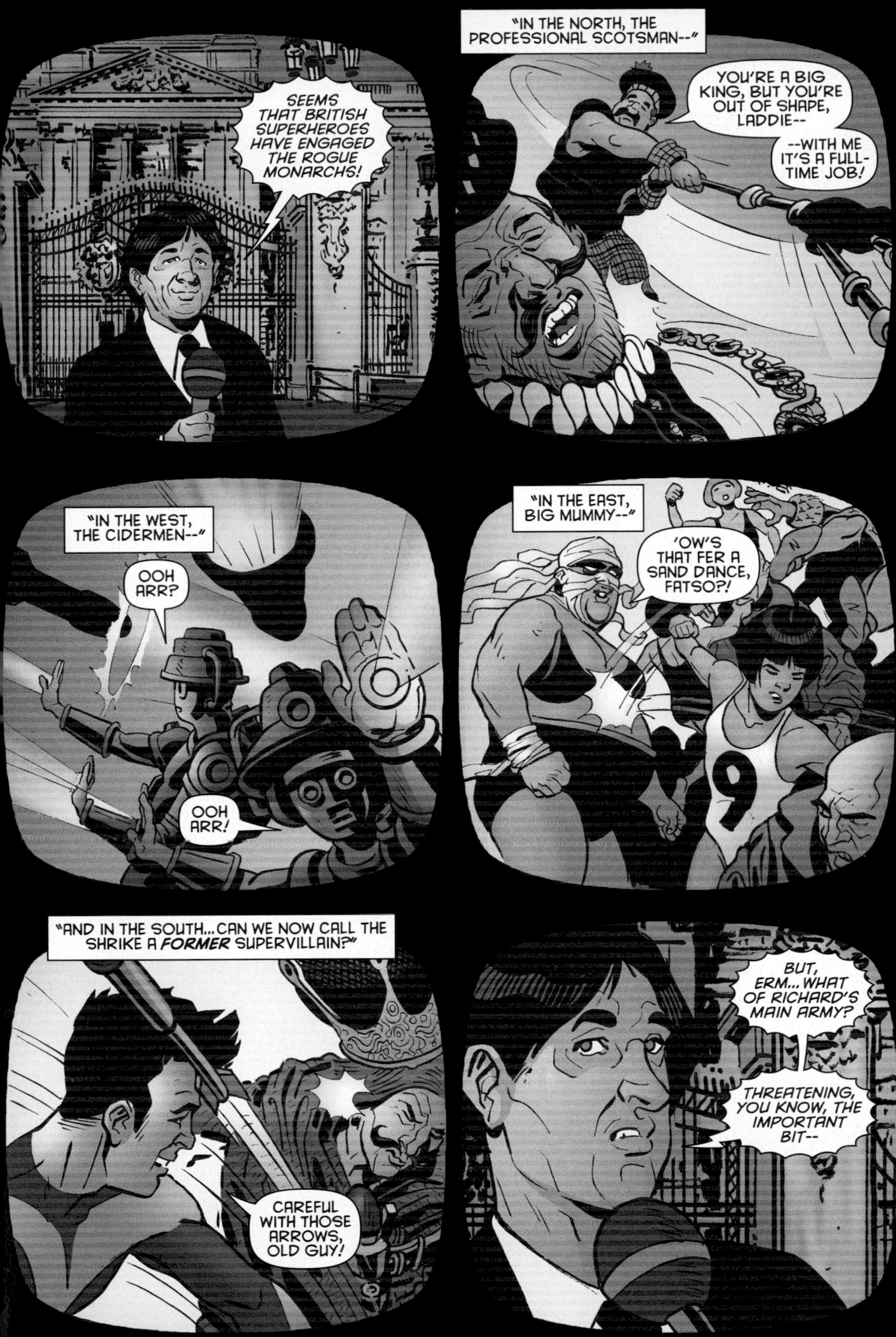
SEEMS THAT BRITISH SUPERHEROES HAVE ENGAGED THE ROGUE MONARCHS!
"IN THE NORTH, THE PROFESSIONAL SCOTSMAN--"
YOU'RE A BIG KING, BUT YOU'RE OUT OF SHAPE, LADDIE--
--WITH ME IT'S A FULL-TIME JOB!
"IN THE WEST, THE CIDERMEN--"
OOH ARR?
OOH ARR!
"IN THE EAST, BIG MUMMY--"
'OW'S THAT FER A SAND DANCE, FATSO?!
"AND IN THE SOUTH...CAN WE NOW CALL THE SHRIKE A *FORMER* SUPERVILLAIN?"
CAREFUL WITH THOSE ARROWS, OLD GUY!
BUT, ERM... WHAT OF RICHARD'S MAIN ARMY?
THREATENING, YOU KNOW, THE IMPORTANT BIT--

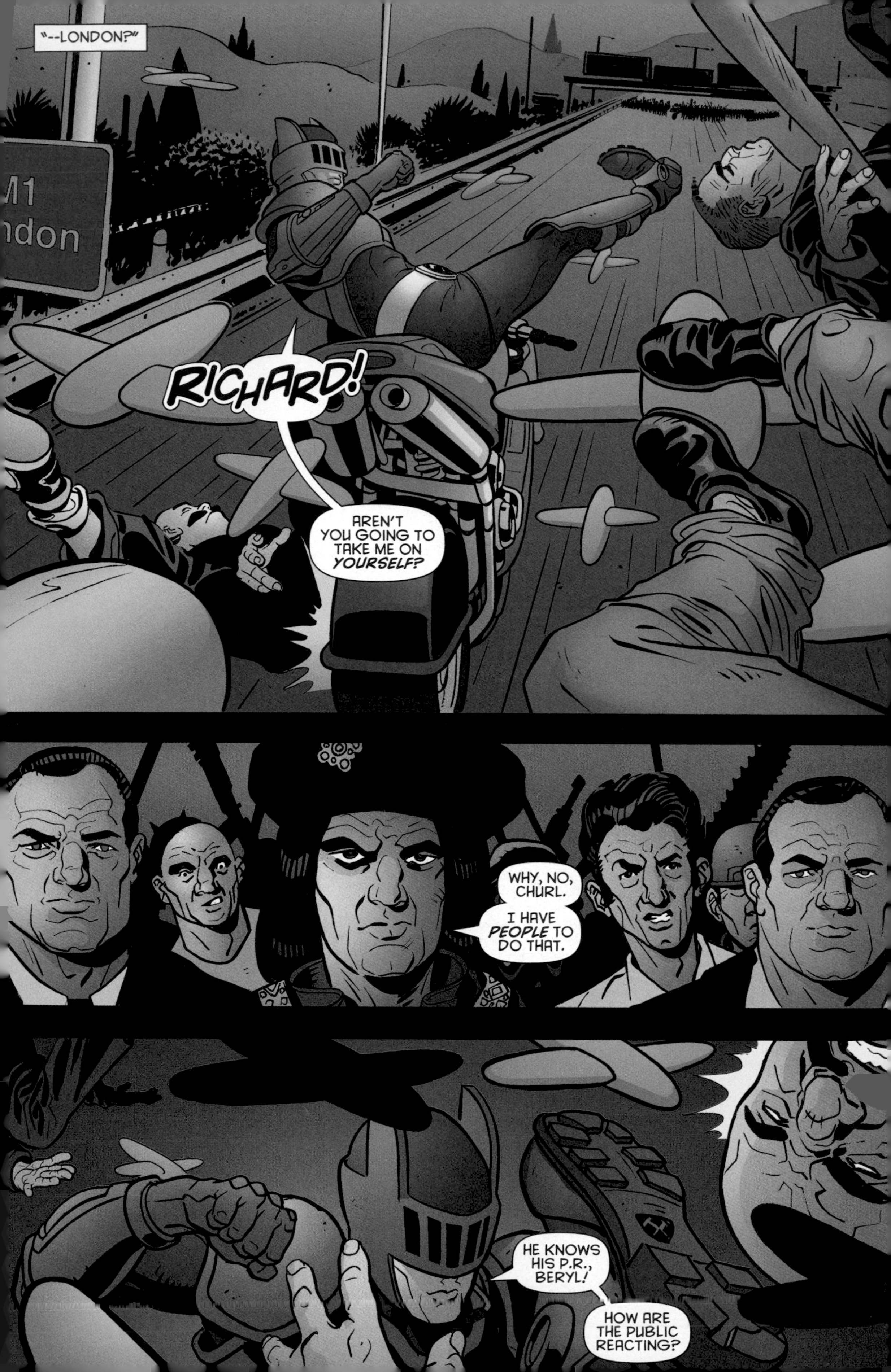
"--LONDON?"
M1
ndon
RICHARD!
AREN'T YOU GOING TO TAKE ME ON YOURSELF?
WHY, NO, CHURL.
I HAVE PEOPLE TO DO THAT.
HE KNOWS HIS P.R., BERYL!
HOW ARE THE PUBLIC REACTING?

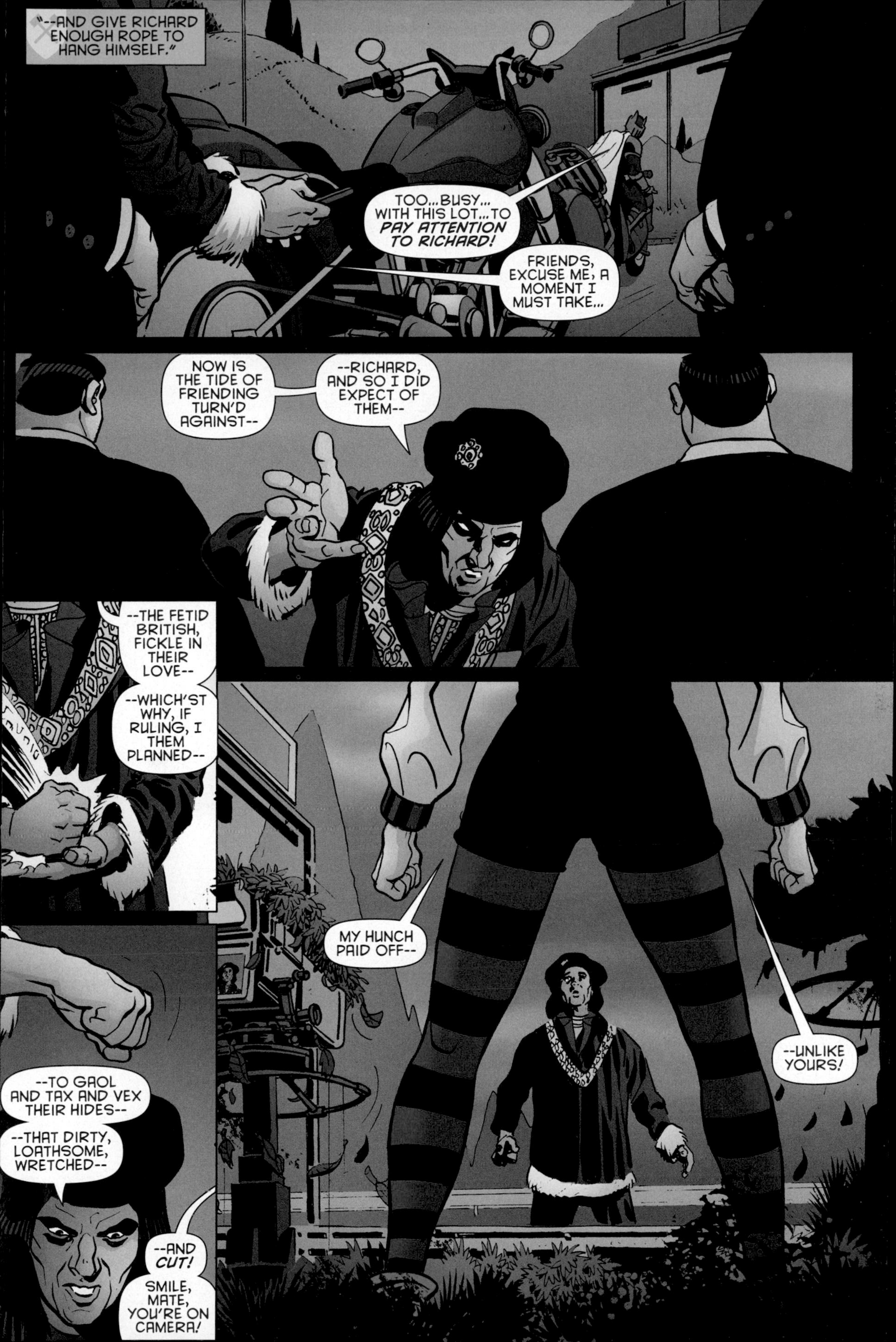
"--AND GIVE RICHARD ENOUGH ROPE TO HANG HIMSELF."
TOO...BUSY... WITH THIS LOT...TO PAY ATTENTION TO RICHARD!
FRIENDS, EXCUSE ME, A MOMENT I MUST TAKE...
NOW IS THE TIDE OF FRIENDING TURN'D AGAINST--
--RICHARD, AND SO I DID EXPECT OF THEM--
--THE FETID BRITISH, FICKLE IN THEIR LOVE--
--WHICH'ST WHY, IF RULING, I THEM PLANNED--
MY HUNCH PAID OFF--
--UNLIKE YOURS!
--TO GAOL AND TAX AND VEX THEIR HIDES--
--THAT DIRTY, LOATHSOME, WRETCHED--
--AND CUT!
SMILE, MATE, YOU'RE ON CAMERA!

Cabbages and Kings

THERE ARE SEVERAL REAL-LIFE GROUPS DEDICATED TO COUNTERING WILLIAM SHAKESPEARE'S SLANDEROUS CLAIMS ABOUT KING RICHARD III, WHOM HE MADE A VILLAIN, SUCH FOLK SAY, IN ORDER TO PLEASE HIS PATRONS. THE REAL RICHARD, THEY ADD, WAS, AS MONARCHS GO, OKAY. AS PER SHAKESPEARE, RICHARD'S DIALOGUE IS IN IAMBIC PENTAMETER (AND YES, THE WHOLE IDEA IS THAT YOU BREAK THE METER FOR DRAMATIC EFFECT, AHEM), AND HE ENDS HIS SCENES IN RHYMING COUPLETS. SHAKESPEARE PROBABLY GAVE HIM HIS HUNCHBACK.

CERYS TWEED'S NAME REFLECTS NOT ONLY A FEW DIFFERENT POP STARS, BUT ALSO HARRIS TWEED, DETECTIVE HERO OF *THE EAGLE,* THE BEST COMIC EVER MADE. JUST 'COS. "COR!" IS AN ANCIENT BRITISH CHILDREN'S COMIC CRY OF JOY. "HE WOULD SAY THAT, WOULDN'T HE?" IS A SLY QUOTE FROM THE PROFUMO AFFAIR, A SCANDAL THAT ROCKED BRITISH POLITICS INTO THE ERA OF ROCK AND ROLL. BRITAIN'S "UNWRITTEN CONSTITUTION" ALLOWS THE BRITISH BODY POLITIC TO DO WHAT IT LIKES, BASICALLY, AS LONG AS IT'S EITHER BEEN DONE BEFORE, OR NOBODY IMPORTANT WILL KICK UP TOO MUCH OF A FUSS. THE GRAY TWINS ARE SATIRICAL VERSIONS OF THE FAMOUS LONDON GANGSTERS, WHO ALSO LIKED TO THINK THEY HOBNOBBED WITH THE GENTRY. "BRUSH UP YOUR SHAKESPEARE" IS A COLE PORTER SONG. OF THE VARIOUS KINGS I'VE SLANDERED, I THINK JOHN IS THE ONE WHO PROBABLY WASN'T AS BAD AS I'VE PAINTED HIM. KNOWING MONARCHS BY JUST A COUPLE OF SALIENT LIBELS IS SOMETHING THE BRITISH PUBLIC DO. THE PROFESSIONAL SCOTSMAN SEEMS TO HAVE WATCHED *GET CARTER* (1971). THE CIDERMEN ARE ACTUALLY QUOTING LINES GIVEN TO PIGBIN JOSH, A COUNTRY FELLOW IN JON PERTWEE ERA *DOCTOR WHO.* BIG DADDY WAS A PROFESSIONAL WRESTLER, ENORMOUS IN THE 1970s.

I LIKE TO THINK OF THIS WHOLE ISSUE AS SOMETHING 1970s BBC COMEDIAN TRIO *THE GOODIES* WOULD HAVE PERFORMED. IF YOU COULD SING THEIR THEME TUNE TO YOURSELF AT THE START AND FINISH, THAT WOULD PLEASE ME A GREAT DEAL. CHEERIO!

UNTIL NEXT ISSUE, CHEERIO!
- PAUL CORNELL

brought to you by KNIGHT AND SQUIRE   ad by Jimmy Broxton   design by SWANDS

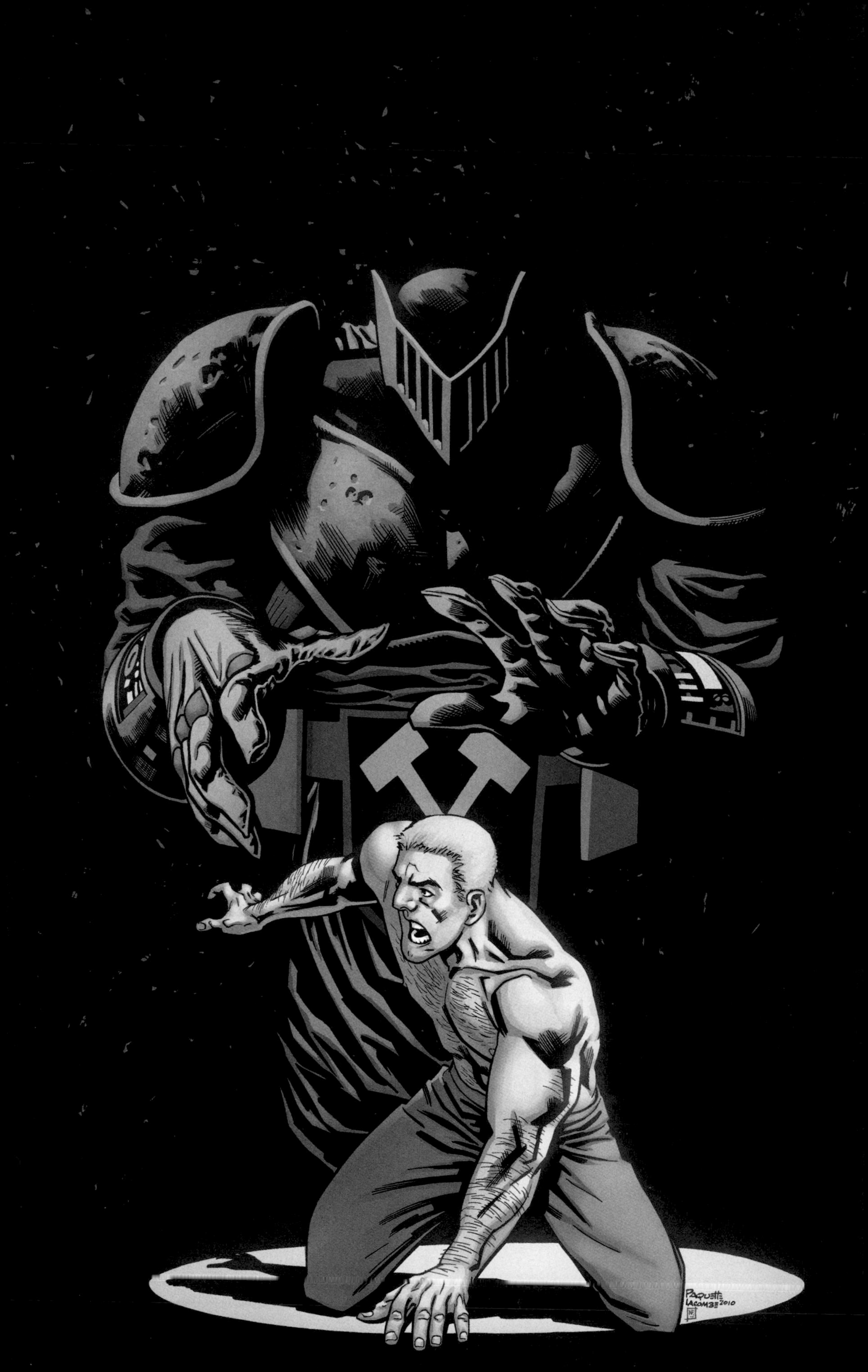
PAQUETTE
LACOMBE 2010

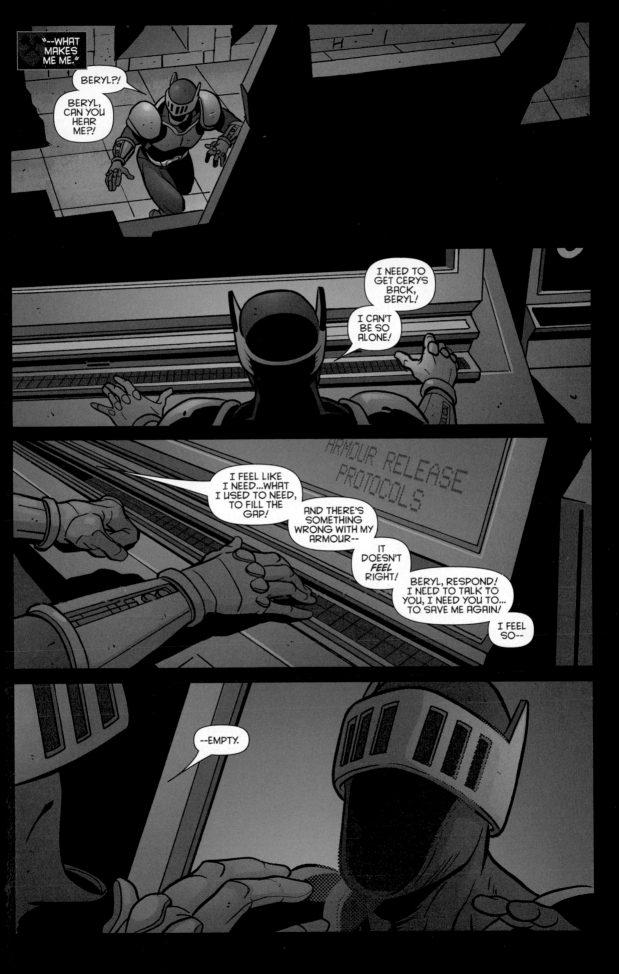

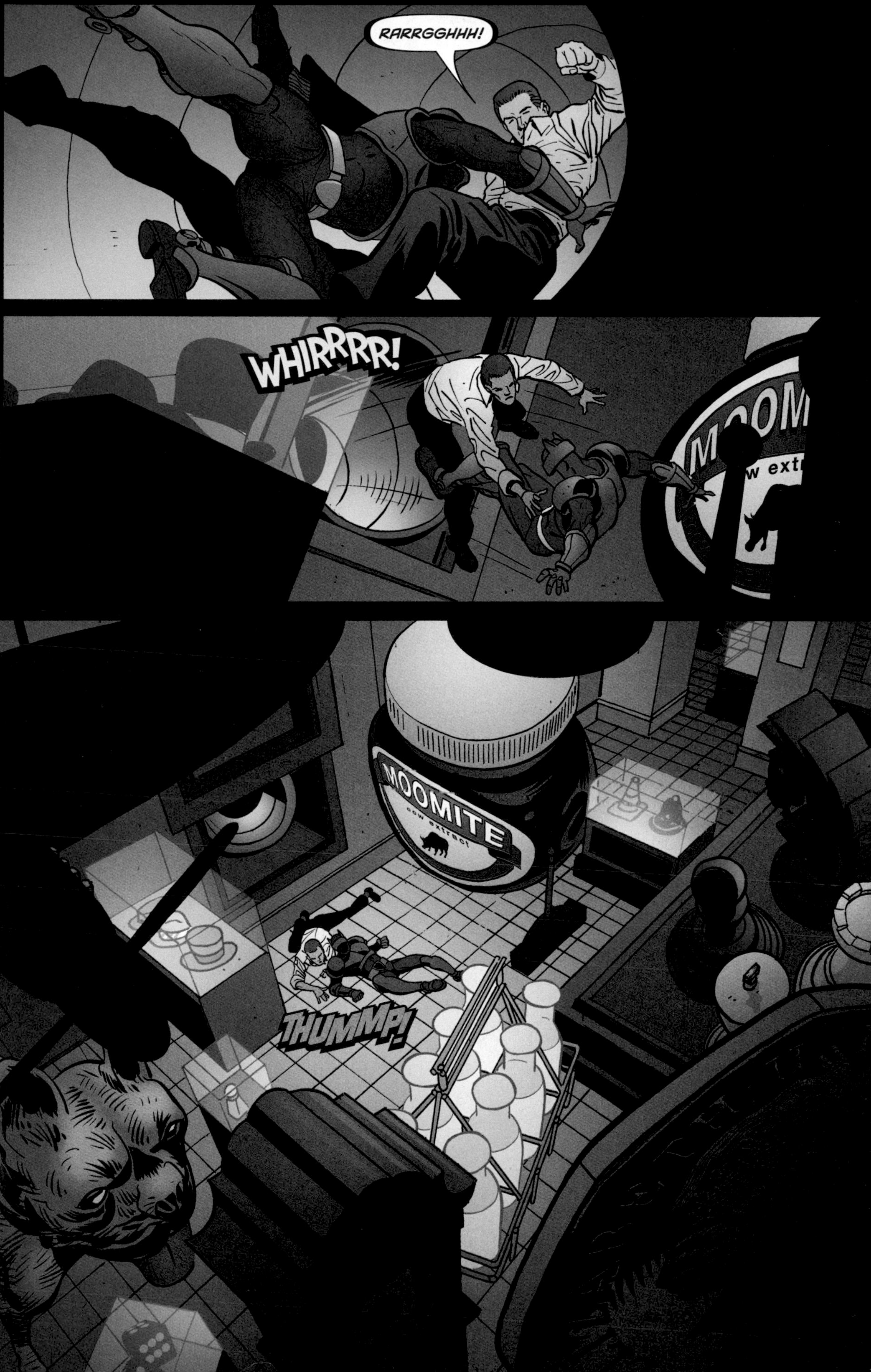
RARRGGHHH!
WHIRRRR!
MOOMITE
cow extract
THUMMP!

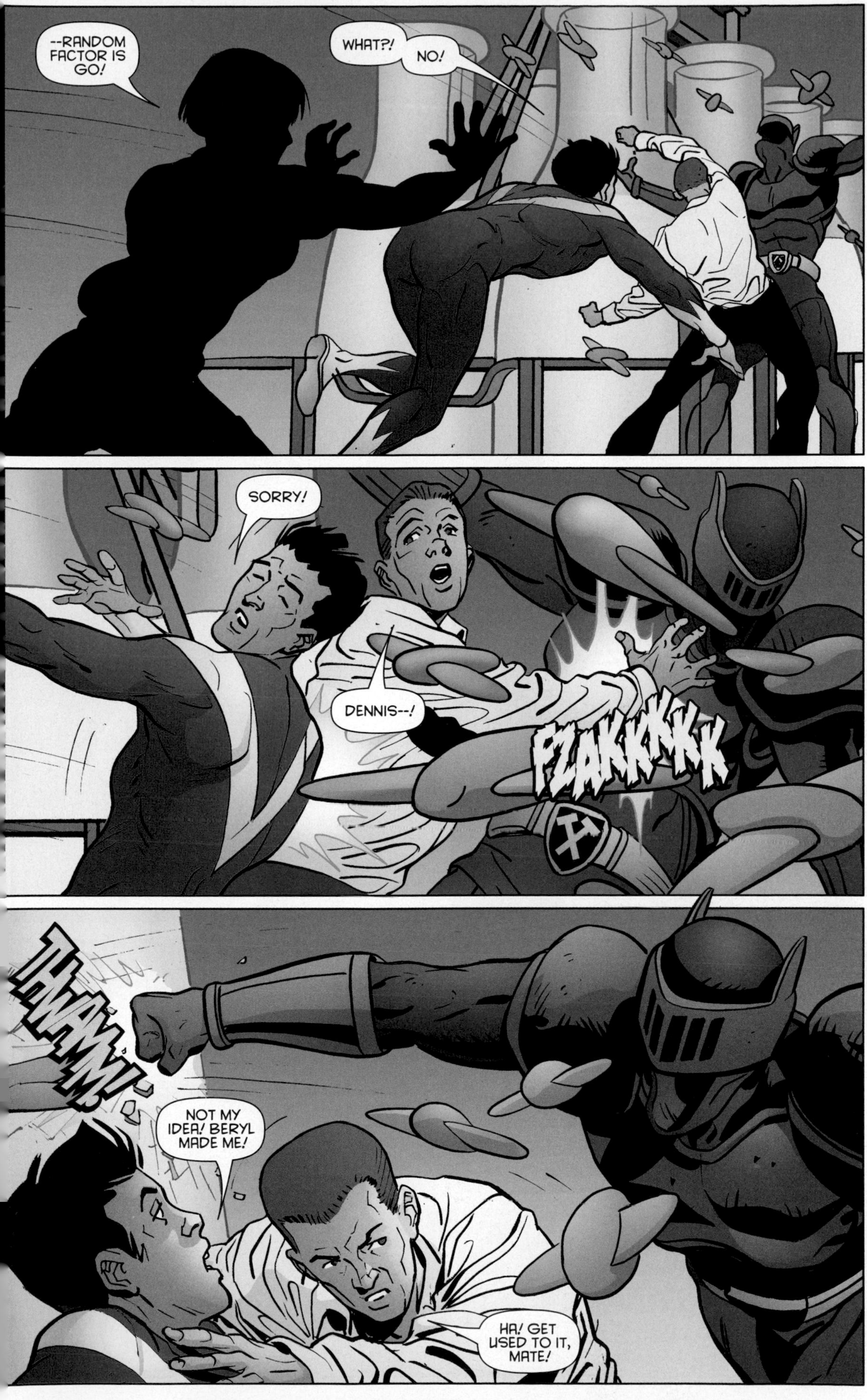
--RANDOM FACTOR IS GO!
WHAT?!
NO!
SORRY!
DENNIS--!
FZAKKKKK
THWAM!
NOT MY IDEA! BERYL MADE ME!
HA! GET USED TO IT, MATE!

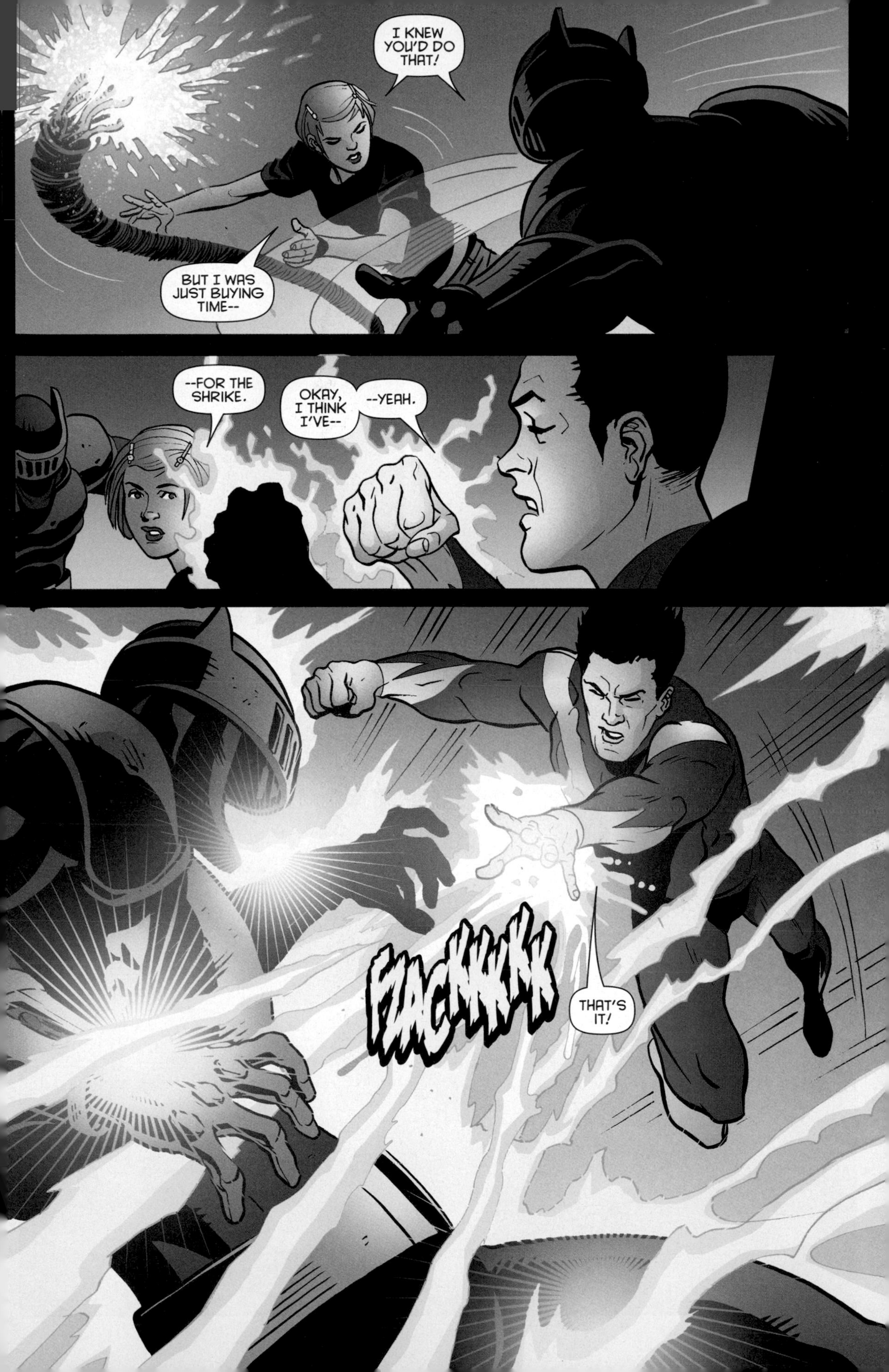
I KNEW YOU'D DO THAT!
BUT I WAS JUST BUYING TIME--
--FOR THE SHRIKE.
OKAY, I THINK I'VE--
--YEAH.
FZACKKKK
THAT'S IT!

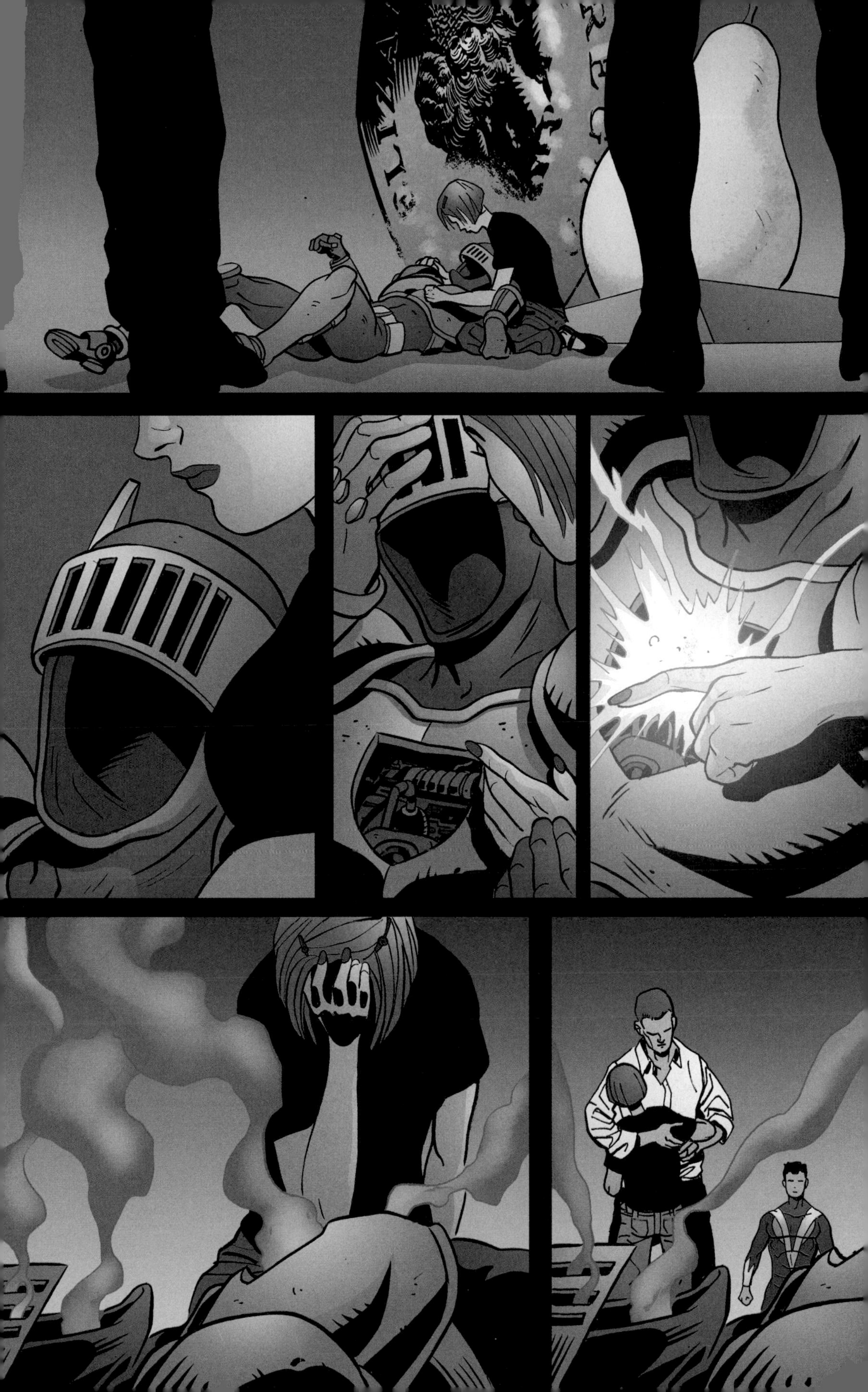

Butlers and Batmen

GIVING BATMAN A BUTLER, IN THE FORM OF ALFRED PENNYWORTH, WAS A GENIUS IDEA: WHO ELSE WOULD KEEP DANGEROUS SECRETS AND OFFER A CALM, FIRM, SECOND OPINION? AND OF COURSE HE WAS BRITISH, THAT'S WHAT BUTLERS ARE. AND IN GENERAL, ALFRED'S BEEN ONE OF THE BEST PORTRAYALS OF A BRITISH PERSON IN COMICS. BUT A BRITISH BUTLER IN *KNIGHT AND SQUIRE* STRUCK ME AS BEING A BIT ORDINARY REALLY. AS BATMAN, INC. EXPANDED ACROSS THE GLOBE, PERHAPS EVERY INTERNATIONAL BATMAN SHOULD HAVE A BUTLER FROM "THE OPPOSITE COUNTRY."

SO THAT'S WHERE HANK HACKENBACKER CAME FROM. (HIS NAME ECHOES THE *NOM DE PLUME* OF BRAINS IN *THUNDERBIRDS*, THAT OTHER VERY BRITISH GAZE AT WHAT AMERICANS MIGHT BE LIKE.) AND WHO KNOWS WHAT PART OF THE STATES HE'S FROM, PERHAPS THAT VAGUELY SOUTHERN OR COWBOY STATE THAT ALL AMERICANS IN UK ADVENTURE SHOWS WERE FROM IN THE 1960s. I LIKE TO THINK HIS ACCENT WAVERS VIOLENTLY AND THAT HE'S PLAYED BY SOMEONE FROM MILTON KEYNES.

BERYL'S "IS GO" IS A NOD TO *THUNDERBIRDS* TOO. THE SHRIKE'S REAL NAME ECHOES THAT OF THE (BRITISH) *DENNIS THE MENACE*, A COMICS CHARACTER OF THE SAME VINTAGE AS BERYL'S INSPIRATION, *BERYL THE PERIL*, AND ALSO DENNIS PENNIS, ALTER EGO OF BRITISH COMEDIAN PAUL KAYE. "THE JUDAS CONTRACT" WAS AN EPIC STORY IN THE WOLFMAN/PEREZ RUN OF *THE NEW TEEN TITANS*, THE CONSEQUENCES OF WHICH I'M SURE EVERY SUPER-HERO WOULD WORRY ABOUT. CAPTAIN HADDOCK WAS TINTIN'S SWEARY SAILOR FRIEND, WHO PERFECTED THE SYMBOLIC SALTY SPEECH.

UNTIL NEXT ISSUE, CHEERIO!
- *PAUL CORNELL*

brought to you by

KNIGHT AND SQUIRE

ad by Jimmy Broxton   design by SWANDS

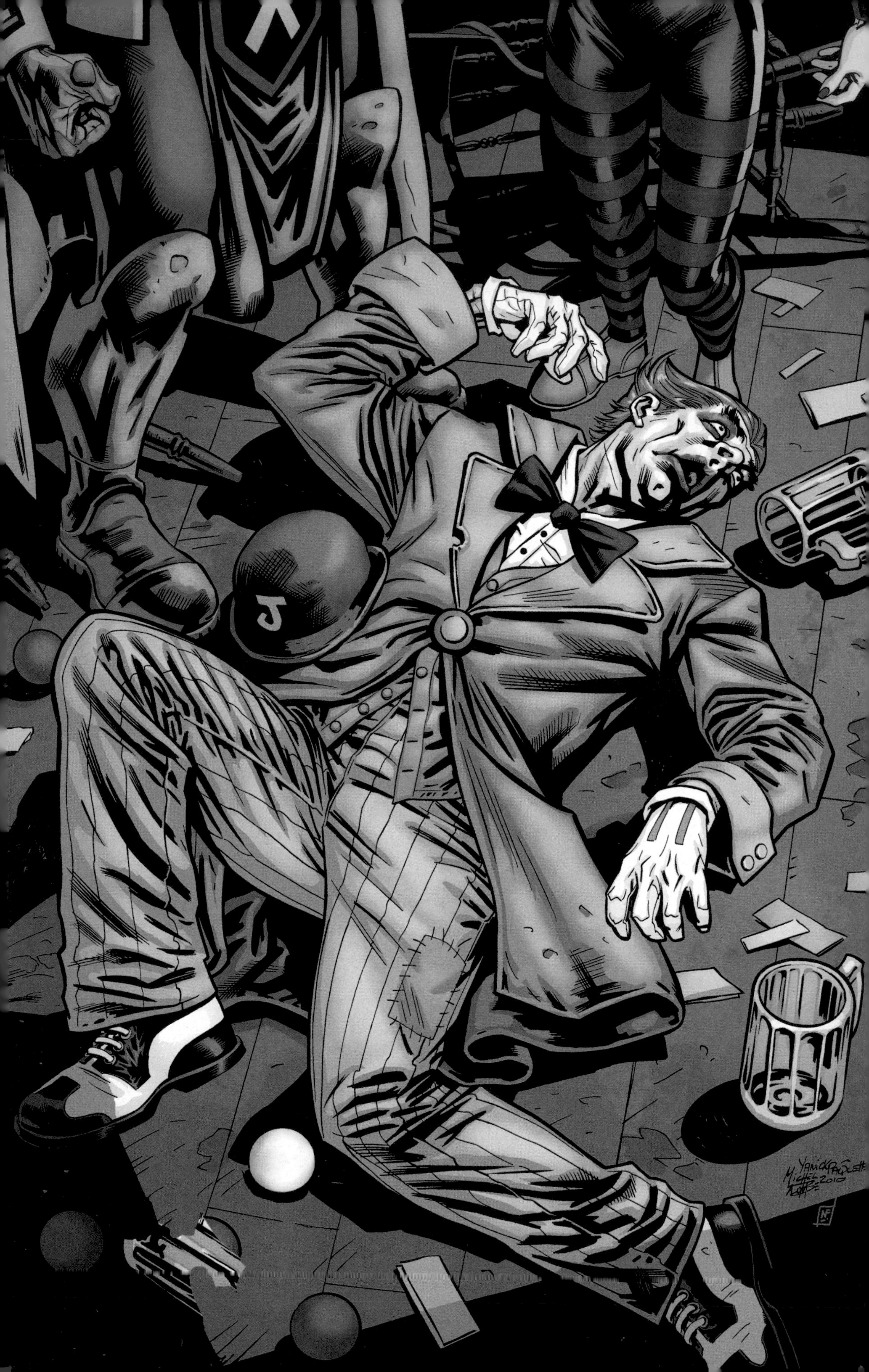
J

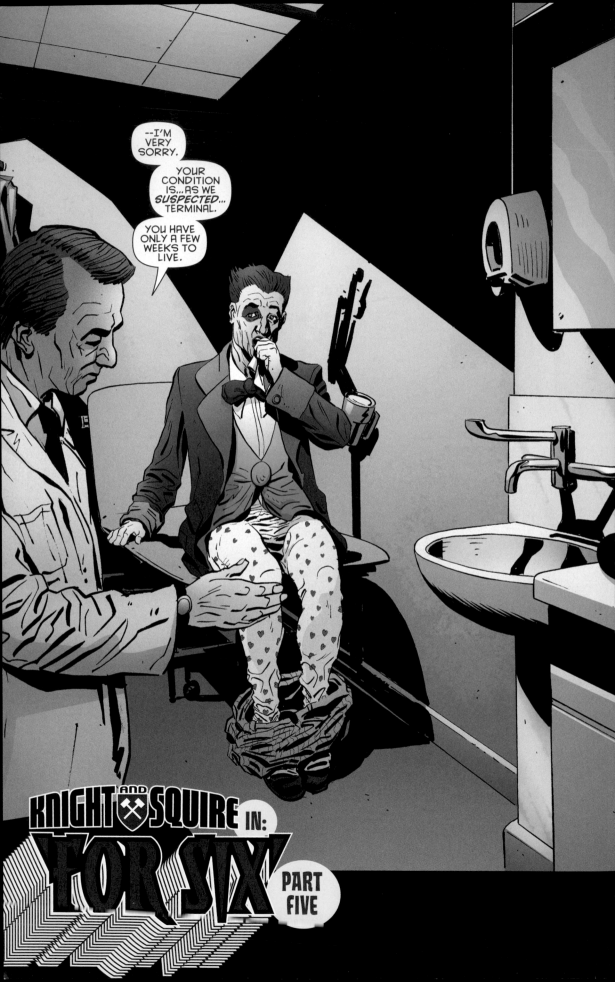

THERE IS NO SIMILARITY BETWEEN THE BRITISH JOKER AND ANY COPYRIGHTED PROPERTIES, IN BRITAIN, THE COMMONWEALTH OR ABROAD.

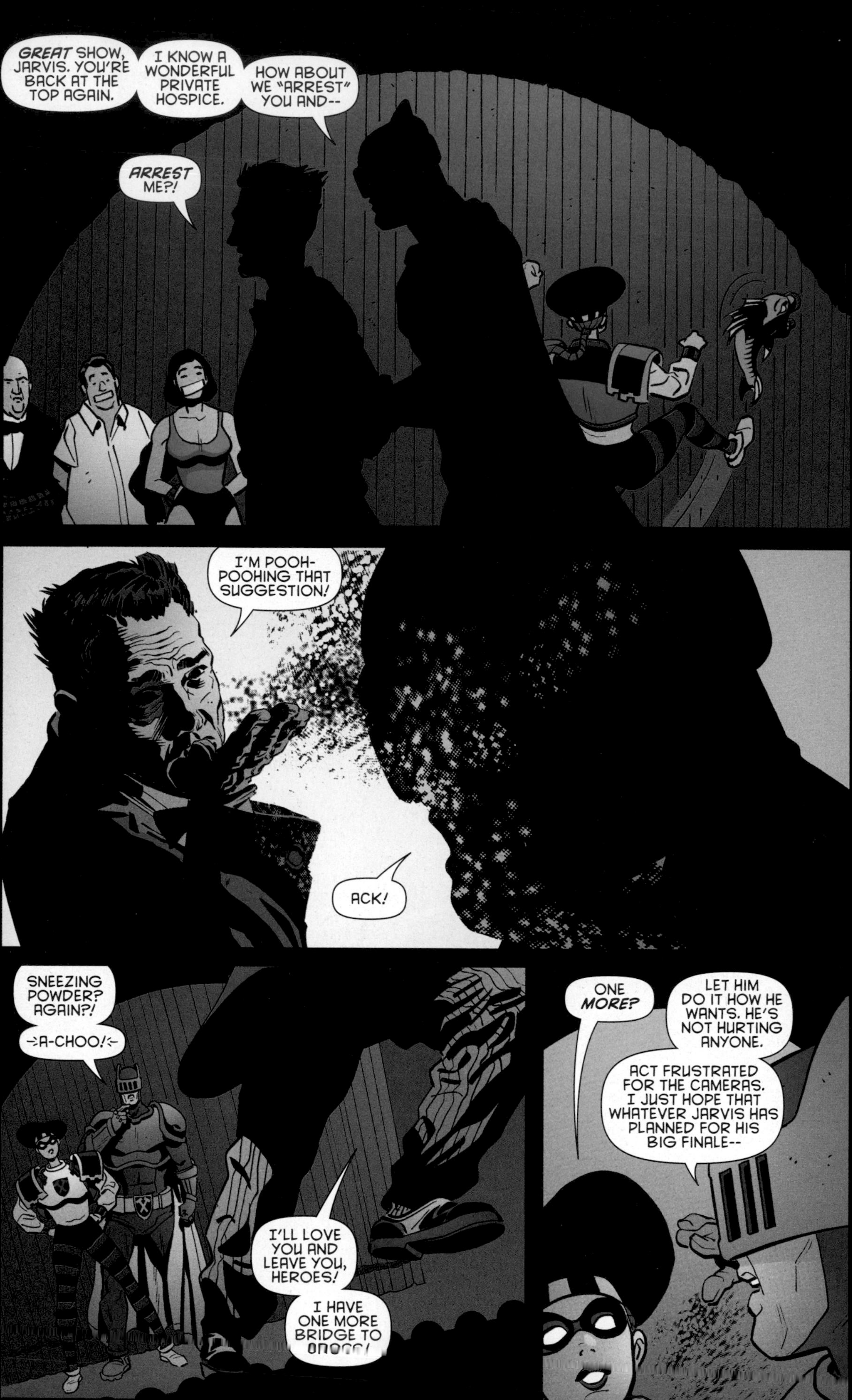
GREAT SHOW, JARVIS. YOU'RE BACK AT THE TOP AGAIN.
I KNOW A WONDERFUL PRIVATE HOSPICE.
HOW ABOUT WE "ARREST" YOU AND--
ARREST ME?!
I'M POOH-POOHING THAT SUGGESTION!
ACK!
SNEEZING POWDER? AGAIN?!
A-CHOO!
I'LL LOVE YOU AND LEAVE YOU, HEROES!
I HAVE ONE MORE BRIDGE TO
ONE MORE?
LET HIM DO IT HOW HE WANTS. HE'S NOT HURTING ANYONE.
ACT FRUSTRATED FOR THE CAMERAS. I JUST HOPE THAT WHATEVER JARVIS HAS PLANNED FOR HIS BIG FINALE--

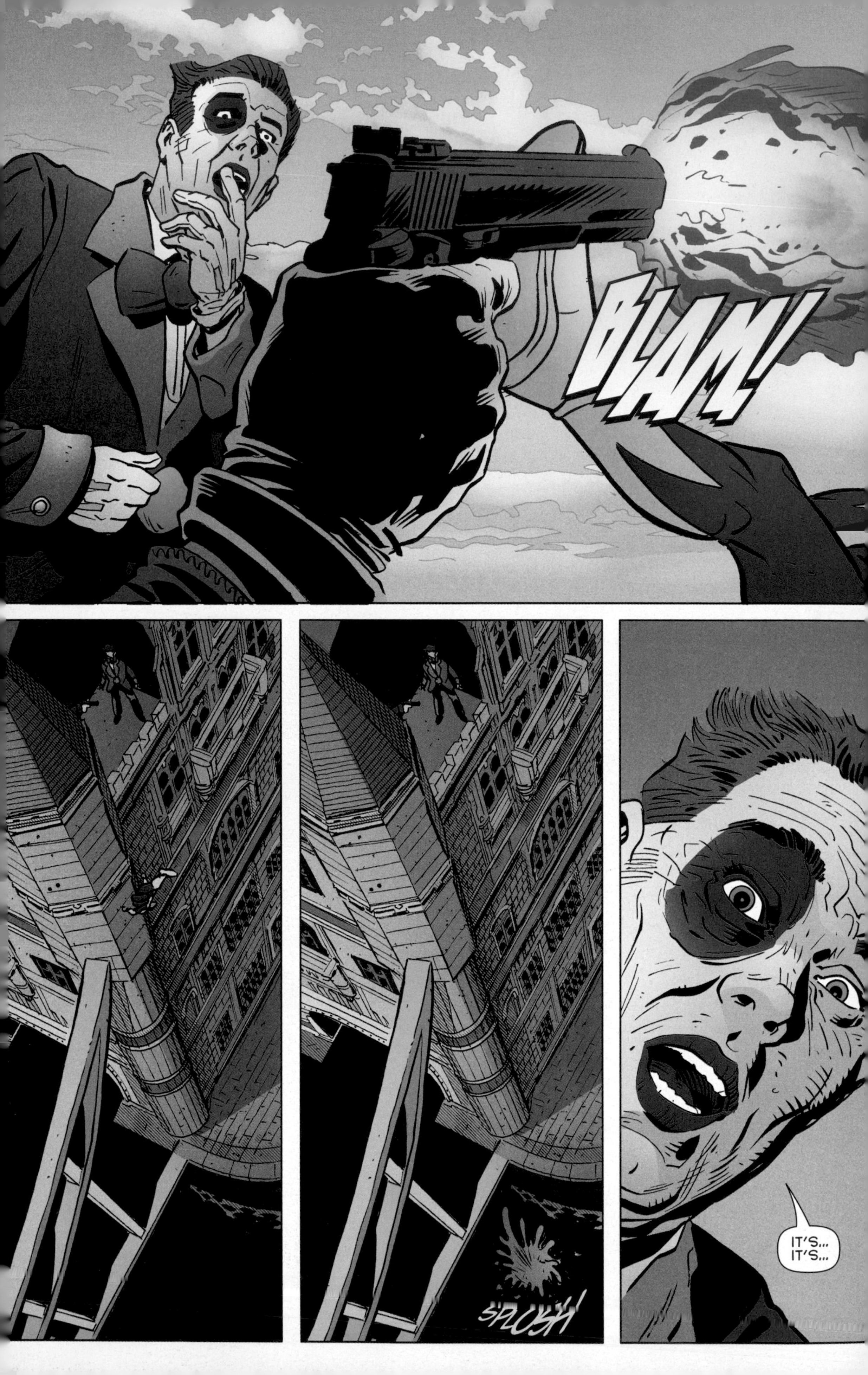
BLAM!
SPLOSH
IT'S... IT'S...

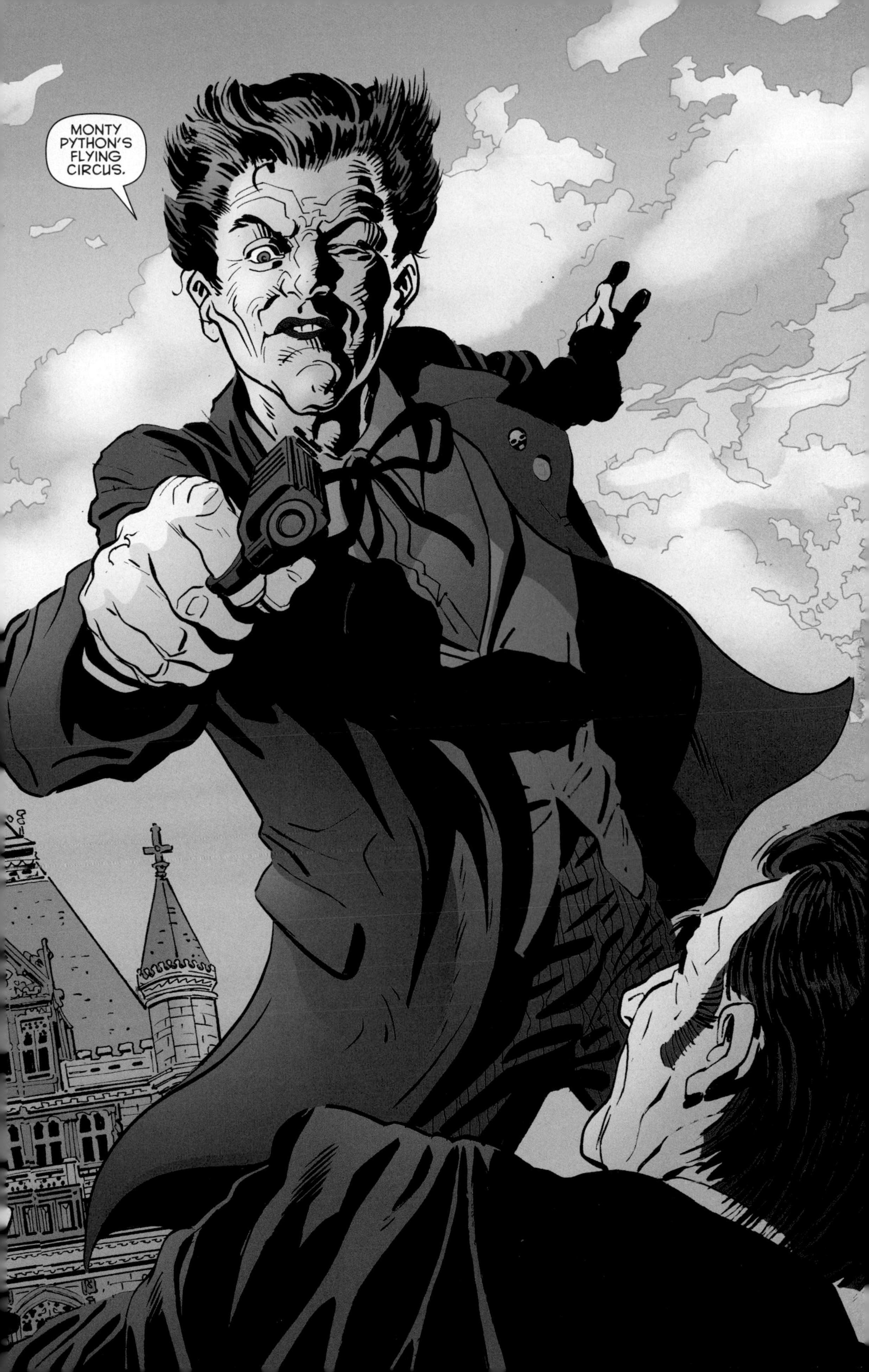
MONTY PYTHON'S FLYING CIRCUS.

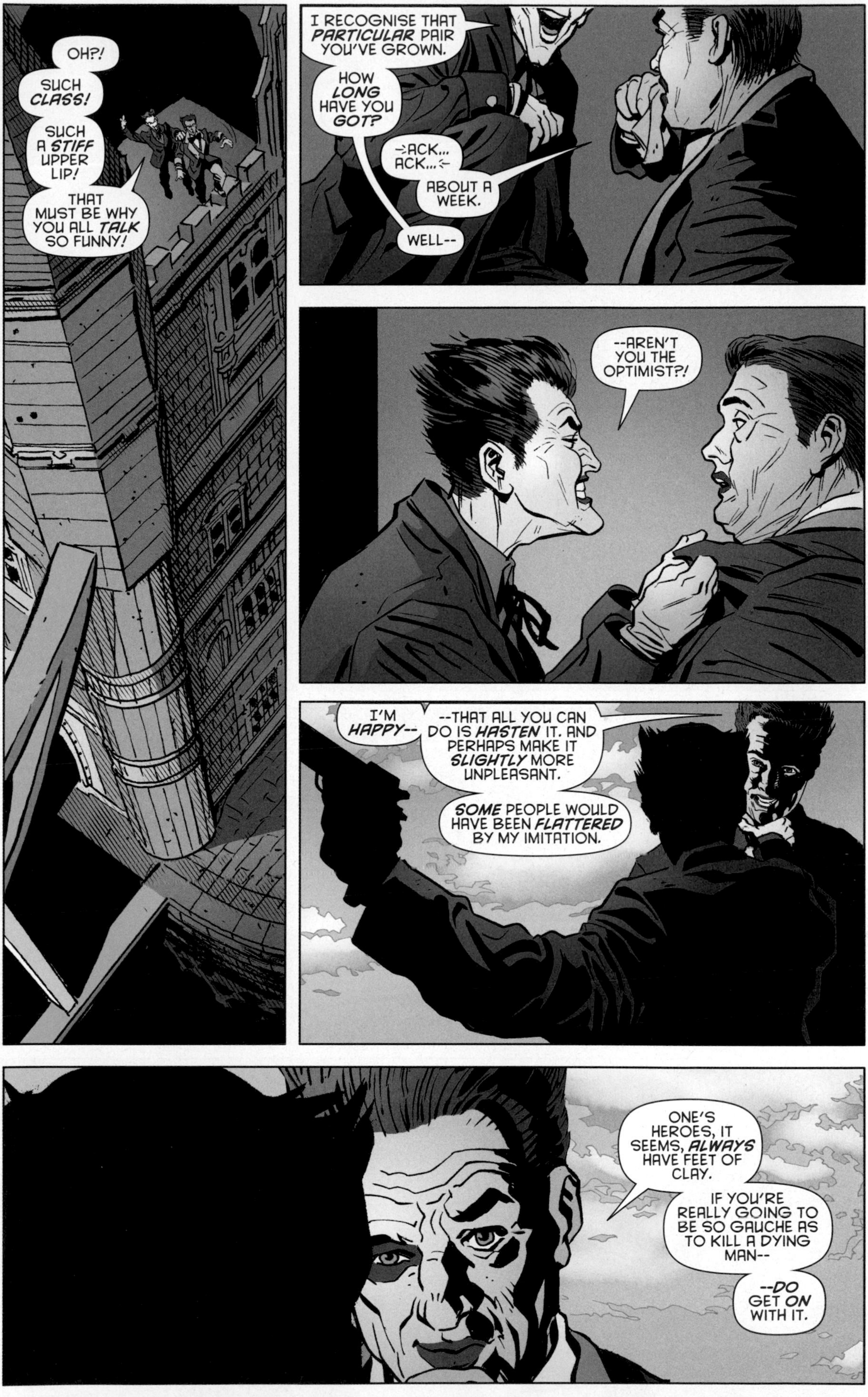
OH?!
SUCH CLASS!
SUCH A STIFF UPPER LIP!
THAT MUST BE WHY YOU ALL TALK SO FUNNY!
I RECOGNISE THAT PARTICULAR PAIR YOU'VE GROWN.
HOW LONG HAVE YOU GOT?
ACK... ACK...
ABOUT A WEEK.
WELL--
--AREN'T YOU THE OPTIMIST?!
I'M HAPPY--
--THAT ALL YOU CAN DO IS HASTEN IT. AND PERHAPS MAKE IT SLIGHTLY MORE UNPLEASANT.
SOME PEOPLE WOULD HAVE BEEN FLATTERED BY MY IMITATION.
ONE'S HEROES, IT SEEMS, ALWAYS HAVE FEET OF CLAY.
IF YOU'RE REALLY GOING TO BE SO GAUCHE AS TO KILL A DYING MAN--
--DO GET ON WITH IT.

The Knight and Squire Character List (Part One)

OKAY, WE HAVE TO LEAVE ASIDE THE BUSINESS OF SINGING FISH AND ODD THINGS WRITTEN ON BRIDGES (LOOK UP BRITISH NOVELTY SONGS ONLINE), SO WE CAN PROVIDE A MASTER LIST OF ALL THE CHARACTERS JAMES AND I CREATED FOR THIS SERIES! STARTING WITH JUST THOSE FROM *ISSUE ONE!*

PAGE 1: ENTERING THE PUB: HAMMER AND TONGS.

PAGE 2: TO THE LEFT OF THE SHRIKE, WHO'S TALKING TO SALT OF THE EARTH AND THE MILKMAN, ARE THE DISTINGUISHED GENTLEMAN (IN TOP HAT), TO HIS RIGHT SPACE CADET (THE GIRL), AND NEXT TO HER THE HAPLESS FORMER WELDER (IN MASK), OXYMORON. FURTHER ALONG THE BAR (WITH AN "O" ON HIS HEAD) IS THE ZERO.

PAGE 3: JARVIS POKER, THE BRITISH JOKER. AND THAT'S OUR FIRST SIGHTING OF THE THREE RUSH HOURS.

PAGE 4: IN PANEL TWO (IN LEOPARD PRINT BRIEFS) LADY VOODOO, AND IN PANEL FIVE (WITH SPIKES AND MACE) THE SETTLER NO.1.

PAGE 5: YOU'RE INTRODUCED TO COALFACE, THE PROFESSIONAL SCOTSMAN, THE BLACK AND WHITE MINSTRELS, TWO TON TED FROM TEDDINGTON AND THE FIRST ELEVEN. IN PANEL THREE (IN THE FOREGROUND WITH POUND SIGN) IS STERLING SILVER.

PAGE 6: CAPTAIN CORNWALL, CORNWALL BOY, DOUBLE ENTENDRE AND FACEOFF. IN PANEL ONE, BEHIND THE RUSH HOURS, ARE PHARAOHS 1 AND 2. AND IN PANEL FIVE, BEHIND FACEOFF, THERE'S THE CHOREOGRAPHER.

PAGE 7: IN PANEL ONE, ABOVE THE SQUIRE'S HAND, THERE'S DEATH CAP AND DRAMA KING. TO THE SHRIKE'S RIGHT IS THE FRO, TO HIS LEFT, THE COUPLE ARE THE GUARDIAN ANGELS (OLD HIPPY TYPES). PLUS CAPTAIN MOONDUST, THE PIRATE ASTRONOMERS, STONE COLD LUKE, DEATH DINOSAUR, BLIND FURY AND THE DARK DRUID.

PAGE 8: IN THE FOREGROUND OF PANEL THREE IS SENIOR CITIZEN. NEXT TO WILDCAT ARE LADY NIGHTINGALE AND SUPER ANNUATOR. BEHIND THE SEAT ARE SETTLER NO. 2 AND (IN ANCIENT EGYPTIAN GEAR) MR. IBIS.

PAGE 9: IN PANEL THREE, BETWEEN WILDCAT AND SHRIKE, IS ORANGE MEDAL. IN PANEL FOUR, NEXT TO CAPTAIN CORNWALL, IN WELDING MASK IS THE MECHANIC, AND NEXT TO HIM (WITH POINTY EARS): COFFIN DWELLER AND THE NAKED WOMAN, BIRTHDAY GIRL.

PAGE 10: IN PANEL TWO, MEET MING DYNASTY WITH THE MANDARIN TWINS, AND ACROSS THE TABLE BIG GAME HUNTER MAJOR HUBERT, STRONGMAN MR GRANITE AND CAVALRY-MAN. IN PANEL THREE WE HAVE BRITISH BULLDOG, THE BLACK COMMANDO AND NEAR MISS, AND IN THE DIVING HELMET, CAPTAIN JAQUES. IN THE BACKGROUND ARE TIN-BIB AND TOXIC TUCKER.

PAGE 11: THE LITTLE GIRL IN PANEL ONE IS THE ONLY CHILD PLUS STRONGMAN MIGHTY MORRIS AND THE FABULOUS BOATER MAN. IN PANEL TWO THAT'S SIXTIES ICONS THE ARRANGERS, AND IN PANEL THREE, MEET THE RAITLES.

PAGE 13: PANEL THREE, BELOW RUSH HOUR'S ARM, THAT'S ILL-INFORMED WHITE GUY, THE YELLOW PERIL AND SETTLER NO. 3.

PAGE 17: IN PANEL TWO, THERE'S SETTLER NO. 4, PLUS, WITH THE FRO AND THE MASK, MOMMA CUSS.

PAGE 19: HOLDING THE GIRL BY THE THROAT, THAT'S SETTLER NO. 5.

WE MAKE THAT *88 NEW CHARACTERS!* A NEW RECORD?

UNTIL NEXT ISSUE, CHEERIO!
- PAUL CORNELL

brought to you by

KNIGHT AND SQUIRE

ad by Jimmy Broxton   design by SWANDS

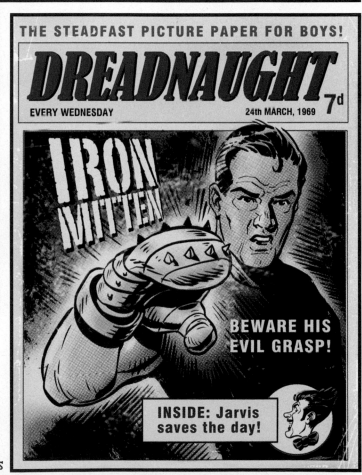

THE STEADFAST PICTURE PAPER FOR BOYS!

DREADNAUGHT 7d

EVERY WEDNESDAY   24th MARCH, 1969

IRON MITTEN

BEWARE HIS EVIL GRASP!

INSIDE: Jarvis saves the day!

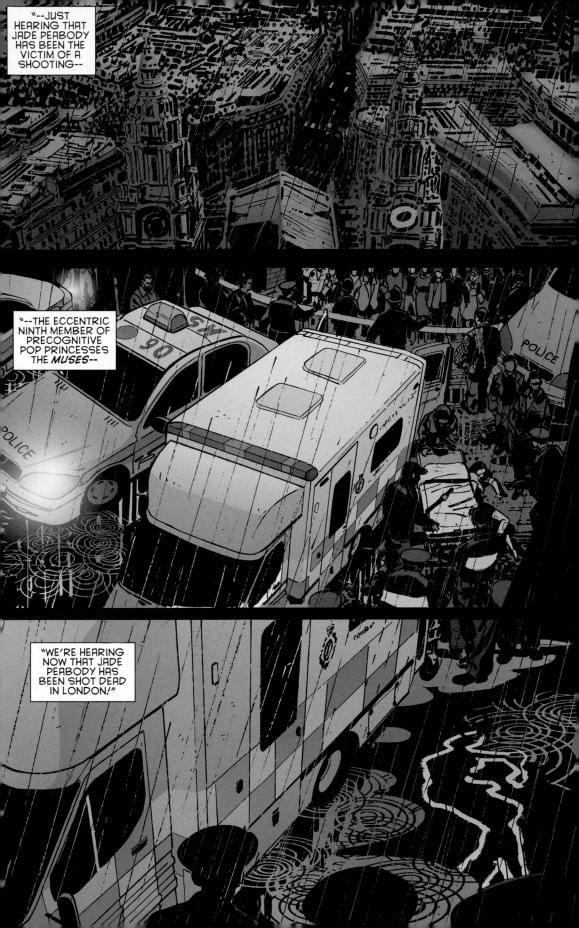

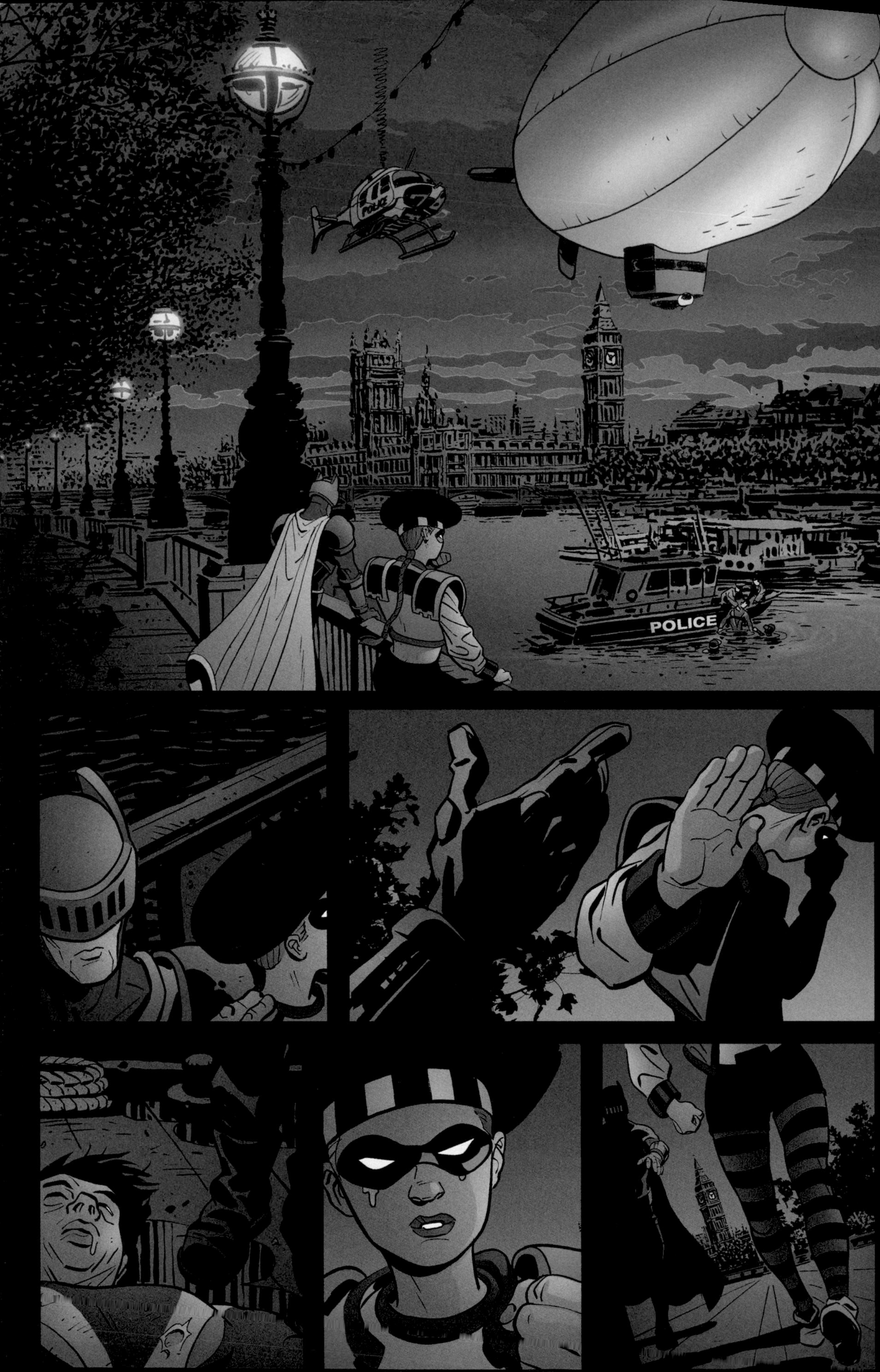
POLICE

IT'S NOT *JARVIS* DOING THIS.

EVEN IN HIS CURRENT SITUATION, IT'S NOT IN HIS NATURE. AND WE HAVE *CCTV* FOOTAGE THAT SUGGESTS HE'S BEEN CAPTURED.

THEN WHO?!

WE'RE FACING THE REAL THING. WORKING THROUGH PROXIES.

I SHOULD HAVE SEEN IT WHEN HE KILLED JADE, THE MUSE WHO ALWAYS FORESAW SUPER VILLAIN'S PLANS--

--BUT I WAS... ANYWAY...

...I THINK I KNOW HOW TO SET A TRAP FOR HIM.

TO MAKE HIM FACE US *IN PERSON.*

WE'RE GOING TO NEED EVERYONE TO... TO STAND WITH...

SAY NO MORE, LOVE--

--YOU TELL US WHAT'S WHAT.

AND WE'LL GET IT *SORTED.*

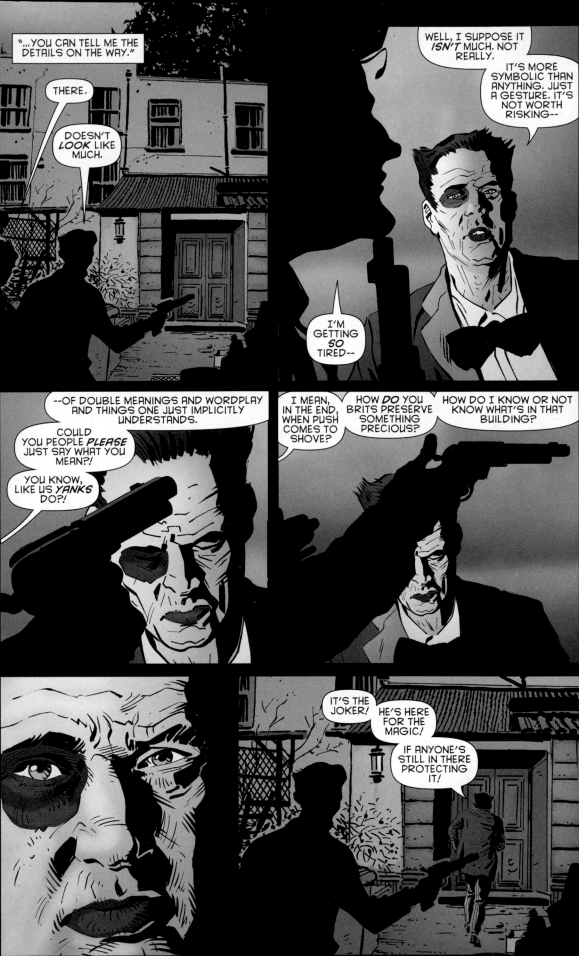

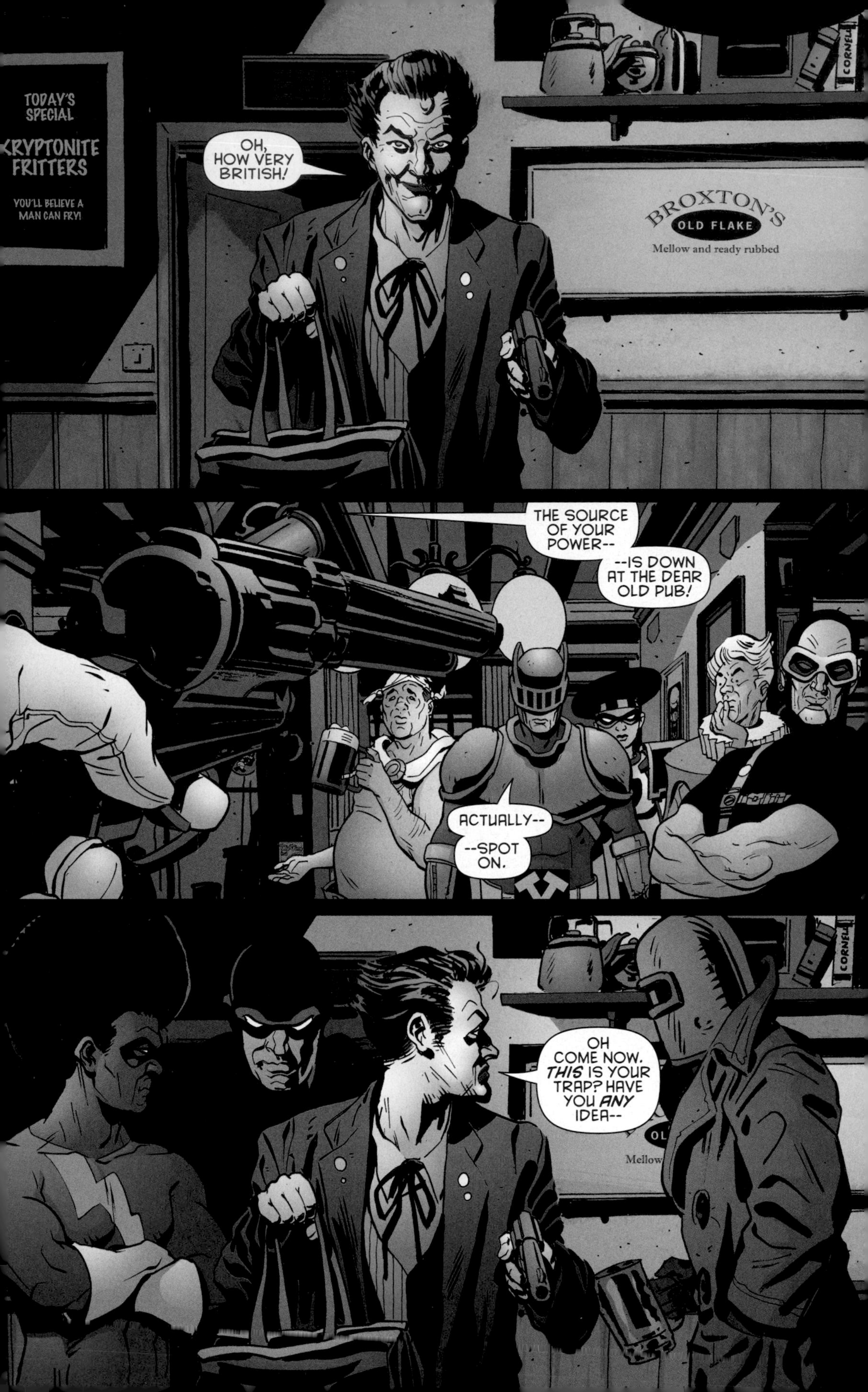
TODAY'S SPECIAL
KRYPTONITE FRITTERS
YOU'LL BELIEVE A MAN CAN FRY!
OH, HOW VERY BRITISH!
BROXTON'S
OLD FLAKE
Mellow and ready rubbed
THE SOURCE OF YOUR POWER--
--IS DOWN AT THE DEAR OLD PUB!
ACTUALLY--
--SPOT ON.
OH COME NOW. *THIS* IS YOUR TRAP? HAVE YOU *ANY* IDEA--

The Knight and Squire Character List (Part Two)

AND NOW, THOSE NEW CHARACTERS WE INTRODUCED IN *KNIGHT & SQUIRE* ISSUES #2-6! IN *#2:* THE ORGAN GRINDER AND HIS MONKEY; MORRIS MAJOR AND THE MORRIS MEN. IN *#3:* THE MUSES (NINE OF THEM), INCLUDING CERYS TWEED AND JADE PEABODY (DECEASED); RICHARD III; EDWARD I; CHARLES I; KING JOHN; WILLIAM II (WELL, WE CREATED THESE VERSIONS OF THEM, BUT YES, THE DIVINE RIGHT AND THE FORCE OF HISTORY DID MOST OF THE WORK); THE CIDERMEN (2); BIG MUMMY AND HER CHILDREN (10). (WE'RE ONLY COUNTING SUPER-HEROES AND VILLAINS HERE, SO THE GRAY TWINS AND HANK DON'T QUITE MAKE IT.) IN *#4:* MAD HAT HARRY AND THE PAPER TIGER. (ONLY SEEN ON A NEWSPAPER COVER, SO THAT'S OUR MOST OBSCURE NEW-COMER.) HARRY IS THE UK COVER VERSION OF THE MAD HATTER, WHILE OWING A BIT TO UNLUCKY LONDON GANGSTER JACK "THE HAT" MCVITIE. WE DIDN'T CREATE ANYONE NEW IN *#5.* (ASSUMING IRON MITTEN ISN'T..."REAL.") AND IN *#6,* WE FIRST WELCOMED THE HEADMASTER; THE GOOD SHEPHERD; ALLY THE CAT. ALL...ERM...DECEASED. IT'S LIKE WE'RE MAKING THESE GUYS UP FOR FUN. ALLY OWES SOMETHING TO BILLY THE CAT, THE BEANO COMIC'S OWN SUPERHERO. THEN ON PANEL ONE OF PAGE TEN, WE ADD, FROM THE LEFT, AMONG OLDER CHARACTERS: LEATHERCHAP (IN CAP); FORK (WITH FORKED HEAD); BAYFRENTOS (PORTLY); BULLFINCH (AS A BIRD); DR. RETINA (THE EYE-BALL); HILT (WITH THE SWORD); THE HOODED HOODIE (ON HIS BIKE); AND SPANGLE (WITH THE BUBBLE HELMET). THAT MAKES 130 NEW BRITISH SUPER-HEROES AND SU-PER-VILLAINS ACROSS THE COURSE OF THE SERIES. SORRY IT WASN'T, AS PROMISED, EXACTLY 100, BUT...YOU KNOW...IT WAS TRICKY ENOUGH AS IT WAS.

A FEW NOTES FROM ISSUES *#5* AND *#6:* "A MAN OF INFINITE JEST" IS HOW HAMLET DESCRIBES YORICK THE JESTER, OR HIS SKULL, ANYWAY. "THE FOG ON THE TYNE," "COMBINE HARVESTER," "RABBIT" AND "ON ILKLEY MOOR" ARE ALL COMIC SONGS, SOME MORE HOMESPUN THAN OTHERS, APPROPRIATE TO THE LOCATIONS OF THE BRIDGES. THE DREADNAUGHT COMIC JARVIS FEATURED IN IS RATHER LIKE 1970S UK COMICS, SUCH AS VALIANT AND HOTSPUR. HIS DIALOGUE THEREIN REFERENCES OSCAR WILDE, AND BRITISH CAMP ICONS LARRY GRAYSON AND JULIAN AND SANDY FROM THE RADIO SERIES ROUND THE HORNE. BRITOVISION MIGHT REMIND US OF THE EUROVI-SION SONG CONTEST (LOOK IT UP, YOU WON'T BELIEVE IT), TWO OF THE WINNERS OF WHICH ARE BEING SUNG BY THOSE FISH. "IT'S..." WAS HOW MANY EPISODES OF MONTY PYTHON'S FLYING CIRCUS BEGAN. GOLD TOP IS THE CREAMIEST (AND MOST DEADLY) SORT OF MILK. DEATH DINOSAUR TALKS A BIT LIKE THE ACTOR TERRY THOMAS. OBVIOUSLY.

JIMMY AND I WOULD LIKE TO THANK EVERYONE WHO'S STUCK WITH US THROUGH THIS WHOLE SERIES. IT'S SOME-THING I'M IMMENSELY PROUD OF AND THINK OF AS SOME OF MY BEST WORK. THANKS MUST GO TO EDITOR JANELLE SIEGEL AND DC IN GENERAL FOR BEING MAD ENOUGH TO LET US DO THIS.

Below: Make-up variations. Traditional green hair was abandoned early on. Too similar to the Gotham original.

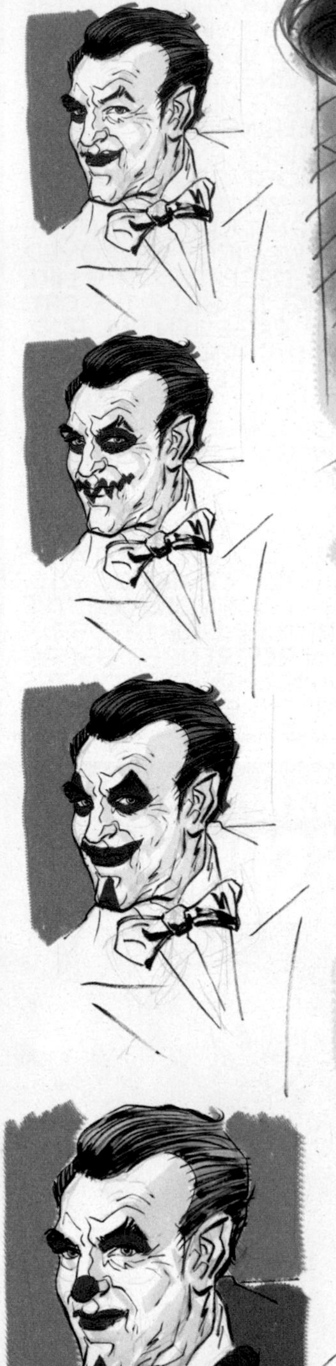
BROX

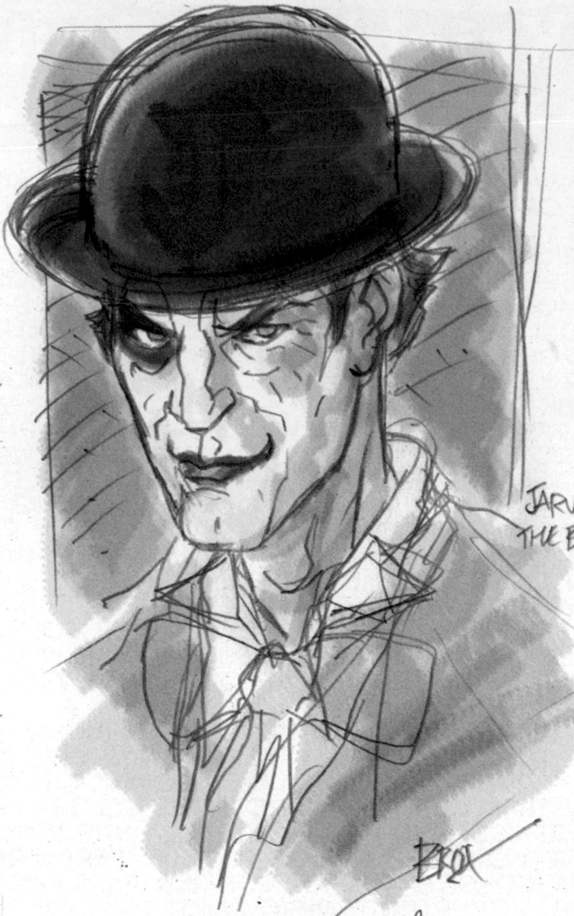
JARVIS:
THE BRITISH
JOKER
BROX

Left: This vicious-looking "droog"-style sketch was at odds with Paul's conception of Jarvis. The bowler, however, was a step in the right direction.

Below: Costume schematic produced as a colour guide. A distinctly "Chaplin-esque" feel is now evident, in honour of Britain's greatest clown. Note the three-fingered "Mickey" gloves, in honour of America's greatest rodent.

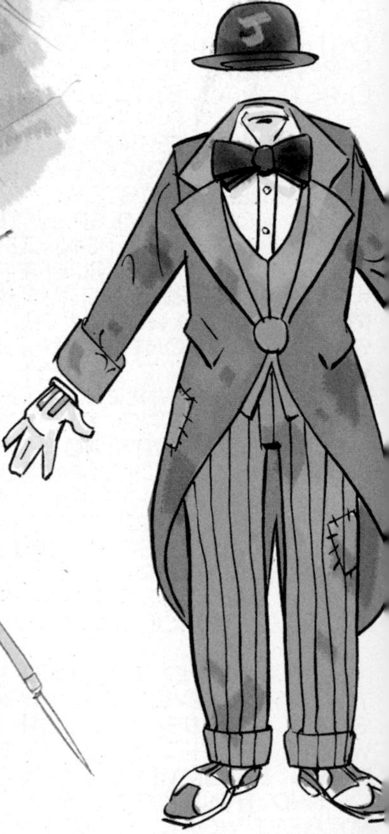

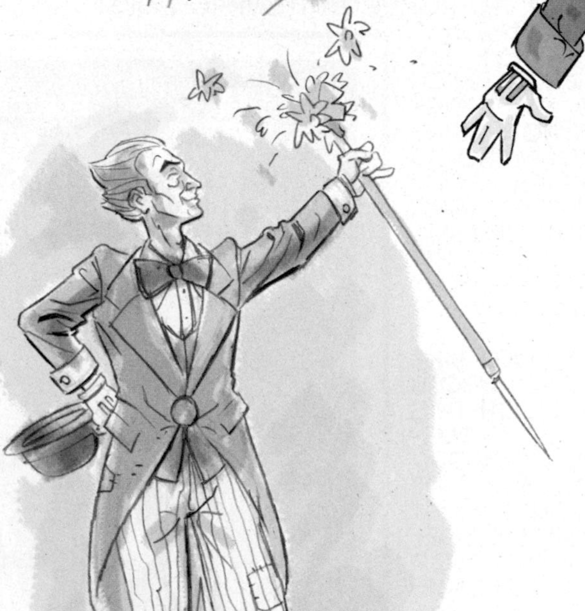
BROX

Above: Our man Jarvis would never kick a bunny, getting close but no cigar.

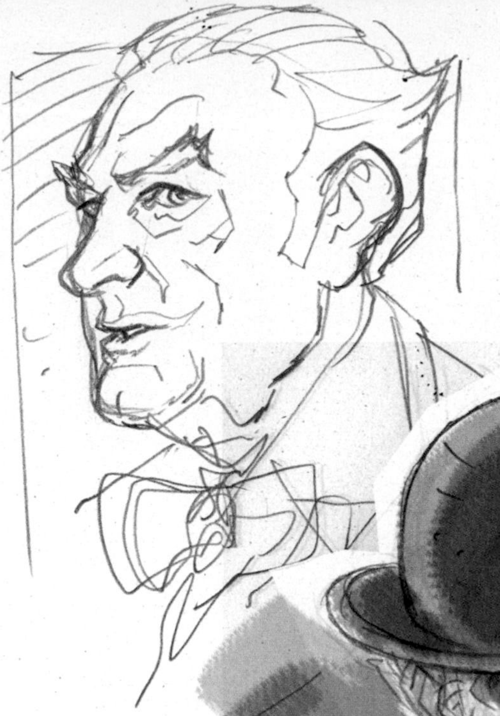

Jarvis Poker, the "British" Joker

Final approved design, now fuller in the face and friendlier. I imagined Jarvis as an ageing matinee idol — handsome but a little worn around the edges, his best years behind him, forced now to play character roles for comedic relief. As tragic as he is funny, in the tradition of all great clowns. Note the bunny, no longer getting a kicking.

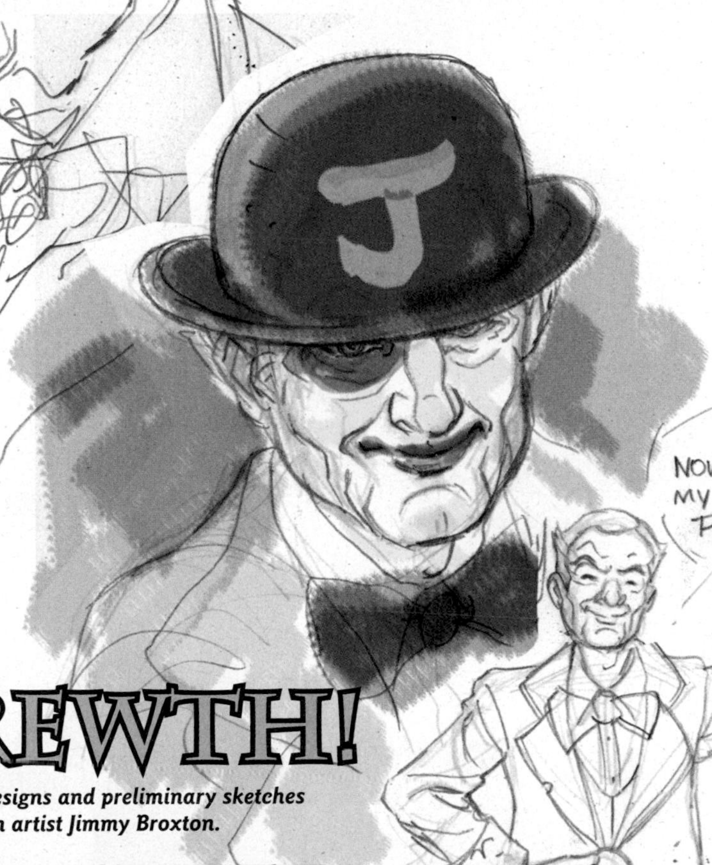

STREWTH!

Character designs and preliminary sketches from artist Jimmy Broxton.

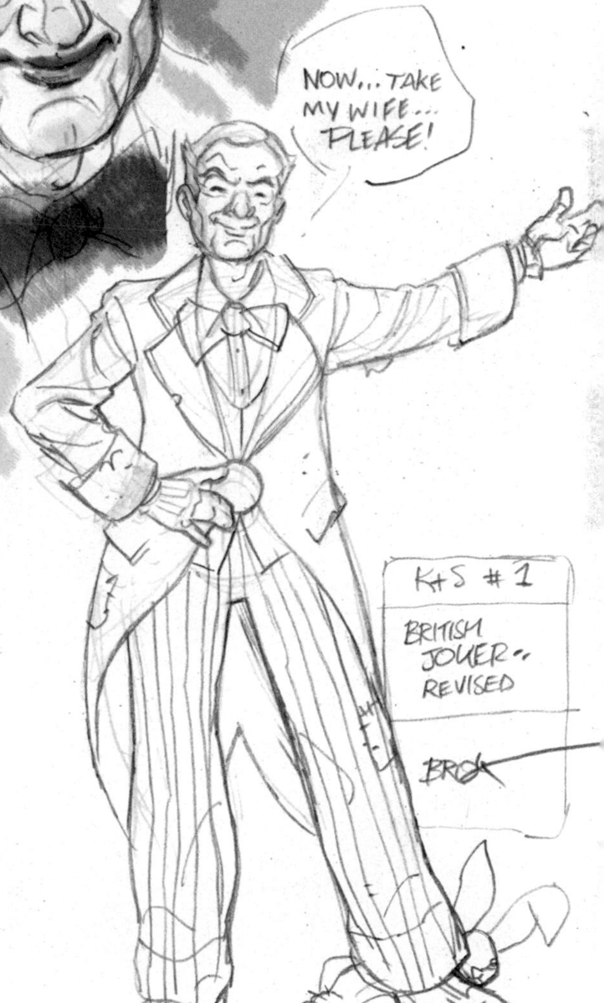
NOW... TAKE MY WIFE... PLEASE!
K+S #1
BRITISH JOKER.. REVISED
BROX

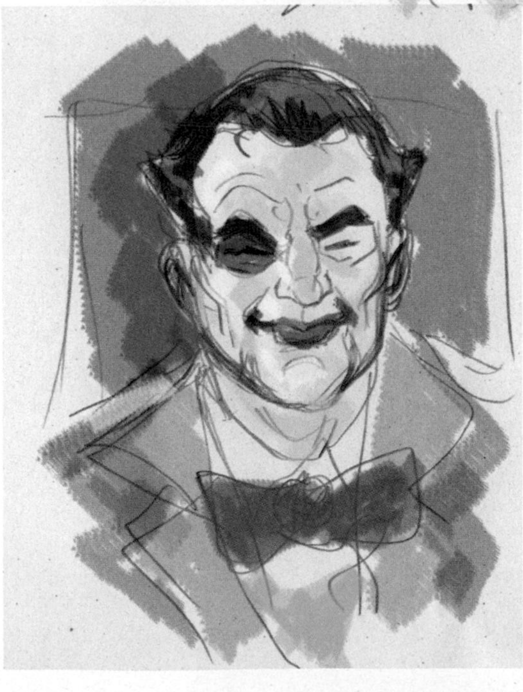

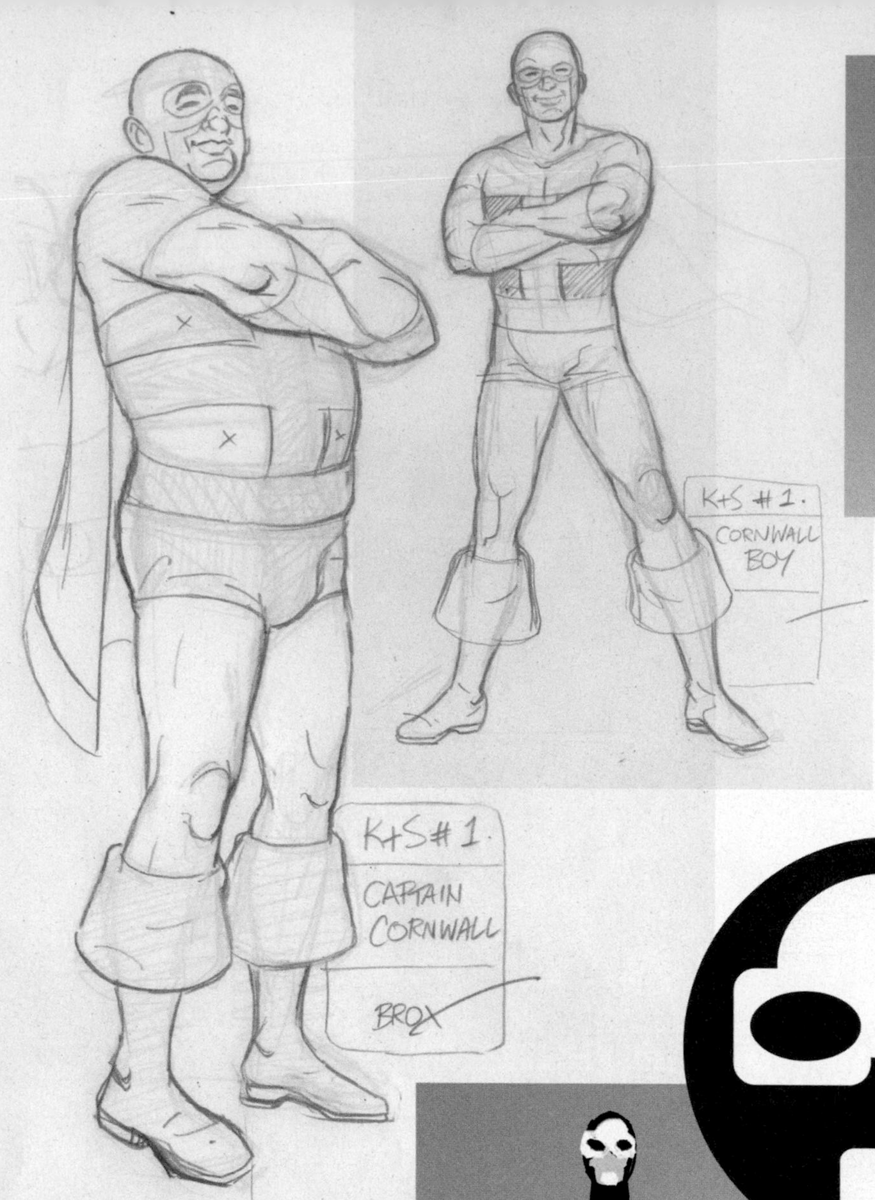
K+S #1
CORNWALL BOY
K+S #1
CAPTAIN CORNWALL
BROX

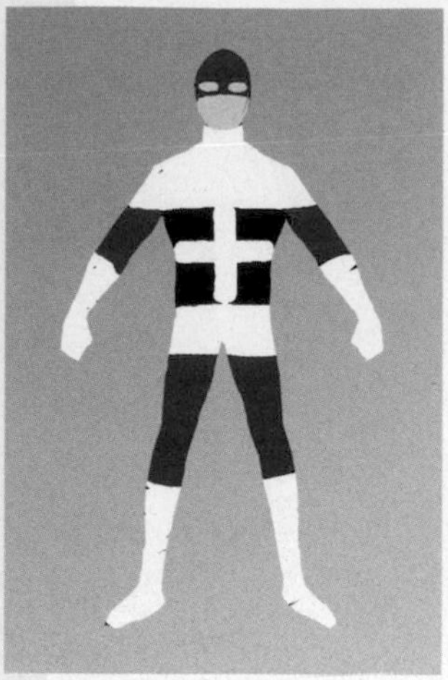

Above and Left: Sketches and colour guide for Captain Cornwall and Cornwall Boy, in all their Cornish glory.

Below: Final designs and badge graphic for Face-Off: everyone's favourite gay, urban, costumed vigilante.

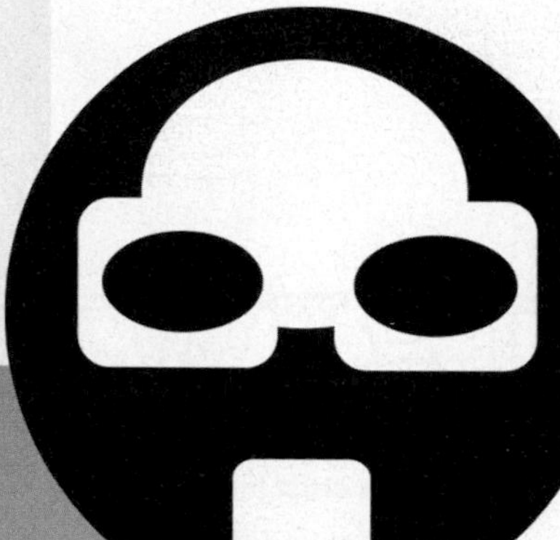

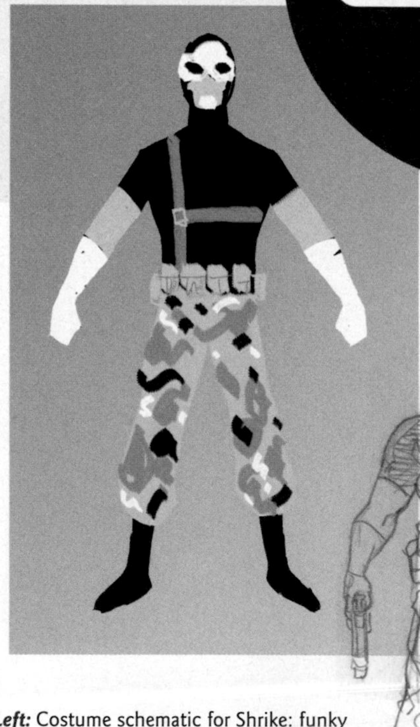

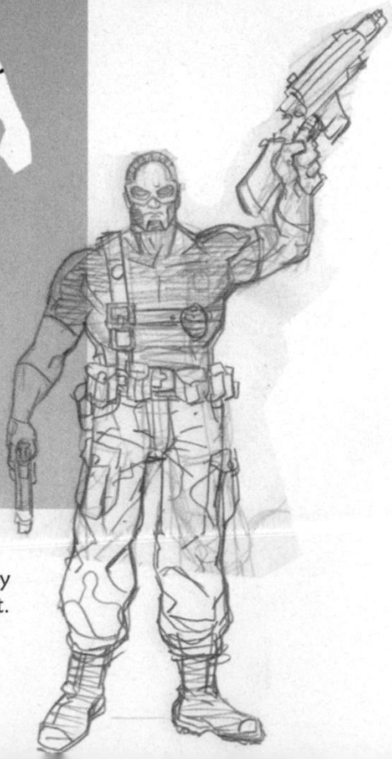

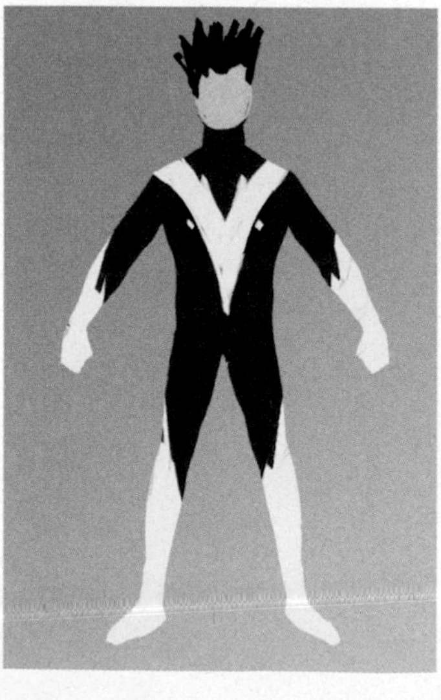

Left: Costume schematic for Shrike: funky dude, love interest and tragic protagonist.

Above: A "single" entendre.

Above: Got some crime that needs fighting? This chap delivers.

Above: Coming to a picket-line near you: Coalface!

Above: An ordinary man with an extraordinary job (and pants). This sketch courtesy of "er indoors."

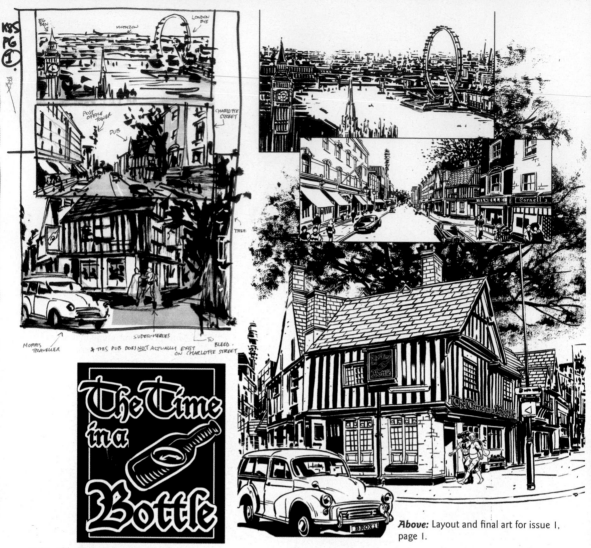

Above: Layout and final art for issue 1, page 1.

Below: Thursday night is all right for fighting. Pencil layout for pages 14 and 15 from the same issue.

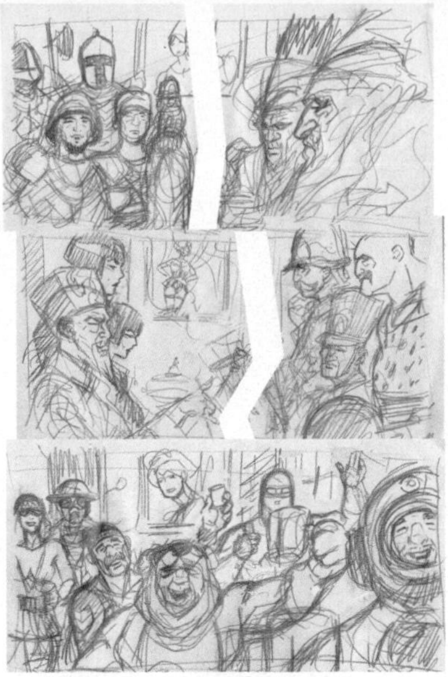

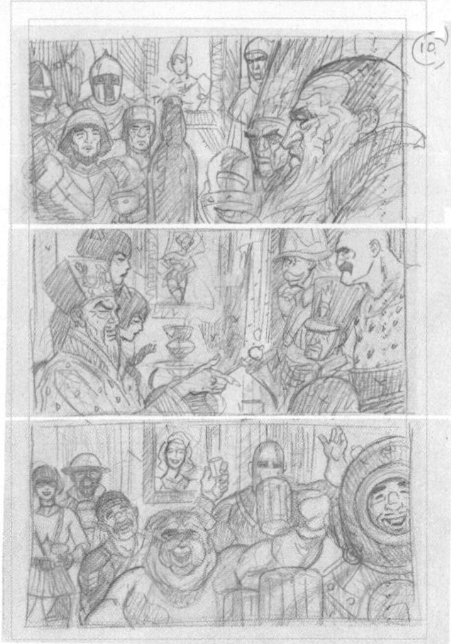

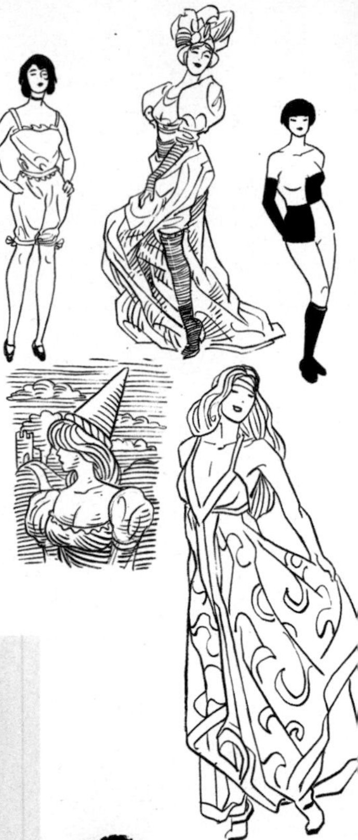

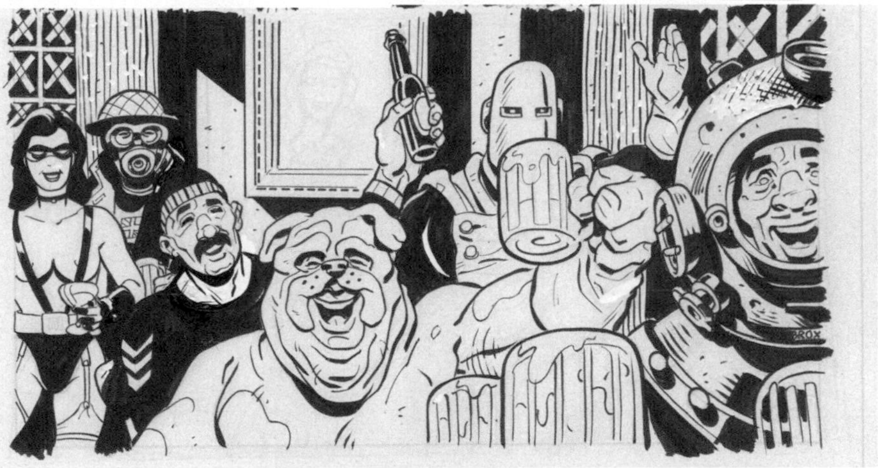

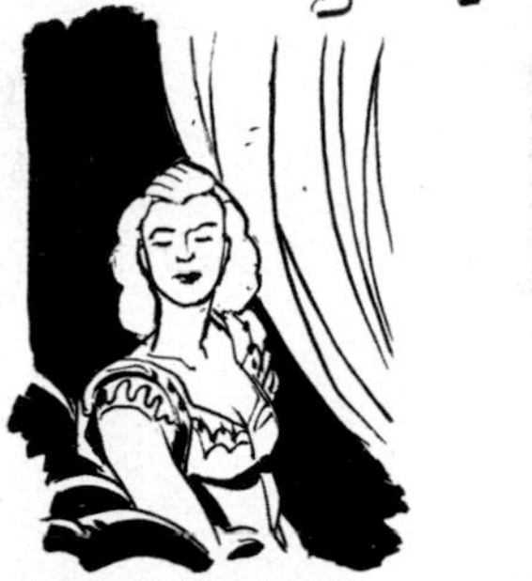

Above: Layout, final pencil and ink detail from issue 1, page 10.

Below: Your guess is as good as mine, but this stuff is in the book somewhere.

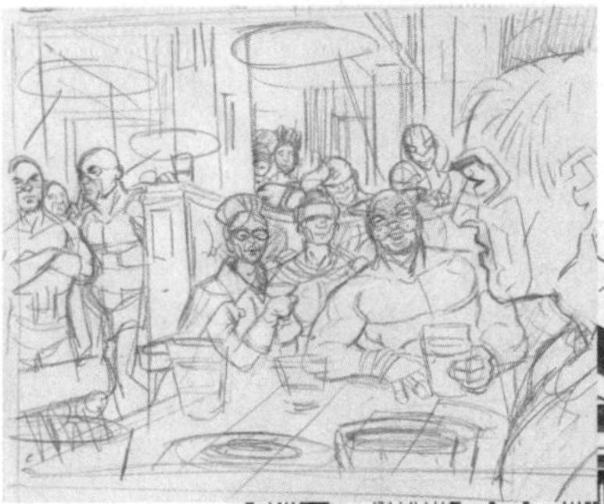

Above right: From wimpled damsels to miniskirted '60s misses, the Time in a Bottle has seen it all.

Left and below: Wildcat gets to feel younger, in pencil and ink.

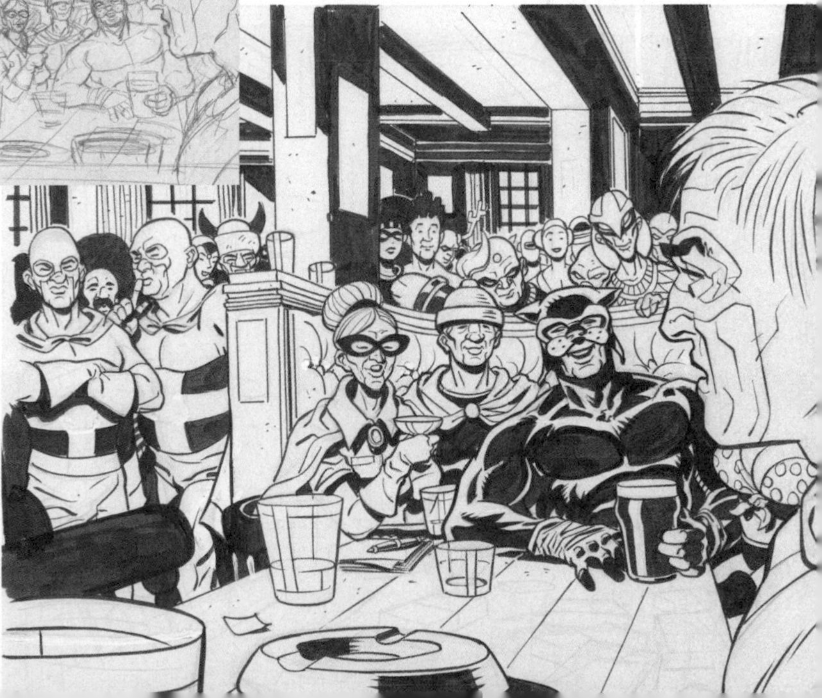

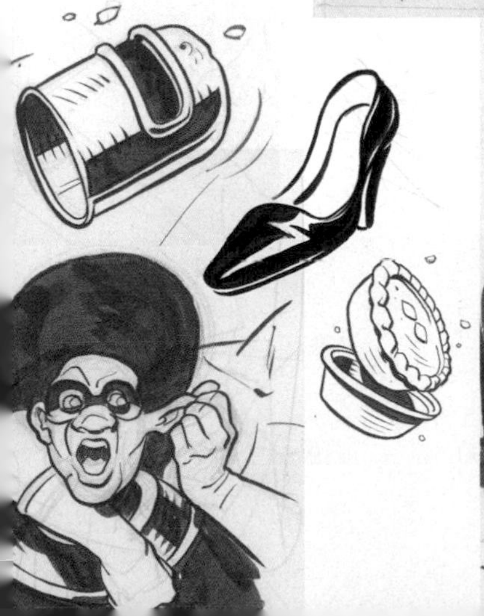

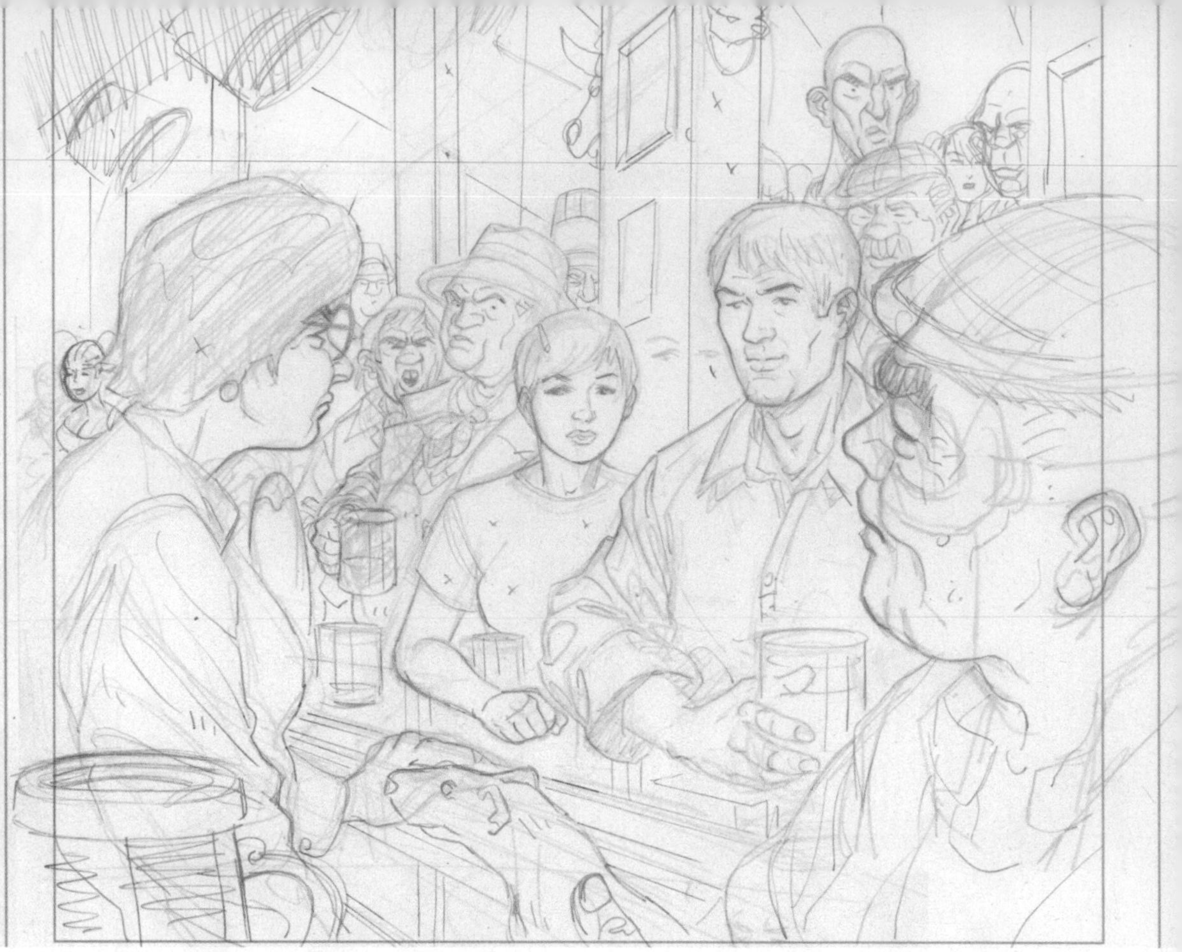

Above: The Wicker Man interior and pencils from issue 2. Different pub, "different" clientele.

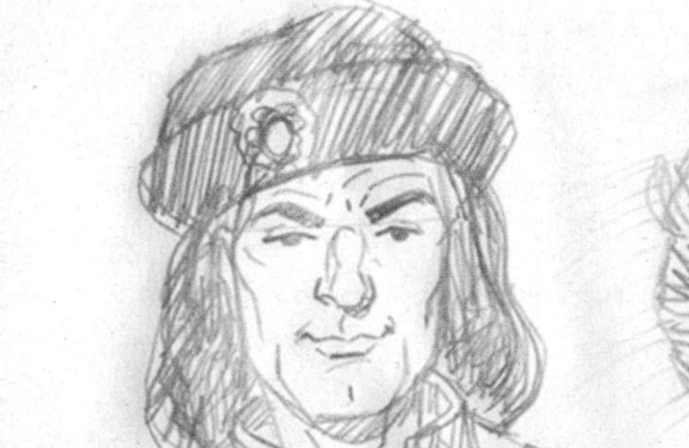

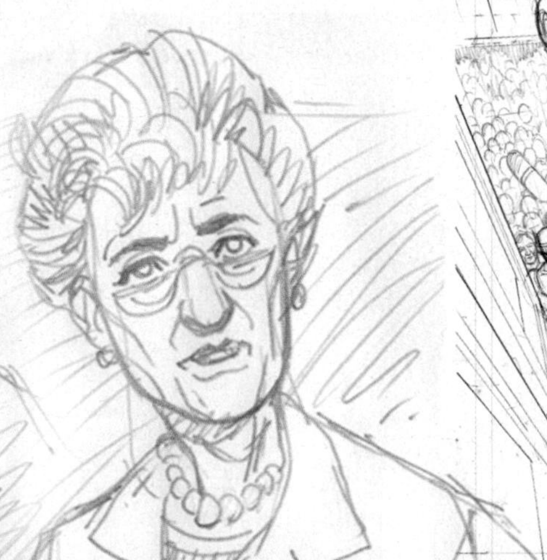

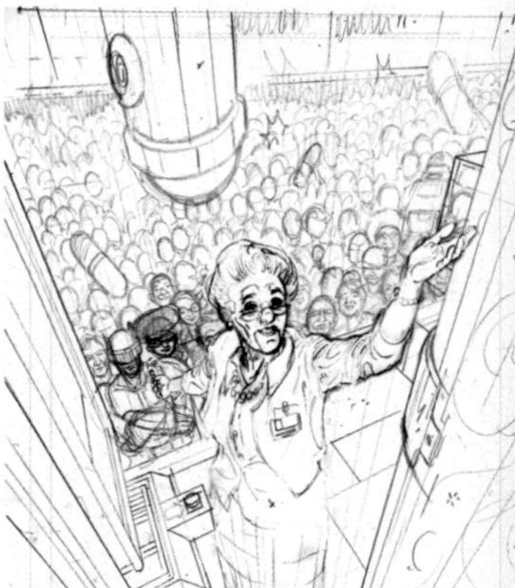

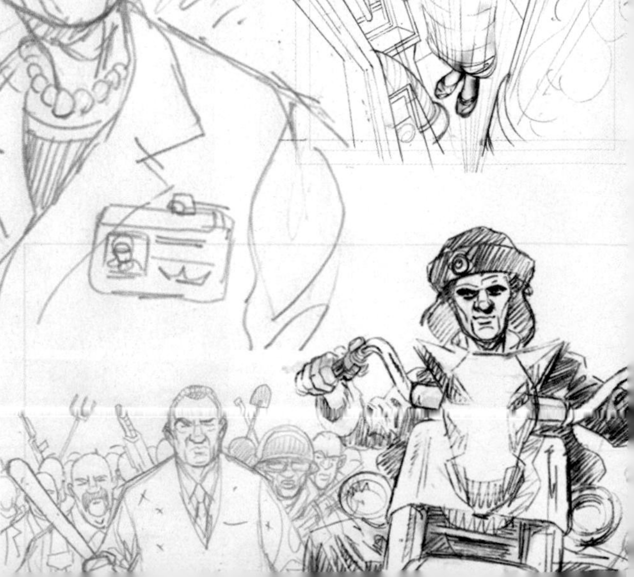

Above: Richard III, modelled on a young Olivier.

Above right: Prof. Merryweather, modelled on a man in a dress. Continuing the great theatrical tradition of men assuming female roles, from Pantomime Dames to the Ealing Comedies of the '40s and '50s up to *Monty Python's Flying Circus* and beyond. We're an eccentric lot, us Brits.

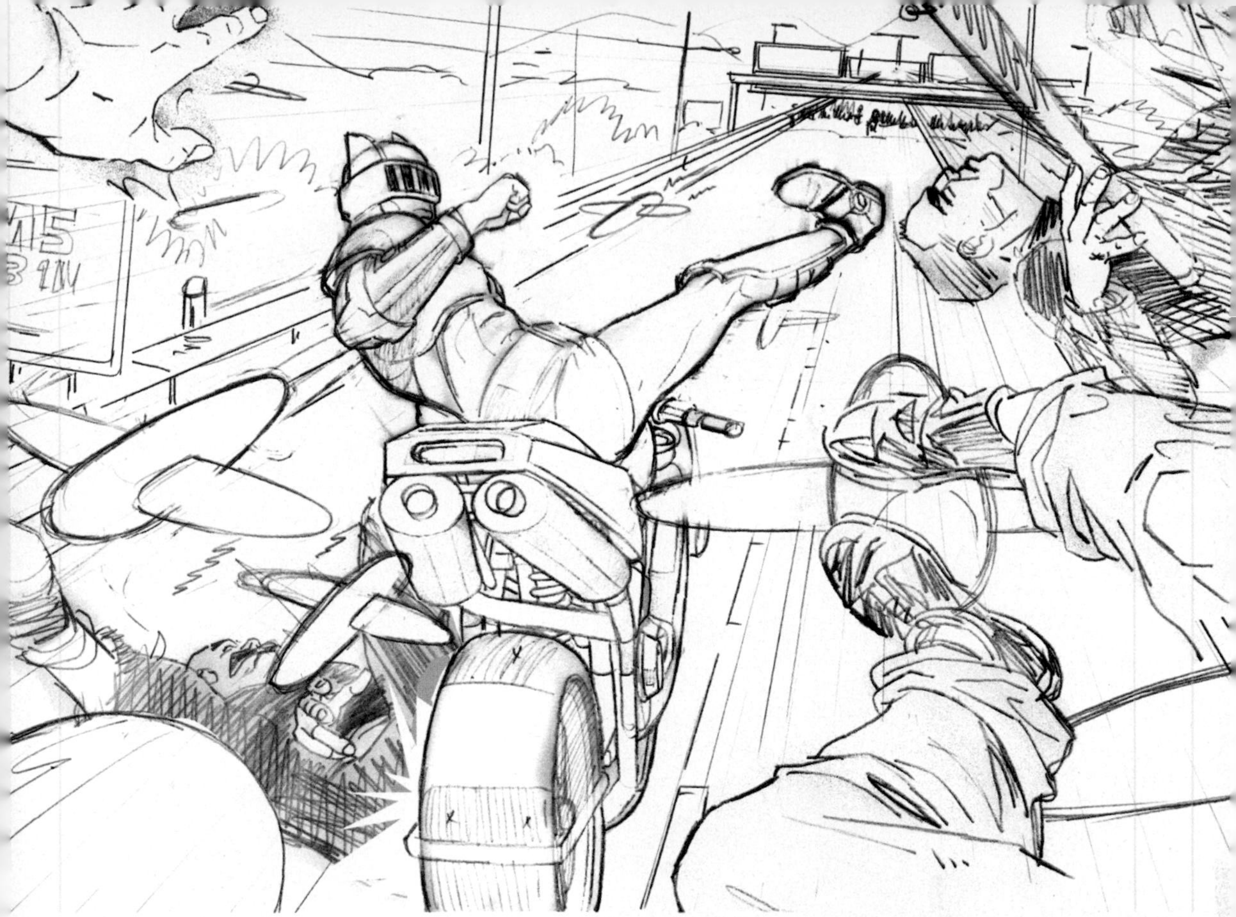

Above and below: Traffic-calming measures on the M1. Pencils and inks from issue 3. Oh, the joys of the English motorway network.

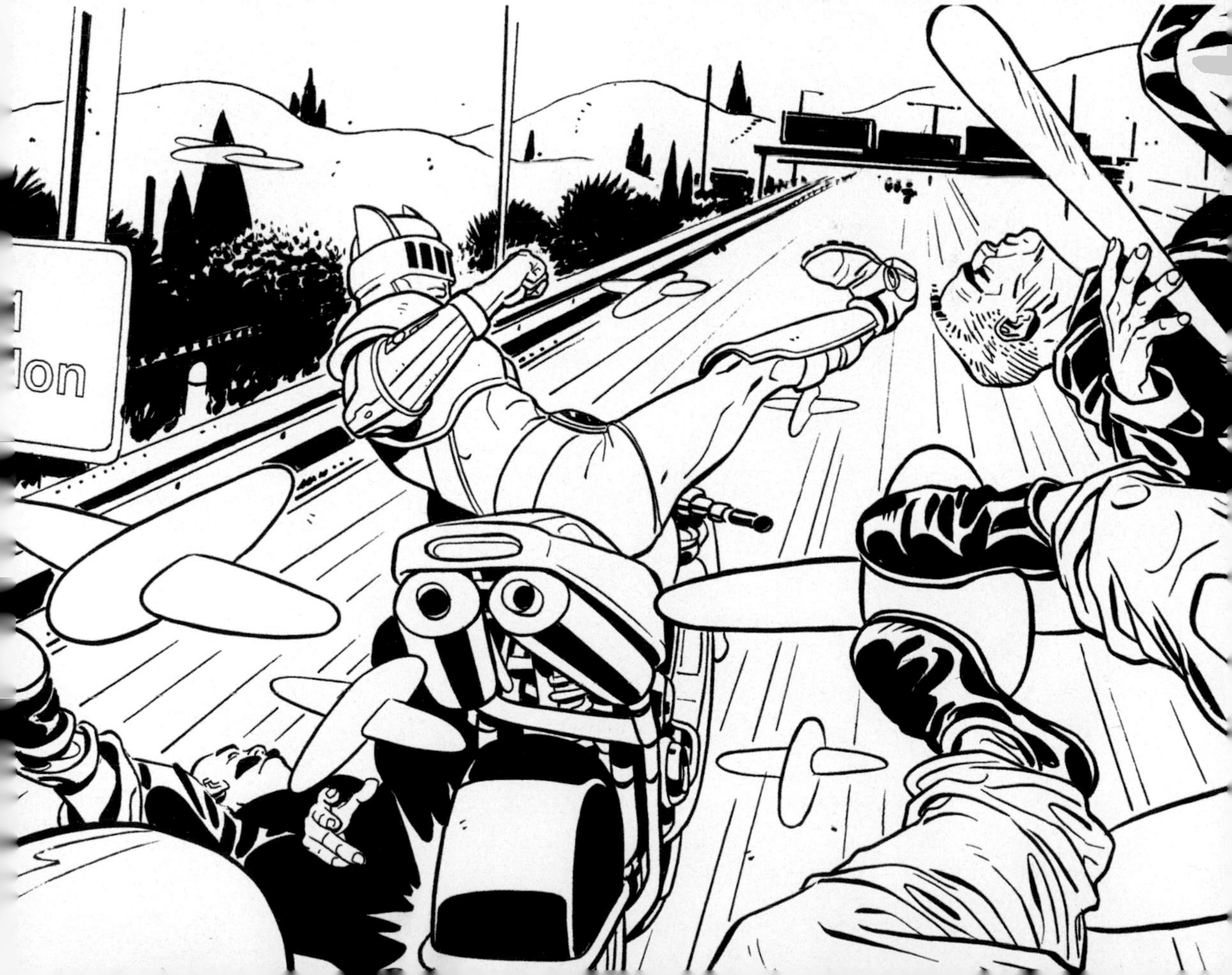

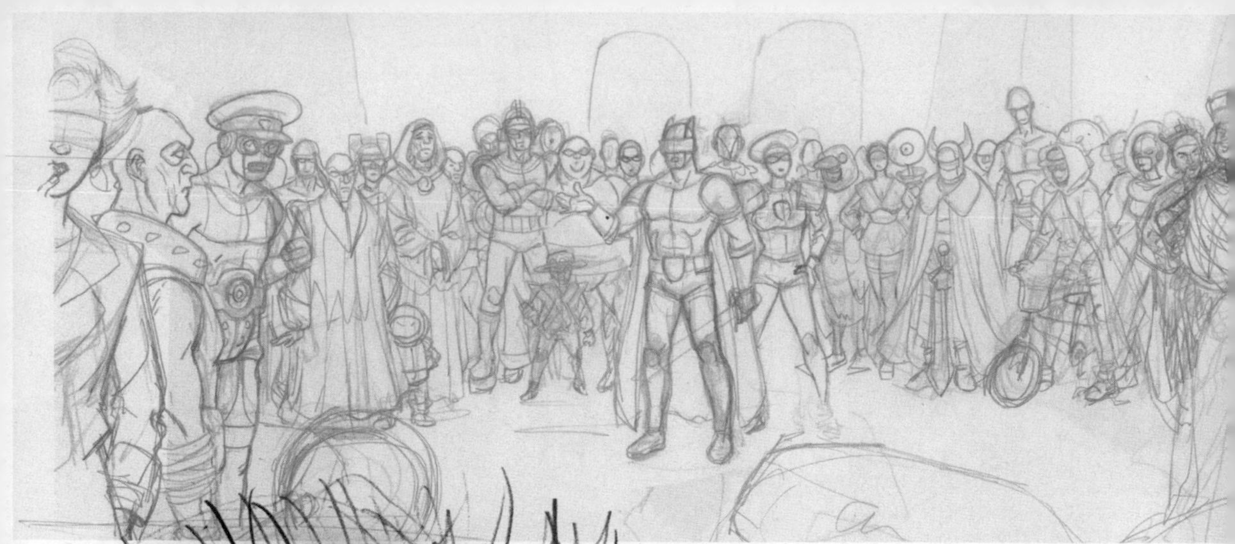

Above: Over 130 new characters were created for the series. This pencil layout for issue 6 features just 27 of them.

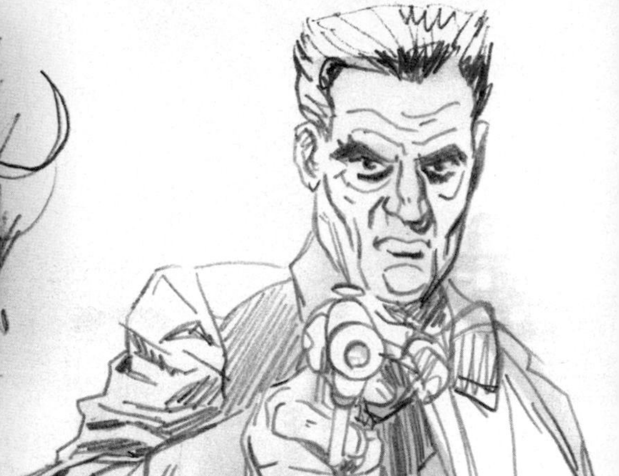

Above: When Jarvis reappears in issue 5 he is noticeably leaner. Alas, despite his best efforts, he is no meaner.

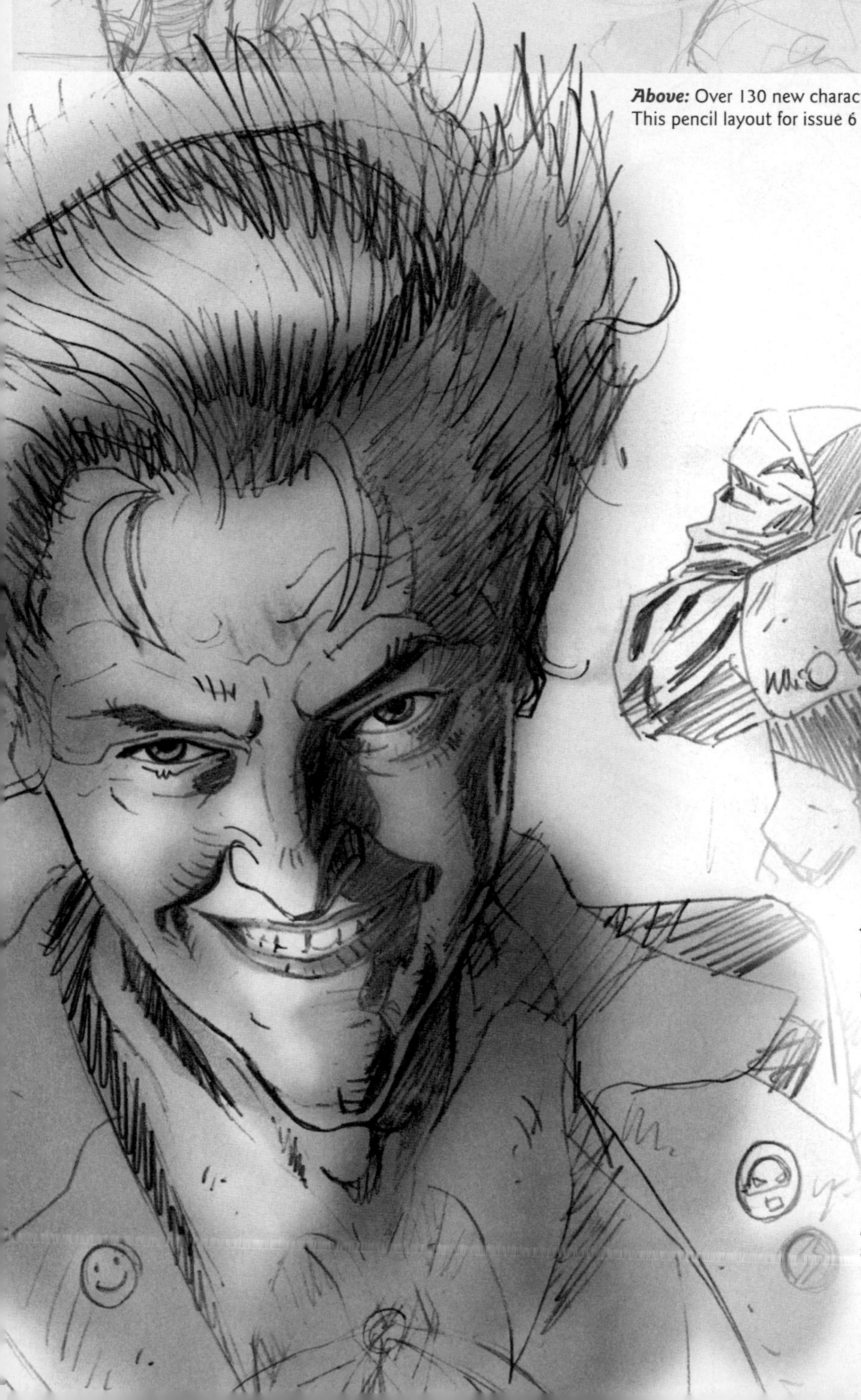

Left: When the "actual" Joker appears in the same issue, he has no such difficulties.

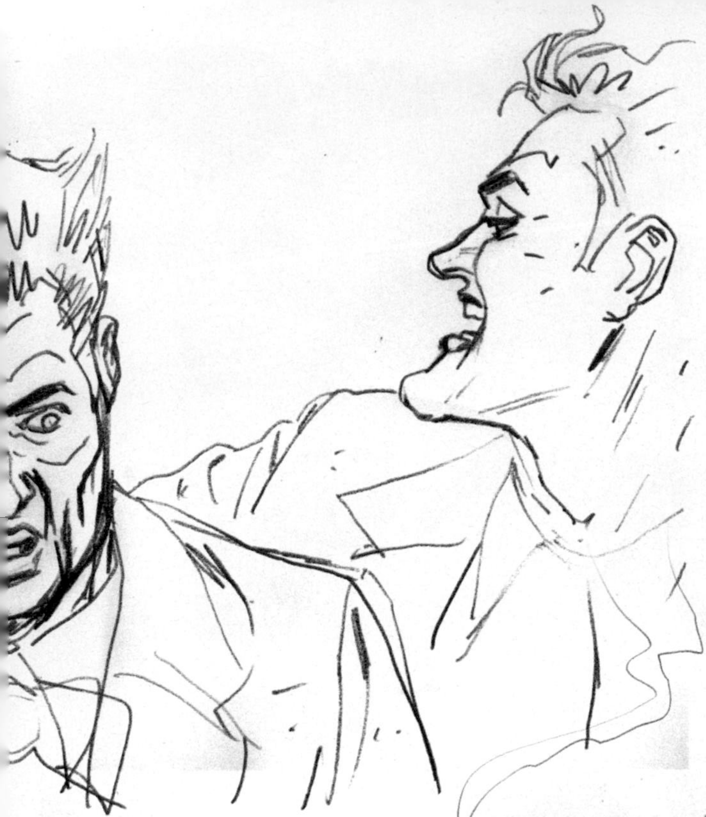

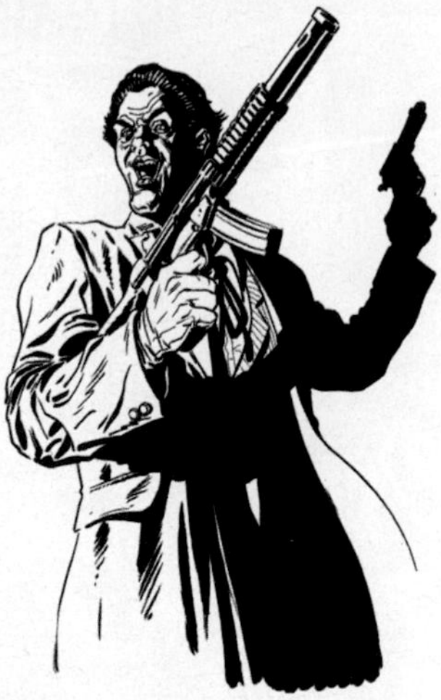

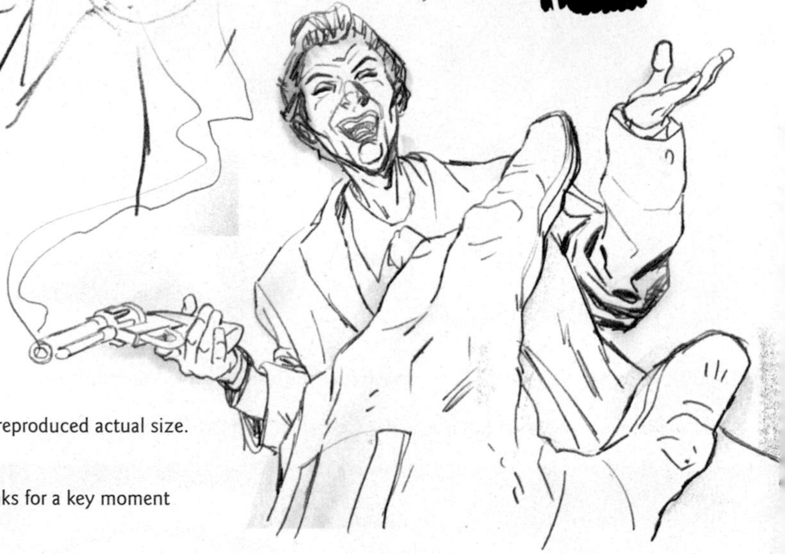

Above: Pencil sketch for a pair of "Jokers," reproduced actual size.

Below and right: Preliminary pencils and inks for a key moment in the story.

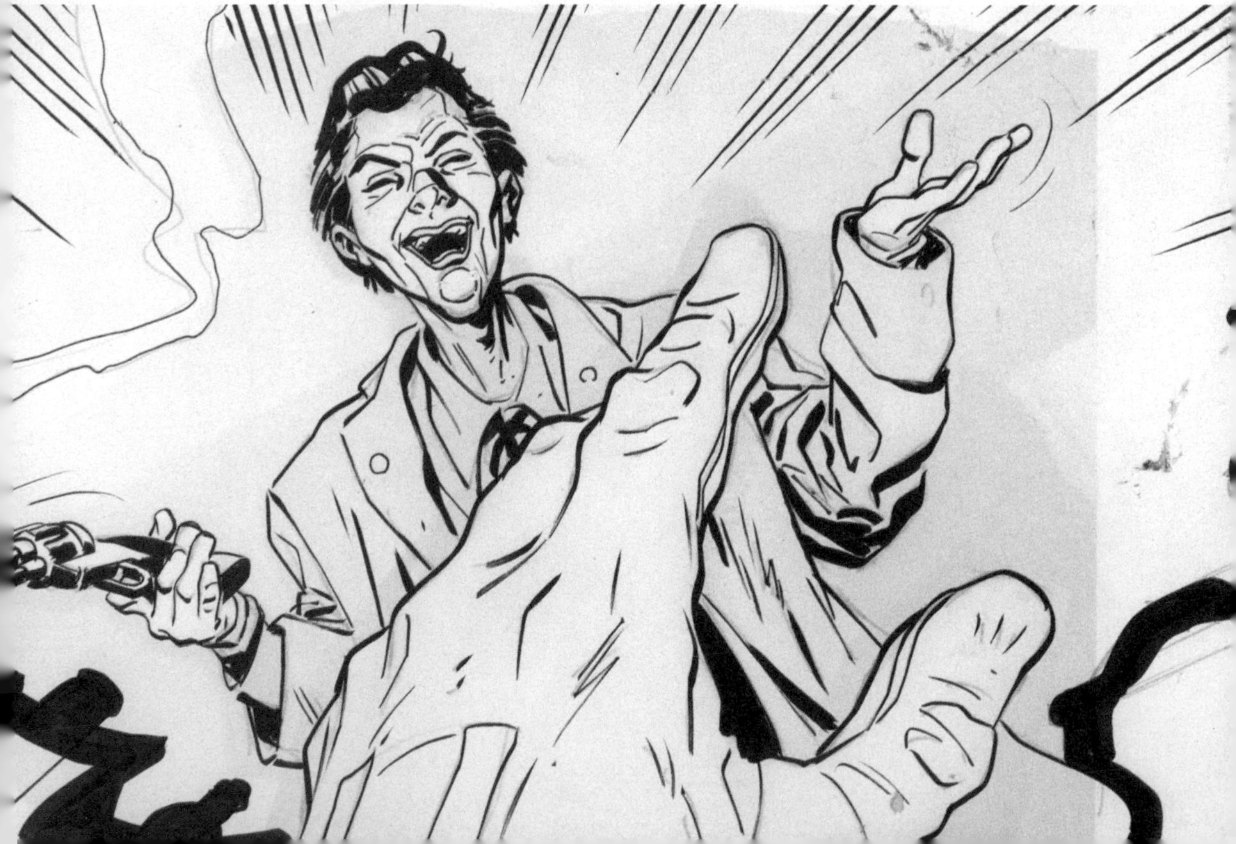

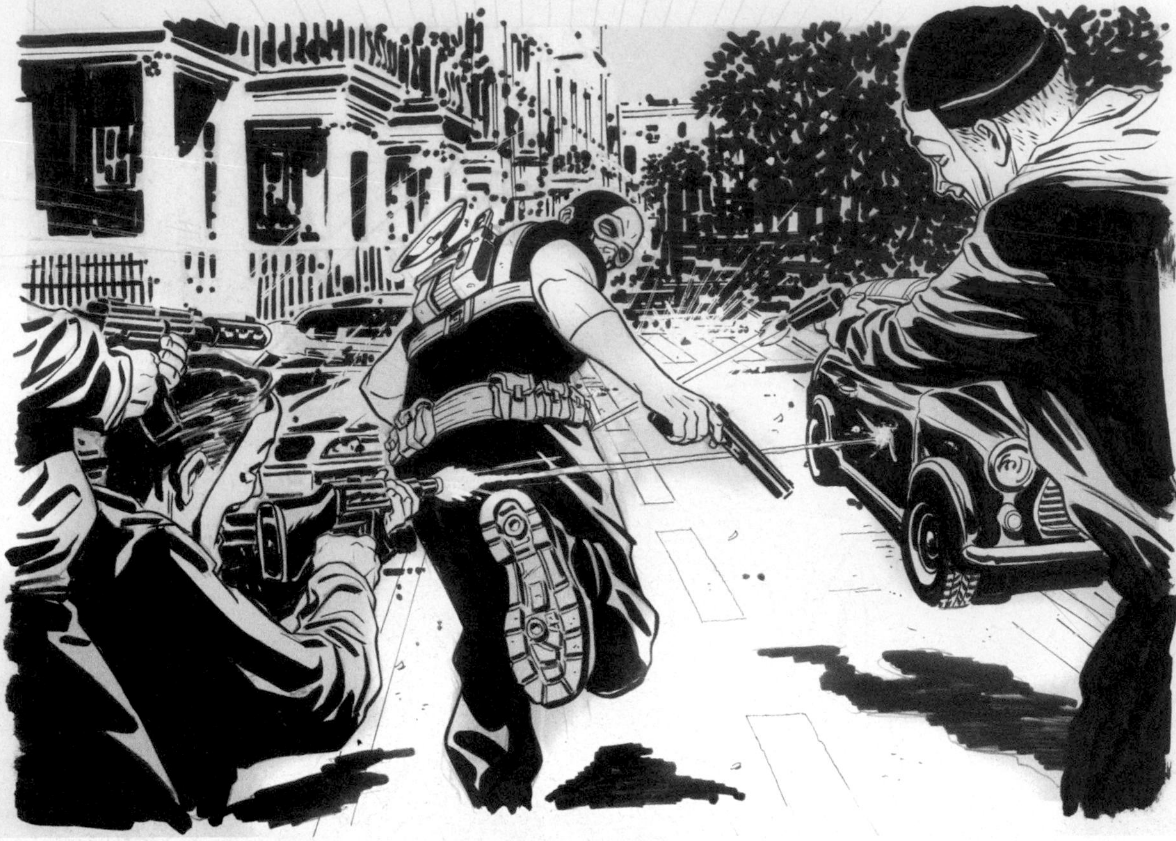

Above: Raw, uncorrected inks for an assault from the rear. Note the iconic British car, drawn way smaller than it should be — a mini-"Mini."

Below: More raw inks showcasing a motley crew with "Birthday Girl" centre stage, complete with "modesty balloons."

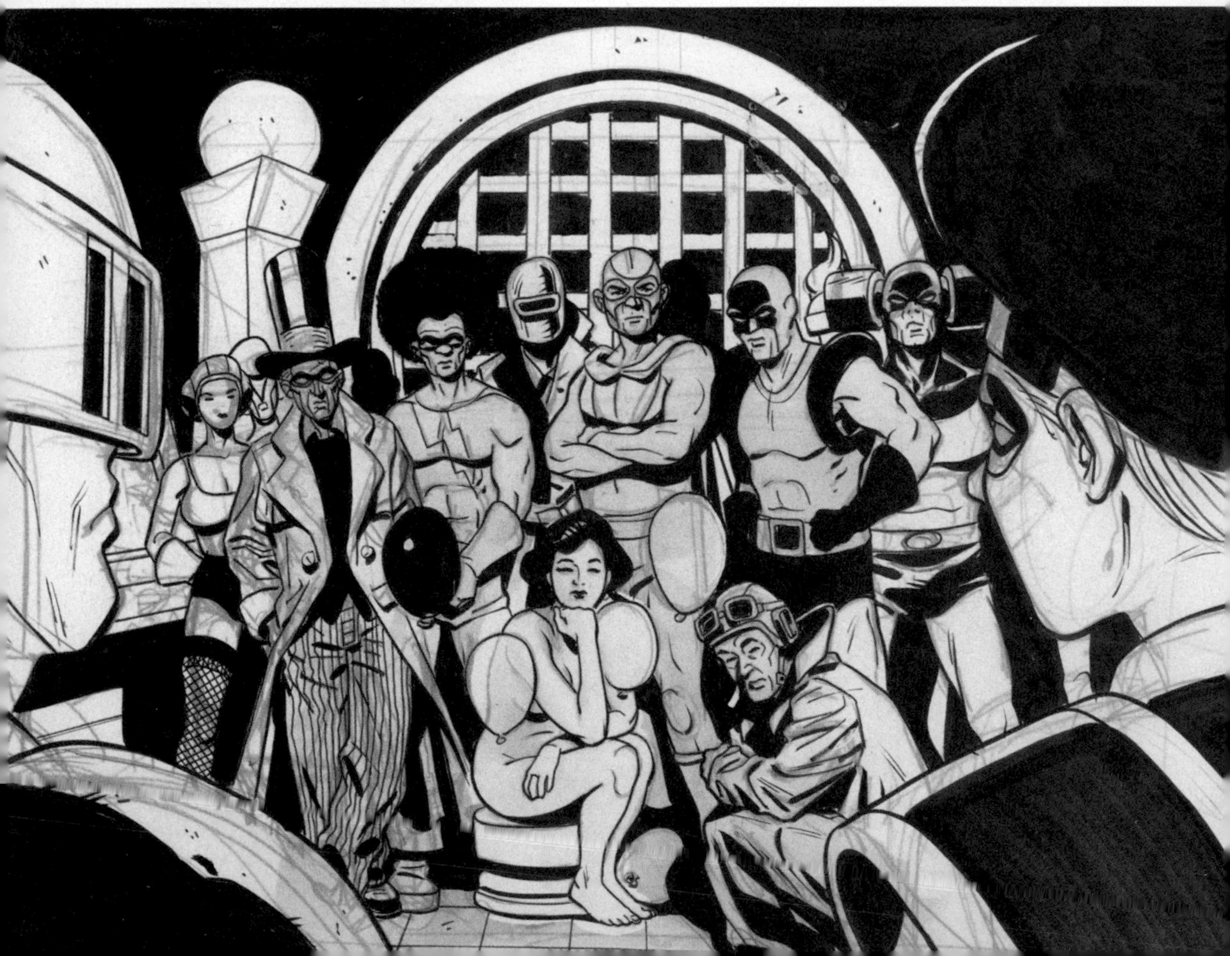

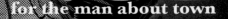

Geezer

for the man about town

JARVIS POKER 1943-2011
The man, the myth, the mirth

His final interview.
The great man talks about his life, his loves, his legacy, his shirts.

Above: Unpublished art for a spoof magazine cover, which was to have been the final ad in issue 6. R.I.P. Jarvis.

Hope you enjoyed the behind-the-scenes look at our little piece of Britain!

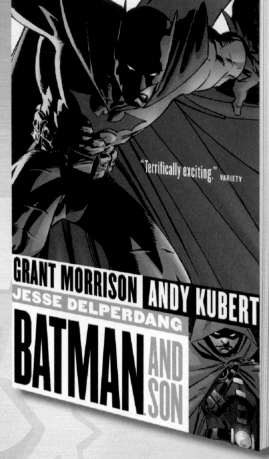

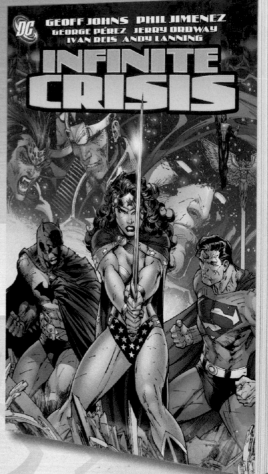
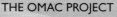